A SOVIET ODYSSEY
Suzanne Rosenberg

D1065793

Penguin Books

PENGUIN BOOKS
Published by the Penguin Group
Penguin Books Canada Ltd, 10 Alcorn Avenue, Toronto,
Ontario, Canada M4V 1E4
Penguin Books Ltd, 27 Wrights Lane, London W8 5TZ, England
Penguin Books USA Inc., 375 Hudson Street, New York,
New York 10014, U.S.A.
Penguin Books Australia Ltd, Ringwood, Victoria, Australia
Penguin Books (NZ) Ltd, 182-190 Wairau Road, Auckland 10,
New Zealand

Penguin Books Ltd, Registered Offices: Harmondsworth,
Middlesex, England

First published by Oxford University Press, 1988

Published in Penguin Books, 1991

10 9 8 7 6 5 4 3 2 1

Manufactured in Canada

Canadian Cataloguing in Publication Data

Rosenberg, Suzanne, 1915-1988
  A Soviet Odyssey

Includes index.
ISBN 0-14-012927-8

1. Rosenberg, Suzanne, 1915-1988. 2. Women political
prisoners—Soviet Union—Biography. 3. Soviet Union—
History—1925-1953. 4. Soviet Union—Intellectual life—1917-
1970. 5. Canadians—Soviet Union—Biography. I. Title.

DK268.R68A3 1991   947.084'2'092   C90-095719-0

American Library of Congress Cataloguing in Publication Data
Available

For Vicky,
and to the memory of the millions
killed under the Stalin regime

Acknowledgments

A number of people, among them Irving Layton, Earle Birney, Gerald Hallowell, Linda Schachter, Vivian Felsen, Sarah Grosberg, Lou and Helen Poch, Ruth Pressman, and Lionel and June Albert, read the manuscript in draft form, and I wish to thank them for their encouragement. I am also grateful for the grant I received from the Ontario Arts Council.

. I wish to express special thanks to my devoted friends Anne and Sam Madras, whose confidence in my ability to complete the manuscript never wavered. Finally, I am most indebted to Richard Teleky of the Oxford University Press for his enthusiasm for the book, and to him and Sally Livingston for their meticulous editing.

Throughout my writing I was fortunate to have the material and moral support of my daughter Vicky and my son-in-law, Timothy Walsh.

Contents

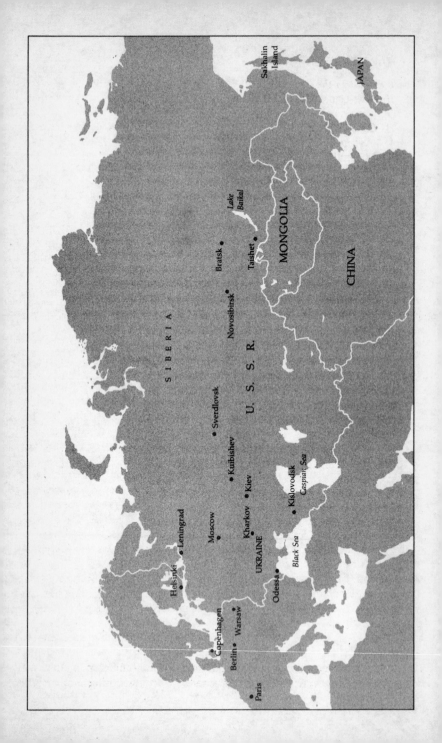

ONE

I On my tracks

In the mid-twentieth century a new wave of terror spills over into all sections of the population. It hits hardest the intellectuals. Many of my Moscow friends, colleagues, and family, who escaped death on the battlefronts of World War II, are now being struck down by it. My husband is a prisoner at Lubyanka, headquarters of the dreaded Ministry of State Security, precursor of the KGB.

At a loss to explain such vagaries of the state, I am torn between despair and hope, the selfish hope that I may be spared the fate of my husband and of those many other unfortunates. My little daughter is staying with my mother in the country. I feel stifled within the massive walls of the building in which we occupy a single room.

Languidly the spring day draws to a close. I long to get out into the big city, its streets and lanes converging into breezy squares where every stone bears witness to the turbulent and tragic past of this country.

I dart down the ancient stairs, slip through the brick gates, onto the newly-built Embankment. To raise my spirits the Moscow River blows its freshness into my face.

Startled, I halt. There is the same young man standing on the corner. Tall, debonair, with good features and a beguiling smile. He has been shadowing me day after day. Instead of feeling scared, I am amused. He does not match the part. I speculate who he might be: a law student making extra money, or a prospective interrogator in training?

I board a streetcar, make my way up to the front—and turn to look. He is there, cheery, snug against a railing. The sleuthing is quite brazen. In a way it is comic; on one bus ride, the flicker of a smile passes between us. Life can be funny and grotesque, even when you walk on thin ice.

After this prepossessing young man, no doubt with a brilliant future before him, has tailed me for about a fortnight, he disappears. Having yielded no results, the sleuthing is discontinued. The next step is to send a well-briefed provocateur to trap me into a political indiscretion.

I am sitting at the Central Telegraph Office on Gorky Street waiting for a long-distance call from my brother Shurri, a lieutenant in the Far Eastern Army. Though scheduled for eleven, the call will not come through until one in the morning. I have not been inside the building for more than a few minutes when a runty man in a greasy suit ambles towards my bench and flops down on the empty seat beside me.

He prattles. I remain silent and aloof. I have a feeling that I have seen him before; for the life of me I cannot remember where. I move to the end of the bench. That only makes him bolder. He sidles closer, but his head lolls forward as though he has difficulty holding it up. Out of his pocket protrudes a copy of *Vechernaya Moskva*, which he now produces. Fluttering it in front of me, he points to an item on the back page. I glance through it and learn that Moscow's world-famous Jewish Theater has been shut down.

"What do you make of that?" he sputters. "And of the killing of its director, the shooting and arrests of the actors?"

"Nothing!" I am on my guard, aware he is out to catch me in a "thought crime."

I need only intimate in some way that I deplore the closure of the theater and the killing of its founder for him to have fulfilled his purpose: file a report to the secret police that would put me in grave trouble.

But I know the game. It is played with people of every nationality. The mother of a Ukrainian friend of mine was sentenced to ten years for just such a thought on the persecution of two Kiev actors. I am not nationalistic; I grieve for Solomon Mikhoels, but I also grieve for the non-Jewish Vsevolod Meyerhold and the Armenian Tairov, all three master spirits of the theater who have been disposed of by Stalin in various brutal ways.

I now suddenly recall where I have seen the man—at the publishing house in Zubovskaya Street for which I translate; he sat in a niche, dictating to a typist. A translator like myself, he is a salaried agent of the MGB.* A common informer does not get an assignment that takes up hours of his time and requires sedulous coaching.

After my call comes through, I walk briskly out of the building and practically jog to the street corner. Red Square, which I have to cross on my way home, opens up before me, vast, frowning, crawling with shadows. I have a vision of St. Basil's breaking away from its solid foundations and sailing upwards, the cupolas vanishing behind the low-drifting clouds. Everything else in the square remains rock-firm, though mantled in darkness. I meet the stony stare of Lenin's granite tomb. The voice of the man who is following me pierces the dusk.

He shoots at me what I know is the crucial question: "Would you like to go back to Canada or live in some other Western country?"

Knowing it to be a crime even to speak favorably of anything foreign, I reply as coolly as I can: "I do not care to go to any country. I wish to stay where I am, in the Soviet Union."

I know exactly what answer to give.

Somewhat earlier, a similar question had been posed to my mother, but under quite different circumstances. It was put to her in a friendly tone, dropped casually, in the office where she worked, by Comrade Pavlov. In charge of a government cartography department, he valued her greatly for her good education and knowledge of European languages.

"Would you go to the new Palestine?" Pavlov asked cordially, as he always spoke to her.

Suspecting nothing, she replied with only that degree of caution which we knew we must exercise at all times.

"Yes, if it were a socialist state."

Unlike my mother, I give a safe answer. The man who has followed me to the Telegraph Office, pestering me with questions, could not be a satisfactory witness against me; a certain legality is observed.

I look now to see if he is still keeping in step with me. No—he has been swallowed up by the warm May night.

On a sweltering Sunday afternoon in June of the same year I have another encounter with a police spy. But this time I sense danger at once. A man of powerful physique, he has a face so coarse and depraved that I am relieved he is following me into a crowded suburban train rather than along a poorly lit Moscow street. His purpose is not to trap me into making a seditious statement, but to show me up as a woman of loose morals.

Bounding into the train after me, he elbows his way through the

---

* Ministry of State Security (1946–53), later the KGB.

crowd to grab a seat across from me. Reeking of alcohol and sweat, he drops a few lewd remarks. I note the gray gabardine slacks, Ministry of State Security issue; the shirt he wears is open at the front, revealing sweaty clumps of sandy hair.

When it becomes obvious that there is little chance of luring me to a dacha where we can have "lots of fun and plenty of drinks," he gets off long before the station he named.

From the train I walk to my mother's home on the outskirts of Moscow, where my little daughter Vicky is staying. We sit around the table in the tiny quarters she now shares with my brother's family.

I do not mention the various games the security hirelings are playing with me. All our faces, even the children's, are clouded. My brother tries to cheer us up by cracking jokes. I cannot relax and enjoy the company of my dear ones. I am tense and nervous. I hardly play with Vicky at all, giving her less attention than on my previous visits. I do not know that I will not see her again for another three years, and my beloved brother never.

II Arrest

Having absorbed the daytime heat, the massive walls of the house where I live, across the river from the Kremlin, exude it into the night. June is a sultry month; Moscow has sunk into a drowsy languor, allaying my fears. I am not suspicious, dismissing the watch kept over me by the security detectives as a necessary precaution following my husband's incarceration. I am in no danger. I have never committed a disloyal action, never let drop an imprudent word.

On the last day of June at about eight in the evening, remembering I had run out of bread, I stepped out of my room, locked the door, and strolled down the dim hall. Two tall, hefty men in gray suits approached, ranging themselves in full strength before me. Both were swarthy, with the flat faces and slanting eyes that suggested Tartar origins. One of them I recognized at once as the man who ten months before had told me: "Last night we arrested your husband."

I noticed then, and now too, his long muscular arms and strong square hands.

"You're going out? Where?" he demanded.

My heart thumped with the wildest premonitions.

"To the corner bakery."

"You can go tomorrow morning," he said lightly. "We have a search warrant in your husband's name. We won't keep you long."

It was a lie. There was no search warrant. Inside his breast pocket lay the warrant for my arrest. It was dated July 1; they had come to arrest me on the evening of June 30, so the warrant would not be valid until after midnight. It was then, when the four-hour search was almost over, that the manner of the two men changed.

A few minutes earlier, after they had gone through all my belongings, missing no scrap of paper, shaking out the books, turning every piece of apparel inside out, I said: "You can see for yourselves there is nothing in my home of the least interest to state security. Could you please leave—it will take me the rest of the night to tidy up the place."

They shot me a curious glance, thinking me, I suppose, an idiot.

"Stop playing the innocent!" snapped the one who had done all the talking. The other man had hardly uttered a word. He had a lumpy, pock-marked face and a vacant stare.

Up to this moment I did not believe that I was in any danger. Now I felt wooden. Everything around me seemed to crumble away. There was only blackness, no yesterday, no tomorrow.

My mouth was parched. Mechanically I turned in the direction of the tiny improvised kitchen to get myself a drink out of a pail (there was no running water).

"Not another step! Stay where you are!"

"I'm not under arrest . . ."

"Yes you are!" He looked at his watch and, fumbling in his pocket, produced the warrant for my arrest.

I cannot remember whether I read it there and then or about twenty hours later when I faced my interrogator for the first time at Lubyanka. But the contents, word for word, are there before my eyes even today. And when, in my foolish credulity and vain hope for justice, I wrote appeals to the Supreme Soviet, which never went further than the camp commandant's office, I remembered it well enough.

In disbelief I read the two charges against me. The first was treason, specified as "espionage activities against the U.S.S.R.," and the second "anti-Soviet agitation among friends." The accusation of espionage rested on three counts: "acquaintance with the notorious American spy Anna Louise Strong"; "a suspicious encounter with Boris Victorov, agent of an American firm"; and "arrests in Canada allegedly for distribution of communist leaflets and participation in anti-fascist demonstrations." The second charge merely cited "anti-Soviet conversations over many years."

It was around two o'clock in the morning when I was led away. Two neighbors dared stare after me. One was Georgi Mikhailov, a colleague who many years later became my husband. Our eyes met. I was afraid to utter a single word, but I knew words were unnecessary. The next morning, without fail, he would get in touch with my mother—I never suspected she was arrested the same night—and brother to tell them what had happened. The other was Vasili Stepanovich. He opened his door wide and stood there with a poignant sadness in his pale eyes. In the seven years that we had been neighbors, I had hardly exchanged two words with Vasili Stepanovich.

Often it happened to me, and I am sure it happened to others, that in a single glance the human eyes conveyed more than long hours of conversation. The look Vasili Stepanovich gave me was one of deep shame. Shame because he was a former factory worker, a member of the Communist Party, who had hailed the revolution as the greatest blessing of mankind. He was a good and upright man, poles apart from the police thugs who were taking me away from normal life, confident that I would now be buried amidst millions of others, behind the barbed wires and watch towers of the strict-regime camps.

Instead of the usual black maria, a black limousine waited for me downstairs, for some reason not in front of the house but half a block away. The limousine moved proudly through the dark streets. We did not have far to go. The car pulled up in front of the heavy iron-wrought gates on the left side of the Lubyanka building. Momentarily the gates swung open and as momentarily shut.

My two escorts led me down a narrow, bare corridor and handed me over to a guard. I was shoved into a cubby hole and frisked. Along with my bra and garters, the pins from my hair (piled on top of my head, in the fashion of the time) were taken away. Hanging breasts—I had the misfortune of being fullbreasted—falling stockings, and long dishevelled hair, besides adding to the discomforts of prison life, were meant to embarrass me and weaken my defenses in the battle with my interrogator.

I was thrust into a detention box, my eyes blinking in the glare of the 200-watt overhead bulb. The "box" was about two feet by four and had a hard, veneered bench fitted into the wall. For a few minutes there was a tomb-like silence, soon replaced by a deafening roar of the most devilish noises pummelling my ears. The box vibrated with the improvised clatter of torture racks.

Moans of torment and a wild screeching followed. I tingled with fear and bewilderment. At first I did not know what to make of it all. But after a few hours I realized it was some sort of machinery, combined, perhaps, with phonograph recordings, all meant to strike terror into the prisoner, muddle his thinking, prepare him to "confess" to his crimes, as the interrogators demanded.

"We know about your subversion against the Soviet state," my interrogator Major Porunov said, when I was ushered by the prison guard into his office. "Speak up! There is nothing you can hide from us."

The interrogator placed before me my first deposition, with his questions and my answers below each one, as he had written them down. It was a double sheet of coarse bluish-gray paper. Before signing it, I caught sight of the heading on the first page: "File No. 3868. Third Directorate, Ministry of State Security."

A second night of questioning. Major Porunov repeated the charges stated in the warrant for my arrest.

I had never been even on nodding terms with Anna Louise Strong. The name Boris Victorov meant nothing to me—nor to my interrogator. I had always avoided conversations on political topics, as did most people I knew. Never had I uttered anything that could in any way be interpreted as "anti-Soviet." The sole grain of truth in the warrant was that I had been arrested, though not convicted, in Canada. But why "allegedly" for distributing communist leaflets? It was outright lunacy; everything that followed was devoid of logic.

Was this really happening to me? Was it really I who was sitting on the prisoner's bench in the dreaded Lubyanka?

The interrogator kept shooting questions at me. What espionage assignments had I carried out? With what foreign intelligence had I been involved? Did I realize what a charge of treason meant?

Indeed I did not. I was in a state of shock. Major Porunov now handed me a blank sheet of paper and told me to write down the names of all my friends and acquaintances. I was too frightened to refuse and decided it best not to confine myself to a few names, but to make the list as long as possible.

Back to a different box with a seat instead of a shelf. I had no idea how long I had been awake. There were no windows anywhere. Soon I was taken by a guard into a small elevator. It creaked to a stop on the fifth landing.

After passing through a narrow deserted hallway I was brought into a small office with a single desk behind which sat a grubby man with a gray blob for a face; not a muscle twitched, the eyes gave no sign of life. He did not look at me when he took hold of my thumb, twisting it now to one side, now to the other, as he pressed it against an ink pad. It was a new and degrading sensation to be treated like a criminal. I could not stop the tears that rolled down my face and showed on the photographs presently taken to attach to my file, which for all time was to be kept in the vaults of the MGB.

The interrogation continued. I was told: "Only a full confession of your criminal activities against the Soviet state will save you and your child."

Unexpectedly there was a two-day break in the nightly questionings. On the third night Major Porunov surprised me with questions concerning my mother's past.

"Did your mother have Trotskyite leanings?"

I was taken aback, alarmed. What could be more perilous than to have Trotskyite leanings? Who dared even to pronounce Trotsky's name?

"No, my mother never had any such leanings!"

"How could you know, you were only thirteen at the time Trotsky was expelled from the Party, and both you and your mother were living in Canada."

I wanted to say: Then why ask the question? But I merely repeated the answer I had already given.

"Your mother, a supposed Bolshevik, left this country five years after the revolution. This in itself is an act of treason."

A harsh note crept into his voice. The accusatory statement staggered me. Though I could not for a moment imagine that my mother too was in a prison cell, that she had been arrested the very night I was, I knew my answers could have consequences, and how cautious I must be.

Years later, when I was a hard-bitten convict, I learned it was common practice for a mother to testify against a daughter, for a husband to be tricked into making incriminating statements against his wife, a sister against a brother.

"My mother left the country legally," I said, with all the calm I could muster. "She had the approval of the Soviet government to travel. She returned legally, was welcomed, in fact. "

There was a long pause. Rising from his oak and leather armchair, he stopped short, midway between his massive desk and my shaky prisoner's stool, and stormed: "So you deny your mother's Trotskyite connections?" A nasty glint settled in his eyes.

Hell, what sort of act is he putting on, I thought. In all of the later questionings I always had the feeling that we were both acting out some cheap, haphazardly concocted drama.

"What about the Trotsky picture in your Montreal home?" he now asked.

TWO

I Trotsky

The picture! I remembered it well enough. Both my parents were militant Bolsheviks who worked and fought to bring about the Revolution. In my childhood I heard Trotsky's name mentioned as frequently as Lenin's.

It was 1921, a year of famine, requisition of property, homeless children, and death. We were living in Kharkov, a city that before the Revolution and during the Civil War had been the scene of my mother's clandestine activities in support of the Bolsheviks. And now she had lived to see Kharkov the capital of the new Soviet Socialist Republic of the Ukraine. In the government she held a key post at the Commissariat of Foreign Trade.

To be closer to the downtown section of this big industrial city, we abandoned the cozy bungalow we had occupied before the revolution and moved into a single room. A number of families would now be crowded into one flat; it was the beginning of the long era of communal living.

With fuel as scarce as it was in the years that followed the revolution, the shared flat had one advantage: the more huddled together people were, the less firewood was needed to keep them warm. In the middle of our room stood a *bourjouika*, a small cast-iron stove. It took an hour of my mother's time, a box of precious matches, and a goodly amount of no less precious kindling wood to start the fire. For the heat the stove gave off we paid dearly. The long-necked black monster exhaled smoke from all its seams and pores, perhaps because the sections of the tube reaching to the chimney pot did not fit together properly.

My mother cared little for riches or comfort, although she came from a well-to-do home. She had trained herself in a life of austerity, and our dingy surroundings did not seem to bother her. Perhaps she was too immersed in the new life ushered in by the Revolution to even notice them.

Smoke hung in shreds over the room, blurring the air and covering the furniture with soot, collecting in our nostrils, causing our eyes to tear. From our comfortable old home we had brought two high-backed chairs with sea-lions mounted on the top corners and fanciful carvings on the legs, backs, and arm-rests—bourgeois reminders of our former luxury. Frowning down from the wall upon them were two enlarged photo portraits, which accompanied us wherever we moved. One was of Lenin, his eyes shrewdly but good-naturedly squinting at me, the forehead high and serene. The other was of Trotsky, anger flashing in his impatient gaze, the beard jutting menacingly. It was a time when Trotsky was still extremely popular, held in almost the same regard as Lenin.

"Your father knew Trotsky personally and fought under him." my mother said proudly.

It was two years earlier, in 1919, that my father came home late one night on furlough from the Ukrainian front. That was the only time I saw him. He was a stockily built man, with eyes like big dark cherries, neat features, and a small moustache. He appeared to be shorter than my tall, erect mother. Before the outbreak of World War I, his family had emigrated from Russia to Canada, where for long years his father, Rabbi Yudel Rosenberg, was the spiritual head of Montreal's Orthodox Jewish community.

After this brief visit, on returning to his regiment, my father was killed in battle a few miles from the city of Kharkov. He had fought on the side of the Reds in the Civil War that raged for more than three years on Russian territory.

I shall not be wide of the mark in assuming that years later, when my mother joined my father's family in Montreal, she hoped a revolutionary situation would arise in Canada. She may well have hoped too that an industrially advanced Western country would make a better job of revolution than backward, peasant Russia had.

We lived in a roomy flat in Drolet Street. On Saturday nights I would wait up until all hours in our big kitchen for my mother to come home from her weekly Canadian Communist Party meeting. I served her a glass of tea with lemon, Russian style, over which, if she was not too fatigued, we chatted about things far removed from our everyday existence.

On one such night my mother returned later than usual from her meeting. And she did a very unusual thing: she confided her troubled thoughts to me.

"Trotsky was ordered out of the Soviet Union, he's been branded a renegade," she said.

Trotsky being the greatest renegade of all—only shortly to be outdone by Zinoviev, Kamenev, Rykov, and Bukharin, Lenin's closest associates, and a couple of dozen others, later their number running into hundreds of thousands—purges and expulsions were launched in all of the communist parties.

After she had bared her heart, my mother's gaze fell on the portrait that hung next to Lenin's. She did not there and then throw the Trotsky picture into the garbage, as good Party members were doing the world over. (But eventually she did remove it, and it was this argument that saved her from one of the gravest charges that could be brought by a Lubyanka interrogator against a prisoner. But how did the interrogator know about the picture? Either an informer had reported it to the security police long before she was arrested, or the admission had been wrung from a prisoner. Either one must have been a visitor at our home in Montreal.)

The next week on returning from her meeting my mother spoke little, drinking her tea in silence. There was a perplexed look in her eyes. Fear darkened her face and snuffed out momentarily the light that drew people so forcibly towards her. It was the first time I saw my mother afraid.

Idealistic, romantic communism, as embodied in my mother's thinking, proved a potent factor in molding the moral views I have held throughout my life. It was my mother who turned me into a communist. Communism was in the air I breathed from my very early childhood.

II My revolutionary mother

The noble ideals for which my mother fought turned against her and through her against her intimates, her children, and the many persons she influenced. Poland was the home of many revolutionaries. And it was in Poland that my mother grew up. She became a radical in her teens.

To her respectable, middle-class family my mother was an enigma, an embarrassment, a source of great sorrow—and a romantic heroine.

Her father was landlord of several apartment houses in Warsaw and also one of the few Jews to have a position in a bank; her mother was the perfect lady of leisure.

My mother joined militant organizations, among them the Polish Bund, championed women's rights, and finally ended up in the Bolshevik faction of the Russian Social-Democratic Workers Party. For her beliefs she was thrown into prison and exiled for life from Poland. Proudly she claimed to have spent a few months in the same cell of the Schlüsselburg Fortress, outside St. Petersburg, that had been occupied several years earlier by Vera Figner, who plotted the assassination of Tsar Alexander II.

Exile took my mother to Paris around 1912, where she settled with her first husband and two children. There she contacted Russian emigrant revolutionary groups, attended the Sorbonne, and carried out assignments for the Bolshevik cell to which she belonged.

At the start of the First World War the European revolutionary movement split up. Russian and Polish emigrant revolutionaries had all sorts of axes to grind, but for personal reasons my mother remained aloof from the wrangling and theoretical discussions that went on among them at the time in Paris. She was either having her first marriage annulled or procuring a divorce—I do not know which. Her first husband remarried, as I later learned, raised a second family, and met his end in the furnace of Maidanek.

At the cost of separation from her two small children, my mother was able to marry my father. She rarely mentioned this part of her life to me. When, in my early teens, I plucked up the courage to mildly reproach her for having abandoned the two children of her first marriage, she paled and retorted in anger: "Do not judge until you have lived your own life."

She was right, of course. This aspect of her past was a painful subject, thereafter not touched between us.

In the early summer of 1915, the second year of World War I, having received her diploma in mathematics from the Sorbonne, she boarded an eastbound train to give birth to her third child in her parents' Warsaw home. She was in luck: the sentence of banishment that hung over her head was overlooked and permission granted to enter Poland.

A few days later Warsaw fell into enemy hands. With an infant in her arms, a bundle of wet diapers, and a few other belongings my mother fled from the city. Her destination was Kharkov, where on Party orders she was to join the Bolshevik underground and organize meetings of fighters for a revolution in Russia. The train was held up by the Germans; all passengers were ordered out and declared prisoners of war.

The story of the circumstances surrounding my birth I heard told many times. What I remember best is my mother's account of how humane and obliging the Germans were. They went out of their way to arrange sleeping quarters and procure food for her and her baby, were courteous and even apologetic. After being detained for a few days she was allowed to continue her journey.

Once in Kharkov she plunged into the work of the Bolshevik organization in the Ukraine, leaving me in the care of a nanny or with neighbors, and often disappearing for long periods. Upon her return the cellar of our house was turned into a rendezvous for revolutionaries. In the morning the house reeked of tobacco smoke. I watched my mother empty ashtray after ashtray into the flames in the kitchen stove to erase all signs of the previous night's gathering.

Kharkov was the scene of some of the heaviest fighting in the Civil War. The city kept changing hands, now captured by the Reds, now by the Whites, and at times falling prey to the Green or other marauding bands.

Bullets hissed in the air. I saw them blow off the frothy crowns of the acacia bushes that formed a fragrant hedge around the front of our home. I was startled in the night by the gunfire of sudden skirmishes, then lulled back to sleep by the soldiers' drunken chants.

My mother was hopeful and cheerful, a great optimist, a fighter, throughout her life. She would pick me up and hug me, and her rigid face, with sharply etched features and hard-set mouth, broke into smiles. She sang revolutionary songs or recited stirring poetry, often in languages I did not understand. As I listened to Schiller's "Joan of Arc" the German verse rang with the clangor of arms in my ears: *"Sieg! Sieg! Sie entflichen!"*

"Revolutionaries never give up!" my mother would exclaim. "The Reds will conquer. Kharkov is sure to stay under Soviet rule!"

A decanter of lemon-laced vodka gleamed on our dining-room sideboard and everybody helped himself. Mother called it "students' elixir" (a good many of the revolutionaries were university students) and insisted that I too take a sip—which I did, trying hard not to grimace when the liquid scorched my throat.

Grand words hovered around me and I rolled them glibly off my tongue. "Revolution," "intelligentsia," and "communism" were household terms to me from the age of two or three. Religion being the "opium of the people," my mother was furious when she caught my elderly nanny diligently instructing me in the Christian faith.

Making sure we were alone in the house, nanny would open her massive, velvet-bound Old Slavonic Gospel, which was richly illustrated, and declaim from memory story after story. To create the illusion of reading, for she was of course illiterate, she would trace the lines with her plump index finger. It was in the middle of such a session that my mother surprised us. She flew into a rage, making it clear that never again must nanny force religion on me.

After resisting the enemy for several months the Reds abandoned Kharkov. General Denikin was expected to march in with his army at any hour.

My mother carried our entire supply of food and water into the cellar.

"We may have to stay here for quite a while," she said.

Excitement gripped me. I recalled her stories about the many times she had had to hide in the past, make quick getaways through back doors. There were arrests, searches, prison sentences, exile, secret meetings with such well-known revolutionaries as Felix Dzerzhinsky, who fathered the Soviet security apparatus, and Yakir, who was later to become a distinguished general, still later to be purged. My mother's life appeared to me more than ever in an aura of romance.

A few days after Denikin marched into Kharkov my mother was seized. I awoke in time to see her prodded out by two uniformed men. Some neighbors took me into their home. People spoke in whispers. Nobody dared venture into the streets; morning after morning new bodies swung from the lamp-post across the lane in the back of the house where I now lived.

"Goodness knows if her mother will ever come back," I heard the people who befriended me say.

The day Kharkov was recaptured by the Reds, my mother walked into the house.

Breathlessly she told her story: "Twenty-five of us, all Bolsheviks, were rounded up the same night. We were held in a shed for about two days. There followed a brief trial. We were sentenced to be hanged by General Denikin's staff, with 'sixty ramrod blows to be delivered before death.'"The hanging started at dusk, which sets in abruptly in the Ukraine. And it was a pitch-black night, as only Ukrainian nights can be. The condemned Bolsheviks sat huddled behind a knoll, on the outskirts of the city, where a gallows had been erected. Crouching behind a bush, she watched her comrades, one by one, being led to their death. She was the last, and when her turn came Denikin's soldiers had forgotten about her. Afraid to stir, even to breathe, she remained sitting in the grass until dawn and only then made her way into the woods.

I could not believe that the woman muffled in a dark, bedraggled shawl over a long, frayed trench coat was my mother. She looked old and haggard. Her nose seemed to have grown longer, her lips thinner; the eyes had sunk deep into their sockets.

No, this was an imposter! I darted out of the house and ran blindly through the streets. My mother's friend went after me and brought me home. A few nights later I watched my mother undress. The fresh welts of the blows dealt her by Denikin's thugs stared reproachfully at me from across her shoulders and, when she turned to face me, from her smooth white breasts.

By the end of 1920 the Civil War was, in the main, over. It ended in victory for the communist forces. But the utter collapse of the economy resulted in many years of hunger and deprivation, which took an enormous toll of the population, especially children. My own hungry childhood in the Ukraine during and after the Civil War is still vivid in my memory.

The thawing snow gleamed mysteriously at me and the wind blew in warm gusts. Famine stalked the city, mocking the festoons of bright lights in the windows of newly opened confectionery shops. Dumfounded, I stared at layer upon layer of creamy pastry and snow-white icing tapering to a pyramid adorned with rosettes and chocolate figures. Private enterprise was encouraged in 1921. Most of the new commercial ventures were started and patronized by resourceful profiteers.

Only a block away from the confectionery the winter twilight illuminated a dead boy, a few years older than myself. He lay propped against a fence, body swollen out of all proportion. His grimy trousers had slit open under the torn quilted jacket, uncovering his bloated belly and blue-veined genitals with stiff frozen hairs around them.

As I ran from the sight, the words of a neighbor, addressed to my mother only the day before, rang in my ears: "People are dying like flies, mostly children. If the bodies are not cleared away quickly, we're in for an epidemic in the spring."

My mother gave a shrug. She looked pale and worried.

I was drawn aside by the same neighbor two months later.

"You have a little brother," she told me in a half-whisper. "He was born prematurely. Goodness knows if he is going to live."

I was surprised. I did not see any connection between the grave-looking stranger who had been a frequent visitor at our home during the past year and the birth of my brother. Nor had I noticed any change in my mother's appearance. If anything, she had grown thinner, smoked more; at times I caught an apprehensive look in her eyes. I was very sensitive to my mother's moods and had a dozen tricks to lighten them. But of late nothing had worked; she remained troubled and withdrawn. I longed for her to confide in me, but she rarely did. Throughout her life she was extremely reticent, in fact far too proud to discuss her personal affairs with anyone.

Well ahead of time for visiting hours, I started out for the hospital. It was early May. The cobblestone sidewalks sparkled with sunlight. On my way I took a peek into an open bakery. There twinkling at me were buns and rolls of all shapes—glossy, sugar-coated, with golden crusts down the middle. They were not for us. We could never afford the sky-high prices of the few privately owned shops, spawn of the New Economic Policy, introduced by Lenin to spur economic recovery.

As I stood inhaling the heavenly smells, the portly Armenian who owned the bakery poked out his head, with a face as rosy and shiny as the nicest of the buns. A pleasant face, wreathed in smiles and billows of fat.

"Come on in, little girl," he said.

Timidly I crossed the threshold. Pride restrained me from ever showing that I was hungry, and now, to conceal how I ached for the rolls, I put on an air of indifference, trying to keep my eyes averted from the counters. The proprietor dug his hand into a mountain of rolls. His long meaty nose, huge ears, and tremendous midriff made him resemble a good-natured elephant. With a gracious smile and a wink of one dark eye, he held out a most appetizing golden bun.

"Take it, pretty child." He thrust it into my hand.

I thanked him in a voice I tried to keep even, and in a happy trance trotted out of the bakery. How tempted I was to take a bite of the roll. But I knew that even if it burned a hole in my hand I would not touch it.

My mother looked very pale and raised her head with difficulty from the gray pillow. There were five other patients in the ward and a strong odor of carbolic acid. I handed the roll to her. She could not have been more astonished if I had brought her a baby kangaroo. I smiled when she asked how I had come by it and begged her to eat it.

She broke off a tiny piece from the top crust, then from the whole. A few crumbs dropped into her hand; she picked them up one by one, and ate them slowly, watering them with her tears.

My brother Shurri and I grew up to be loving companions, with many views and tastes in common. But in the days following my mother's return from the maternity hospital this illegitimate child aroused a good deal of snickering among the neighbors. There were taunts and insinuations.

Who is his father? Has he turned up? Not daring to pose these questions to my aloof mother, they tried to pry the answers out of me.

Shurri's father! One day, shortly after my little brother's birth, he arrived with a valise. But a quarrel ensued, what about I do not know. My mother showed him the door. He left, never again to reappear in our lives. Years afterwards I noted the resemblance between my brother's eyes, the most beautiful in the world to me—velvety, almond-shaped, with sweeping dark lashes—and the eyes of my mother's lover who inspired me with jealousy and unreasonable hatred.

Kharkov was full of homeless, starving children who turned to thievery. Teenage prostitution was rife owing to the appearance of the new rich after free enterprise became a temporary feature of Soviet reality. My mother was pained, shocked, deeply concerned.

The cold weather had come to stay, and our stove was once again filling the room with its acrid fumes. There was little to eat but millet gruel, which yellowed our complexions, the rare bit of bread, rarer still sugar.

A friend pleaded with my mother: "You hold an important post—demand a ration, or you'll lose your children!"

"Why should my children be treated any different from others?" Lamely she added: "Everybody is starving."

After work she would pick up waifs and young prostitutes off the streets and bring them into our tiny quarters. Then she would spend much of her energy finding homes for them or getting them accepted into one of the communes for juvenile delinquents that were springing up in the country.

"You care for others more than for your own flesh and blood" was an accusation frequently hurled at my mother.

"But that is the essence of being a communist," she would argue.

Indeed, throughout her life she was so eager to help others that the needs of her immediate family rarely came first.

One evening she arrived with a beautiful young girl, heavily rouged, eyes outlined with charcoal, wearing a fur coat that was falling apart in shreds. She slept that night on our floor and woke up the next morning with a high fever. All day she tossed about and was delirious.

My mother went for a doctor. "Typhus again," he lamented.

Two weeks later my mother herself landed in a typhus ward where she stayed for almost two months, fighting for her life.

Typically Russian in their generosity, the very neighbors who had taunted me about the birth of my brother, and who had far more contempt than love for my impractical mother, turned from critics into saints. They saw me and Shurri through the difficult period while my mother was away. They cooked better food for us than my mother—how they obtained it in a time of famine I cannot tell—nursed Shurri, cleaned, and even managed to repair our stove so that it rarely smoked.

My mother came home from the hospital greatly weakened, wearing a kerchief to conceal her shorn head.

The neighbors reproached her: "Almost five years since the revolution and there is no end to our sufferings." "We must not lose our faith in communism," she would reply. "We need to be patient. Living conditions will improve."

She sincerely believed what she said. But patience is rarely a virtue of the headstrong, pipe-dreaming revolutionary.

III Travels

The decision my mother took to uproot herself and leave Soviet Russia, for a time or for good, cannot have been made lightly. It must have weighed heavily on her heart.

In the early twenties there were a number of people who took this course. They continued to support the new regime, but they preferred to live abroad. Some may have harbored minor grievances. Others saw the rise of unpleasant forces like the New Economic Policy, which was bringing to the forefront a fresh brand of bourgeoisie, or the terror unleashed by the Cheka, and perhaps felt intuitively that the ideals for which they had languished in tsarist prisons, as my mother had, and sacrificed so much—my father, his life—were being shortchanged and steered away from their original humanitarian intent.

My father's family were urging my mother to visit them, even to settle in Canada. The Commissariat for Foreign Trade, for which she worked, agreed to send her on a mission to Berlin and Paris. Anguished no doubt by the long separation from her older children, she must have clutched at this rare opportunity to see them, an opportunity, given the isolation of Russia, that might not present itself again.

Her attempts to procure a Polish visa so that she could visit Warsaw, where my half-brother lived with her parents, came to nothing. She arranged to meet her sister Augusta in Danzig, begging her to bring him with her. She was greatly distressed when her sister arrived alone.

Eager to meet the mother he hardly remembered and fearing that his aunt might not take him along, he had left early and tramped all the way from Warsaw to Danzig, arriving in that city hungry, footsore, and moneyless after we had boarded a train for Paris and Aunt Augusta was off home.

In Paris, luckily, the meeting went off smoothly with my half-sister Annette, who had the most gentle brown eyes, longlashed like Shurri's, and lived in a bright clean flat with her young husband. Shortly before our departure from France my mother took us both to a cozy restaurant for a farewell dinner. They chatted gaily, their eyes sparkled, and their faces were flushed from the garnet wine rarely absent from the tables of the eating-places we frequented in Paris.

But beneath the light-hearted chatter I sensed a growing sadness, perhaps caused by a shared presentiment that we might not meet again—and we never did. At the time we took leave of Annette, the pernicious idea of covering the territory of Europe with extermination camps—in one of which, twenty years later, Annette's only child, a boy of thirteen, would be gassed to death—was only half-maturing. Our faces therefore were but slightly clouded. We were smiling. My mother, I could see, was glad and relieved to know that Annette was comfortably settled in life.

THREE

I Canada

On a misty autumn morning our ship sailed into Halifax; from there we journeyed by train to Montreal, where we were met at Windsor Station by my Aunt Lily. She gave a start and opened her eyes wide at the sight of the child in my mother's arms.

There followed an awkward moment. My mother resented prying into her personal life. Moreover, she despised philistine attitudes to children born out of wedlock. In her letters to my grandparents there had never been a word about Shurri. Squaring her shoulders, she jerked a finger in my direction: "This is your brother's little girl." Clearly she was not going to offer explanations.

When I first saw my grandmother she looked like a queen compared to the wizened, wrinkled old grannies I knew in Russia, the few who had survived the revolution, Civil War, and famine.

Framed in the doorway stood my grandfather, a towering figure. He wore a long black robe of shiny material, from under the hem of which peered out the pointed toes of his shining black boots. His great height, the unbelievable length of his straight nose, the end of it almost touching his full upper lip, and his strangely asymmetrical eyes singled him out as a man who resembled nobody I had ever seen.

Afterwards, on being told he was a learned man, a scholar, I had a vision in my childish mind of him sitting at a huge desk and constantly pulling at his nose, which made it grow longer and longer. From the nostrils blew vapors that formed into thoughts, and these he recorded in his big golden book with a quill pen—which he indeed used. My grandfather inspired me with mingled feelings of awe and curiosity.

Lacking the courage to address him directly, I often asked Mother questions about him. She rarely answered, though once it broke from her: "He is a religious fanatic!"

Everything was done in my grandparents' Montreal home to make me feel happy and loved. But one thing was definitely missing. There was no effort to arrive at any sort of an "ideological" understanding and compromise with my mother.

She never concealed that she was a communist; rather, she constantly reminded people of it. It was not hard, therefore, to guess that a confrontation between my religious grandfather and my defiantly irreligious mother was on the cards. When it did occur, it ended in a complete break between her and my father's family.

Some time before this break, however, my grandparents seemed keen on finding a husband for my mother. She was still an attractive woman, having retained her great vivacity, proud bearing, and smooth white skin. But she scoffed at their plans. A marriage of convenience was repugnant to her.

In the background hovered one persistent suitor, a corpulent Englishman whose profession frequently took him away from Montreal. He wrote my mother long epistles, signing them, "Chartered Accountant, Graduate of Cambridge." In all weather he wore a raincoat and carried an umbrella and cane along with his satchel. On leaving he would bow himself out of my mother's presence with brisk backward steps, as though she were royalty.

"What? Marry a man just so he could support me and my children? Never!" my mother repeated proudly.

Her pride and independence were not rooted in egotism, but rather in the perpetual need to reaffirm the free woman in herself. She gave much of her time to spreading among her women friends what she considered to be the most advanced views on sex.

On Sunday afternoons she would read to them, translating at sight, chapters from Madame Kollontai's *Red Love* and Pantelei Romanov's *Without the Birdcherry*, interspersing her reading with comments on the revolutionary "glass of water" theory as opposed to the institution of marriage: having sex should be as simple as downing a glass of water.

With my mother's mind elsewhere—in the higher sphere, so to speak—ours was a very neglected home. The things that least interested my mother were cooking and housework. When she could afford it she engaged a maid or cleaning woman. But most of the time we ate cold meals; dust and cobwebs collected on the furniture and in all the corners, without our even noticing them. Not until I was much older did I realize that floors needed frequent sweeping, and furniture dusting.

What my mother most missed in Canada was a position in which she could make use of her professional training. It was not to be had. With no money and two children to support, her job hunt ended in her taking work in the needle trade in sheer desperation. This was a crushing blow to her self-esteem as an educated woman who spoke both English and French fairly well and had a diploma from the Sorbonne and also from the Kharkov College of Civil Railway Engineering.

At some point in her search, she applied for a post with the Canadian Pacific Railway Company. She was happy when sporadic assignments from that company came her way. Often she sat up all night over a folio of blueprints and next morning sang and smiled as she prepared our breakfast.

My mother was a splendid speaker, with a strong, well-modulated voice that carried to the last seat in a large auditorium. I often heard her address meetings both in the Soviet Union and in Montreal. She possessed a phenomenal memory and could recite long poems by heart in many different languages. Two of her great favorites were Mickiewicz and Lermontov. On Sunday mornings she would recite works from these poets as she did the laundry, scrubbing the clothes on the washboard to the rhythm of the verse and pausing to smoke her home-stuffed cigarettes in a long ebony holder.

I believe we were both of a strangely romantic frame of mind. I often pondered on how empty and commonplace our life in Canada was in contrast to the dramatic happenings of my Russian childhood. My mother, too, must have felt a spiritual void, which she filled by becoming ever more active in the Canadian Communist Party.

During one of our first summers in Canada my mother sent me and Shurri to a Catholic convent. It rained a great deal that summer, and I still remember the afternoon naps in the damp rooms, bare, uninviting, with stone floors and hard wooden boards to sleep on. There were no toys to play with. The life was Spartan, but the convent's atmosphere was one of kindness, tolerance, and understanding of children's feelings, with no gimmicks, no "fun," no comfort to detract from it—an atmosphere not so much of religion as of the spirit.

My brother and I were not requested to participate in the religious services or scriptural readings, out of respect for my mother's different views. Apparently we all came from poor families or broken homes. The meals served to us were frugal and the whole institution smelled of poverty. But somehow the lack of externals, the stark, massive walls within which we rested or slept in the afternoon and had our meals, the orderliness of our existence, the green grounds and the sky overhead, combined with our simple, unplanned pastimes, were conducive to thought and reflection.

The peace and serenity of the convent were in striking contrast to the uninhibited, boisterous play that went on in the streets and yards of Montreal. My mother was away for most of the day. Unable to resist the temptation of going outdoors, I would lock Shurri up in our mouse-infested toilet and dash out into the yard for as long as I could. As captain of a gang of wild kids, mostly boys, and with the skirmishes I had witnessed as a child in the Civil War vivid in my memory, I would get them to lie in ambush, waiting for the appearance of the "enemy" to make sudden sallies into their "territory."

And now a change came over me. A calm elation possessed me. There were times when I wanted to be more alone with myself, with my thoughts, longing to devote myself to some romantic ideal. The pugilistic phase was over. I abdicated my captaincy, often not even answering the doorbell when former playmates called.

My Canadian peers were too flighty and mindless for my taste. They had not the slightest interest in the problems that fascinated me. None of them had heard of Spartacus, my great hero; the name Lenin meant nothing to them. And when I held forth on the Russian Revolution, of which after all I had firsthand knowledge, they ran off to play baseball or read the comics. I succeeded in summoning a more sympathetic audience when I acted out scenes from Russia's past. Perversely enough, instead of impersonating revolutionaries, I made up little sketches about the royal families and, draped in old curtains, cast myself as a princess. My young spectators nicknamed me "Russian princess," which, surprisingly, I did not take as an insult.

Poor as we were, there were always plenty of books in our house or to be borrowed from the lending library. I recall one summer devoted solely to the French authors. I read them in alphabetical order; from Balzac and Daudet I went all the way to Voltaire, rounding off the season with Zola. I was intoxicated with the philosophical discourses in Anatole France. *Thaïs* supported me in the atheism ingrained by my mother. The line "Nothing is true except life on earth and carnal love" became a motto to me, although I had not the faintest idea what carnal love meant.

Victor Hugo's *Les Misérables* and the works of Charles Dickens made me ponder the misery of the world. I discussed the books I read with my mother, who blamed the capitalist system for all social ills. I was firmly convinced that once capitalism was overthrown, the world would be a true paradise.

To work for the overthrow of capitalism I joined the Young Pioneers and later was graduated to the Young Communist League. How seriously I took my membership in the League!

Studies of communism made life more purposeful, and I am thankful for the stimulation I received from them. But it was often in parrot-like fashion that I reeled off the communist stock phrases; on many issues, especially those concerning literature, I was greatly confused.

I recall a discussion about Shakespeare's place in literature I had with Irving Layton, who later became one of Canada's leading poets. I repeated the current communist view expounded by left-wing critics: that Shakespeare embodied the pessimism and collapse of the feudal system. At first somewhat stunned by my words, Irving soon saw how absurd they were.

"What about the exuberance and optimism of Shakespeare's comedies?" he parried.

Many figures in literature were branded "bourgeois" in Soviet Russia, among them the poets Pushkin and Lermontov. If these two freedom-loving bards were mostly seen as the exponents of bourgeois ideology, why should Shakespeare have fared any better? (Later such views were dropped and qualified as "vulgarization" of the literary heritage.)

From the age of about fourteen, most likely because of my good command of English and resonant voice, I was assigned to speak in front of large groups of workers. One of my audiences was the workers at Montreal's Northern Electric Plant. They were men well past their youth, and from their accents, good figures, and easy, pleasant manner I judged them to be Anglo-Saxons. I saw few French Canadians at the big industrial plants, and still fewer immigrants.

I would saunter into the factory yard during the meal break. With their lunch boxes and milk bottles on their laps, the workers sat on crates or logs. They welcomed the diversion of a young girl getting up to speak and telling them to unite against their bosses.

Knowing nothing of their conditions or grievances, I had three subjects to choose from: the international situation, the doom of capitalist society—"the capitalists are digging their own grave, imperialism sounds the death knell of capitalism"—and China, the latter being the most topical and the one with which I felt most at home. I would climb on top of a crate and from all sides came the greeting: "Hello, Rosie, how is China getting on?"

"Rosie" because of my pink cheeks, I was a plump, well-fed high-school girl talking to these seasoned workers about the downtrodden masses of China with the cocky assurance of ignorant youth. They listened with amusement, grinning and joking.

When the time of Depression and lay-offs set in, nobody grinned. Nor were the workers in any mood to listen to speeches—they wanted jobs. I brimmed with new hope. It was good to be a communist. I imagined I already heard the death rattle of capitalism, and that revolution in Canada was just around the corner.

II Irving

Most of the friends I made I tried to convert to communism and draw into the League. Among them was Irving, a tousled, bright-eyed boy with a jutting chin and a firm, generous mouth. When it came to political arguments, I met more than my match in him. We both enjoyed arguing immensely.

I first saw Irving when I was nine years old. Not being able to afford help, my working mother kept me away from school for a whole year to mind my little brother. One rainy morning I was keeping Shurri amused when the doorbell rang and a delivery boy came in, wheeling groceries on a small platform cart with a long handle. Irving was about twelve, and there was a haughty air about him that told me he hated his dull job no less than I resented being turned into a nanny, rather than learning at school and playing with my peers. My gaze caught the intensity in his deep azure eyes and for long afterwards I was haunted by it.

We did not meet again until a few years later, when we were both students at Montreal's Baron Byng High School.

Irving and I would often spend our evenings arguing about politics at Horn's Cafeteria on St. Lawrence Street over a single five-cent cup of coffee. There were times when I did not wish to be seen in his company because he was on the other side of the fence, so to speak, and my comrades, particularly the "leaders," regarded the relationship with disapproval. But Irving and I were in love.

Irving's sympathies lay with the socialists rather than the communists. Loud fulmination against the Second International was as much part of the life of the Canadian Communist Party and Young Communist League as it was of the communist movement all over the world.

But now there was a sudden change of directive from the Party. Members of the Young Communist League were instructed to penetrate the socialist ranks and try to wean the youth away. I was chosen to "infiltrate" the Young People's Socialist League in Montreal, whose meetings were often chaired by David Lewis, destined later to become a prominent Canadian politician. In a British accent I admired greatly, he would tell his audience that "the workers need to be educated before they take power and are able to rule."

What gibberish, I thought, education for the workers will be made possible only with a dictatorship of the proletariat, which will create economic conditions favorable enough for the common people to fill the universities. The dictatorship of the proletariat, with Stalin and men of his ilk at its head! How was I to know that only a decade or two later I would see with my own eyes thousands of wonderful people, among them my own family, crushed like insects beneath its heel?

On my birthday Irving gave me a volume of Shaw's plays and H.G. Wells' *Outline of History*. These two writers were our mentors. We were romantics, we hoped for a better world. Enchanted by his humanitarian views and faith in science, with Wells we believed that national and racial feelings would gradually vanish and that the world was heading for a single language, for harmony, understanding, and peace. These were the illusions we labored under in the early part of the century, when we would have done better to accept Lenin's appraisal of the times we lived in as "the age of wars and revolutions."

An English company was presenting *The Apple Cart* in Montreal and, knowing my admiration for Shaw, Irving bought tickets for the play. Years afterwards I found Shaw's mockeries distasteful; moreover, had he and other eminent men of letters been less supportive of Stalin, perhaps millions of lives might have been spared. But in my youth I was one of his votaries. To see a play by Shaw was a real treat, and I enjoyed every minute of it—except that my own behavior, which later gave me food for thought, cast a shadow on the evening. Not even the box of chocolates Irving produced could ease my mood.

The band struck up the tune of "God Save the King." Everybody rose; I alone sat through the entire anthem, despite hostile stares from the people around me. Later, on probing my motives, I saw that I had succumbed to a kind of childish exhibitionism. I knew then that I would not gain sympathy for my cause but would repel people from it. The idea of paying blind homage to a sovereign or a political leader has always been repugnant to me, but to show my feelings in this vulgar manner seemed equally unworthy.

Yet I had the choice. I sat through the entire anthem without any fear of consequences. Later, in Moscow, how I would have liked not to suffer the indignity of being forced to jump to my feet, as everybody did, and applaud each time the name of Stalin, or some subsequent wise father of the nation, was mentioned.

During my youth in Canada I was articulate; I had no inhibitions, no fears about voicing my thoughts. Irving and I would talk our heads off about literature, politics, and philosophy, though when it came to communism we quarrelled bitterly. I gave him a copy of Bogdanov's *ABC of Communism*, and after reading it he challenged the ideas that were so deeply ingrained in my heart. I remember my association with Irving best for our unrestrained exchange of thought, the clash and stimulation of our two minds, and also for his warmth and tolerance as opposed to my own antagonism and bigotry.

What marked my later love life was a constant suppression of thought. Neither I nor the partner to whom I gave my love dared to trust one another with our thoughts. Strangely, so strangely, there was always between us, even in the bed we shared, the shadow of the prying state security—the all-seeing eye and the all-hearing ear, as Pushkin even in his time called the secret police.

The tiny room Irving rented in downtown Montreal had a small bookcase; books were piled high on the table, too, and spilling out on the bed. He bought them second-hand with the money earned by private tutoring. From the age of fourteen I also was able to earn a little money by teaching English to immigrants. Always generous, even in those poverty-stricken days, Irving gave me richly bound books as gifts, each with a new poem of his on the front page. I took these books to Moscow, but when I was hard up I sold them to a second-hand dealer, long before my childhood friend began to publish his poetry.

After our fill of arguing at Horn's Cafeteria, we would round off the evening by taking a long walk in the somber little streets that ended abruptly in a steep mountain slope. Behind tall forbidding fences stood the villas of the rich. The rich! They will be expropriated—both Irving and I agreed on that measure. Neither a socialist nor a Bolshevik government could tolerate such indecent class distinctions. But years later I was to see even taller and more massive fences in Moscow, one close to Lenin Hills, my own neighborhood, others in Kislovodsk, Sukhumi, Sochi, Yalta, and in hosts of other places, owned by Stalin, Beria, and their many underlings; they are

still in existence today, with the same fences, armed men guarding
the gates, big shepherd dogs lurking behind.

Moonlight silvered the shadows and illumined the fluffy crown of
a lilac tree. Irving climbed the spiked fence, helped himself to the
flowers and, jumping down, handed me a huge bouquet, looking
like a knight out of a fairy tale.

Back in the downtown section of Montreal, I noticed in the street
light that he had a big tear in the seat of his trousers, possibly the
only pair he owned. On my doorstep he blurted out that he was
famished. He had not eaten anything that day and had no money.
We too were so hard up that I knew there was little food in the house.
If I were to take the last morsel and give it to my starving sweetheart,
I would have to face my stern mother and listen to a cascade of
reproaches.

Shamefacedly, angry at myself and at him for the dilemma thrust
on me, I turned away and quickly vanished into the house. I felt
terrible. A beautiful day was wrecked—because we were so poor.
Because of our economic state, I thought bitterly, I was forced to deny
food to a dear person. Would he forgive me?

Next morning Irving came to see me as though nothing had happened. He possessed that breadth of heart and mind from which
trifling things were hastily dismissed. And that endeared him to me
more than any other characteristic.

I owe much to Irving Layton. Through him I was able to see far
beyond the world of communist ideas in which I lived. Methodically
expanding his knowledge of English, he imbued me with his love of
language. Even in those years, at the dawn of his poetic ambitions,
he was never in the clouds, as were my mother and myself; like
Antaeus he drew his strength from the earth, and was opening himself up to the realities of living. Happily our romantic love ended as
it did, and Irving, much as he desired to at the time, did not follow
me into the unknown in the socialist land. If he had, he would have
surely ended his life in a Siberian prison camp, and Canada would
never have heard of him.

III Uprooted

After distributing communist leaflets one day I found myself in the
detention room of the local police station. Into the gloomy cell, with
its porous cement floor, young girls and women were being shoved
in one after another. From their appearance I could easily guess who
they were: the police had raided a section of Montreal's notorious

red-light district, close to the harbor. The arrested women kept to themselves; I was too shy to talk to them.

Mugs of murky, sugarless tea and thick square slices of well-buttered, though stale, white bread were handed out. I did not have to touch the prison fare, because my comrades brought me appetizing pie, hot coffee, and chocolate bars. I was not insulted or manhandled. When I look back at it, by comparison with my later experiences the entire arrest was more in the nature of a picnic. Almost immediately I was released on bail, and when I appeared before a judge at the Juvenile Recorder's Court the case was dismissed. It was all a trivial affair, and I would not have given it a thought had it not had repercussions.

With a presentiment of trouble, I went back to classes the next morning. I learned that I had been expelled from Baron Byng High School. I was upset mostly because I knew my mother had sent me to that school, not a commercial high, in the hope that I would go to college. How my impractical mother imagined she would be able to pay the tuition fees was anybody's guess.

My expulsion was a shock to her. Partly she must have felt that she herself was to blame. She had brought me into the communist movement, was proud of my activities, and never chided me for neglecting my school work. She now betook herself to Mr. Astbury, the principal, and pleaded with him to have me reinstated.

Mr. Astbury wanted my mother to assure him that I was not likely to get myself arrested again—in other words, that I would cease to be an active member of the Canadian Young Communist League. This she did, though she knew it to be an empty promise. Much as I loved her, I was furious: she had acted without the Party's blessing, thinking only of our personal interests. Her conduct gave me a sense of guilt. Nothing was more important to me than to meet the Party's expectations. The lofty principles of communism—how dear they were!

My case was brought up at the Board of Education and in a few days I was reinstated. Mr. Astbury called me into his office, assuring me that the teachers were well disposed towards me and pleased with my progress. This was a surprise, because truancy had become part of my life. I continued to skip lessons.

Over the years I have often thought of what I learned from my Baron Byng teachers, most of whom were Englishwomen. There is much good to be said for Soviet education. But had I had Soviet teachers who were obligated to inculcate in their students worship and total acceptance of Stalin's "wisdom," I would have resisted, inwardly of course, this imposition on my mind. I could never have become reconciled to the blind adulation of the leader, the "genius of mankind," as Stalin was called.

I remember the way my Latin teacher, whom I adored, would by little tricks of her own make us see the weakness of a Caesar, a religious dogma, or the prevailing system of values. She would flip up an American coin and with a sardonic grimace say to the class, "In God we trust—for cash." That kind of healthy skepticism was communicated to us. Yet when she said, "Do others or they'll do you!" by her very irony she succeeded, I think, in showing the nobility of the Christian maxim. Similarly, the excerpts of English prose and poetry we discussed with our literature teacher were designed to show us the fallibility of men, the magnitude and diversity of life itself.

Many choices that were crucial to keeping my self-respect as a human being, when it could have been trampled, lay ahead of me. Somehow I owe it to those two teachers, whose names I do not even remember, as well as to the great prophets and moralists of world literature, that I have refrained from adopting courses of action I would have recalled with shame today.

On the other hand, I was never in an extreme situation that would have forced me to commit an ignominious action. I did not stand ankle-deep in water in a small cell with hungry rats around me, as did an elderly fellow prisoner of mine at Lubyanka. Nor was a loaded gun pointed by a Gestapo officer at the temple of a child of mine, as happened to Roslyakova and her little boy during the Nazi occupation of Kiev. This mother of three slept next to me in a prison shed; the officer had threatened to shoot her son if she did not sign a pledge to cooperate with the Gestapo.

I was back at school, but my political life took precedence over my studies. I was arrested again during an anti-fascist demonstration and then a third time, which meant farewell to my education.

We were quite destitute after my mother lost her job during the Depression. But no matter how poor we were, she would never forego her subscription to *Pravda*, which arrived regularly at our home in Montreal. Often she translated to me articles describing Russia's achievements. To us the Soviet Union was a land of justice and equality, if not exactly milk and honey—in any event, of jobs for all who cared to work. My mother believed every word she read.

Canadian newspapers carried headlines of "Forced Labour in Russia," which my mother and other communists pooh-poohed as shameful fabrications. Yet among the small trickle of immigrants from

Russia arriving in Canada my mother ran into a woman from Kharkov, who told her that collectivization had resulted in the deaths, arrests, and deportations of thousands of hard-working peasants who were not kulaks. There was hunger in all parts of the country, and the people with jobs had less to eat than the unemployed in Canada.

My mother must have realized, as I did, that some of the reports in the Canadian press and the accounts of new immigrants from the Soviet Union were not groundless. But being devoted communists we would not admit it, or rather we knew we must not.

Yet in my own mind I was troubled by the rigidity that prevailed in the communist movement in Canada and the acceptance of all acts by the Soviet Union as infallible. I remember a doubt creeping into my mind following a conversation with a Young Communist League leader who had just returned from training at the Lenin School of Moscow. To many of my questions about life in the Soviet Union he avoided giving direct answers. His candid, broad-featured face grew clouded. I sensed that this comrade, whom I believed to be honest, preferred to leave many things unsaid.

Meanwhile a new idea on the further course of communist activities was brewing in my mother's mind. The conclusion she arrived at raised many an eyebrow among her comrades. She now believed, and was quite outspoken about it, that communists the world over, instead of putting so much effort into the futile struggle to gain power in their own lands, would do better to help build socialism in the Soviet Union, which could then become an example to the rest of the world of a flourishing new society. She was convinced of the validity of her view, but the leadership of the Canadian Communist Party was not and warned her to abandon it.

The warning came too late. My mother was in the midst of organizing a group of immigrant Canadians, mostly Ukrainians and Russians, ready to leave Canada and make their home in the Soviet Union. This was in 1931, at the height of the Depression; at that time many workers were driven to seek jobs in the Soviet Union, unemployment in their own countries being as much a motive for them as sympathy for communism. The group consisted of about forty people and their children. Unwilling to go to the socialist land empty-handed, they pooled their meager savings to buy agricultural machinery as a gift.

The Montreal group was following in the footsteps of Ukrainian immigrants from Canada who had gone back to their homeland in the early twenties and taken machinery with them. Settling on the

fertile soil northwest of Odessa, they had founded the Lenin Commune, where the new enthusiasts from Canada hoped to join them.
The entire repatriation scheme proved a disastrous undertaking.

On me it descended like a bolt from the blue; not until a few days
before our departure did I learn of my mother's decision. I regarded
Canada as my homeland. I did not want to be uprooted. At the same
time, I supported the criticism the Party directed at my mother. One's
loyalty was first and foremost to the Party—one of the inhuman twists
that went with fighting for a cause. I wrote a letter to Party leader
Tim Buck: "Canadian communists should be concerned with the
struggle in their own country and not abandon it . . ." I appealed to
him for advice. He never replied.

My legal status as a minor (I was only turning sixteen), combined
with my love for my mother and brother, left me without a choice.
My mother, unlike myself, was happy. She was going back to her
communist country. She was certain an education for her children
was assured there, and the future looked bright. Moreover, she had
nothing to lose. Canada had treated her shabbily.

From New York, where at the Amtorg she arranged for the purchase of the machinery, my mother brought back clothes we needed
badly. Among her buys was a pale green woollen spring coat with
a squirrel collar, now the only coat I possessed. Her own capacious
Persian lamb coat, bought ages ago in Europe, she refused to pack.
It would look too "bourgeois," she claimed, in a land where all were
"equally rich or poor." Both of us would freeze in the long severe
winters to come.

The night before we departed from Montreal I lay awake with a
strange premonition of disaster, weeping hysterically into my pillow.
The good cry relieved my tensions. In the morning I felt a different
person.

Once aboard the ocean liner I gave myself up to happier reflections.
I thrilled to the toil of the billows, making me feel an expansion of
self into the universe. I mused upon the future: I must live with an
overpowering intensity of feeling, thinking, loving, doing. With
these thoughts, foolish, vain, naive, I was leaving my girlhood
behind me, in Canada.

As we sailed into the ports of northern Europe my mood of exhil-
aration faded away. Copenhagen was a cemetery of ships, a sinister
reminder of the Depression. Our vessel stood at anchor. No motion,
no joy. The city crouched in the lap of idleness.

Baltic ports presented an even sorrier sight, teeming with embittered people. Hundreds of men, women, and children had swarmed
into the harbor to beg for food. Apparently every time an ocean liner

docked it was met by the city's destitute inhabitants.

Passengers were soon pitching oranges, bread, and other eatables to the throngs below. But much that was tossed down was caught in the air by the no less famished seagulls. People on deck now wrapped up the food in neat packages with weights strung to them before dropping it down. There was far from enough for everybody. I fled to our cabin. The lunch gong sounded. In the dining-rooms the tables were laden with rich foods. I almost cried.

Sentences from Lenin and Marx condemning the capitalist system raced through my mind. Economic crises, unemployment, the impoverishment of the working-class—yes, these two great men had foreseen it all! A socialist society alone, I told myself, held out the promise of equality, of enough food and clothes for all. Had not Lenin said that under communism we would line the toilet bowls with gold? Spiritual values would take precedence over material greed. Unfettered man, proud man, intellectual man! Thus Marx, Lenin, Maxim Gorky had referred to man under socialism. A thrill ran through me. I was going to the land of socialism; I would be a zealous builder of the new society.

Such were my thoughts as our boat docked at Helsingfors, on a sunny day in late June. The city's thick-walled, craggy buildings shone with amber. In between sightseeing excursions we took refuge from the hissing north wind in the little coffeehouses at the top of the flagstone stairs descending to the waters of the Gulf of Finland.

My escort was a Finn, one of the ship's passengers. The color of his eyes, skin, and hair blended into a rugged gun-metal handsomeness. His sister had come to meet him at the pier, and throughout the day she was my chaperone; in the puritan Finland of the early thirties it was improper for a young girl to be seen alone in male company. In the streets of the Finnish capital I noticed how attractive the men were with their muted coloring and reserved manner. But the women, their calves encased in lisle stockings, their muscular shoulders broader than their hips, looked undesirable, more fit for hard work than sex.

An overnight train was taking us to Leningrad, with a stop at Belo-ostrov, the border point. The trimly buckled Finnish guard who examined our papers eyed me with more than mild surprise. In sign language he conveyed to me that I would find life no picnic on the other side. He drew himself up with that arrogance the Finns were destined to shed after the Second World War and pointed an accusing finger at the territory of the Soviet Union. His eyes became cold and hostile.

FOUR

I I am in a socialist state

We poured out of the train and set foot on Soviet soil. The Russian border guards, gawky country lads, smiled a broad welcome. They were guileless, the soul of hospitality—a far cry from the haughty, dour-faced, suspicious guards I was to encounter decades later on a train from Cologne to Moscow. It was the road traversed by Soviet officials, minor and major: from lowly peasant to arrogant urbanite.

Vasili K., a squat young man with a more refined cut of features than the guards, welcomed our group at the Finlyandsky Railway Station. He was from the Leningrad City Executive Committee, assigned to look after our needs and show us around the fabled city. Vasili had the same gun-metal coloring as the handsome Finn from Helsingfors, but he was more tense, more withdrawn, and there was a hint of caprice and weakness about his mouth and chin. The clothes he wore were typical of the government officials of the period: an ill-cut dark gray tarpaulin coat, a khaki army tunic buttoned up to the top of its stand-up collar, breeches, and army boots. He also carried a bulky dispatch case, with which it seemed he never wanted to part. There was a tight-lipped, dead earnest expression about him, and he rarely smiled.

We were installed in a cheap hotel and given a hearty breakfast of savory freshly baked bread, rather soggy, and plenty of black caviar. The latter, I must say, is an excellent morale booster, putting one in just the right all-receptive, enthusiastic frame of mind to view the achievements of the world's first socialist state.

With no sign of approaching darkness, I could not drop off to sleep on my first night in Leningrad; I was very excited. The next night

Vasili pressed me to go for a walk with him. I had forgotten the Russian I knew as a child. But silence befitted the entrancing scene of a city draped in a violet haze, the stone and granite of its stately buildings melting into the dreamy twilight. It was the magic of the "white nights" of Dostoevsky.

When the time came to say goodbye—we were to board a train for the commune in the south of the Ukraine—Vasili claimed to be in love. I sensed that he was not in love with the real me, but with some romantic vision that his imagination had conjured up in its almost morbid pursuit of forbidden bourgeois beauty.

"I read about the love I now feel in novels, but did not think it could exist," he said.

Later I was to realize, sadly, that it was mainly my "different," non-Soviet appearance, and in a way behavior too, that constituted my attraction for the men I met in the thirties. But for them or me to utter such a thought aloud would have been heresy.

I told Vasili he would get over his love. I smiled. It was nonsense! *Chepukha!*

There was no nonsense about that love when, six weeks later, Vasili turned up at the commune. From there he followed us to Kharkov, where my mother had gone on commune business. He took the revolver he carried out of its holster, clamped the weapon down on the hotel-room table, and threatened to shoot himself if my mother refused to let me go alone with him to Leningrad. Realizing that he meant what he said, and scared out of her wits, she very reluctantly agreed, but not before making him promise that there could be no talk of marriage before I was of age. Our "affair" turned out to be purely platonic and altogether one-sided.

The early thirties were very hungry years. A return to the millet of my childhood did not dampen my enthusiasm for the new order, but it did affect my health, causing skin rashes, boils, and other minor troubles. I tried not to think of food. But I craved a juicy apple and had forgotten the taste of an orange.

For a while I lived at the Oktyabrskaya Hotel near the Moskovsky Railway Station—this was arranged or perhaps wangled by Vasili—and spent a good deal of my time studying Russian. I took lessons from a prim elderly lady who, like the tiny, cluttered room in which she lived on the Petrogradskaya Storona, breathed the mustiness of the old regime. Soon I was able to make myself understood pretty well, but it took another year or more before I acquired a good command of Russian.

I made a few friends, some of them members of the old Russian intelligentsia. The great luxury of the table then was herring and potatoes boiled in their jackets. I was struck by the elegance of the tableware. There were gold-rimmed blue teacups, old silver, plates with hand-painted copies of famous paintings and the monograms of renowned Russian families. Onto these ornate plates we dropped the shrivelled skins as we ate our small hot potatoes with relish, washing down the delicacies with vodka or red wine in massive, exquisitely designed crystal goblets—another legacy of the St. Petersburg aristocrats who had fled abroad.

Vasili had managed to get me a job as a translator at the Leningrad port administrative office, a job I was not doing well at because my written Russian was poor. The work itself was quite simple: translating bills of lading from English, German, and French into Russian. I came to know a few of the top port bureaucrats; some of them had called me into their office just to take a look at the *inostranka*, the foreign girl. Then one afternoon the head of the port administration sent for me.

It was lunch hour and I was quite famished when a deputy of his, a tall man with a satanic air about him, approached and whispered that "Comrade Bronstein" desired a word with me. "But it's lunch hour . . ." Hunger tugged at my insides. "Don't worry about that," he smiled mysteriously.

Glad to escape the tedious bills of lading, I climbed cheerfully up the steep steps that led to the top man's shrine, wondering what the summons was all about. I had never laid eyes on him. I knew only that he was Trotsky's brother.

A door padded in burgundy leather bore the bronze nameplate "Bronstein." I walked in and saw on my left another door. I knocked. A voice said "Come in!" Passing through an anteroom, I stepped into an opulent suite. It was like a corner of the Hermitage—embossed tables, malachite urns, settees and couches upholstered with costly colored brocade. Every piece was genuine, all were well matched. An added luxury were two polar-bear skins on the highly polished parquet floor.

The whole atmosphere was more of a love nest than of a business office. That was my first impression, but on second thought I concluded that perhaps it was an appropriate environment for striking deals with the captains of foreign merchant ships.

Awed by the surroundings, I paused for a few seconds before catching sight of a table in the shadows at the end of the room. It was covered with a snow-white cloth and laden with platters of jellied veal, cold turkey, juicy ham framed in fat, sliced pink sturgeon, and fruit in tall cut-glass bowls. Two bottles of Russian champagne reclined in silverplate ice-buckets.

With an unctuous smile my host came towards me. The moment I saw him I felt an aversion for this man and for everything the scene represented. Gross, with a huge midriff and rolls of fat spilling over the starched white collar onto the nape of his neck, he was no answer to a maiden's prayer. The lascivious gleam in his pale eyes made me tighten inside. He had a bulbous nose, and his pink skin looked powdered. But the domed forehead commanded attention, and later, at a meeting of the harbor employees, I would see the full, sensuous mouth clamp into a firm line.

His eyes softened as he approached me, and the lust in them changed to an expression of surprise when he realized my youth and innocence. Taking my cold hand into his, he held it for a while in the hollow of his plump palm. He moved a chair for me to sit down, peeled an orange, putting it gingerly on my plate, and hovered satyr-like over me. A last glimmer of the brief, wan autumn sunlight flitted across the room.

On a corner table stood a horn gramophone. He put on a record and the strains of a foxtrot floated in the air. With a gallant gesture I found repulsive, my host invited me to dance. Not to seem rude, I went along. What a mockery the scene was! The overfed high executive taking time off his work to indulge his low pleasures, the table laden with rare, exotic foods, when people all over the land were starving.

The atmosphere of *après moi le déluge* shocked me. I said I must go, leaving practically untouched the food he had put on my plate. He escorted me to the door, to my relief pressing no advances, and cordially enough bade me goodbye.

The fate that shortly afterwards befell Trotsky's brother is well known. Had he any premonition of his end? Perhaps he did. Perhaps, too, like so many others in his position, he wished to indulge his appetites, make the most of his power while he possessed it, before his downfall and physical destruction.

I pleaded a headache and left the office a little earlier than usual. Instead of taking the streetcar, I trudged homeward. I paused on a bridge over the Neva River. A fierce wind ruffled the surface of the water. That man was no communist, I thought, he was scum. I tried to regain my composure. The proud sweep of the Admiralty spire on the opposite bank, the glow of sunset in the windows, the austere dignity of the architecture, mitigated a little the shock and disgust I had experienced in Bronstein's company.

Then my thoughts took a general turn: why were these privileges allowed in hungry Leningrad? How skimpily clad the men and women were who passed me in the street. "Fashion" was dictated by the scarcity of manufactured cloth. Young women and girls wore skirts above their knees, faded kerchiefs, flimsy jackets over cotton blouses, while many of the older women walked about in drab home-spun skirts that reached to their ankles. Almost everybody was shod in canvas shoes, poor protection against the cold of approaching winter.

As I peered into the faces of the passersby, some of the old elation returned to me. They shone with idealism and hope. Cheeks were sallow and sunken, but spirit and courage glowed. I noted especially the delicately molded features, the inspired, purposeful expressions; in years to come so many of them would disappear.

Just a few steps away from the home I now shared with Vasili's family was a small bakery. I dropped in to see if I could buy some-thing for tea. But, as could be expected, the bare counters stared mockingly at me. I knew that Vasili's mother would not let me go hungry, though I contributed little to the family budget. She would generously set before me a plate of fried potatoes with sliced pickle, treat me to a little honey for tea.

When I entered the house on Stachek Street, in the newly estab-lished neighborhood close to the Putilov Works, later named the Kirov Plant, I found Vasili locked up in his room with his former lover, Nina. I took this as a matter of course; if anything, I was glad that his romantic mood had ebbed away. The person I most admired in that household was the mother, constantly fighting to keep the family fed. Once a week she drove to a nearby village to barter old uniforms—Vasili's two brothers were army officers—vodka, soap, and other items in short supply for potatoes and honey. She queued up for bread and cereals, mostly millet, and in cooking she employed amazing ingenuity to stretch the rationed groceries. She washed, scrubbed, carried heavy loads, while her menfolk read their news-papers and books, drank vodka, and indulged themselves as they pleased. What went on in the world around her hardly mattered, and women's emancipation was an empty phrase to her.

"What made you leave Canada? Why did you come here?" I was frequently asked. The people who put these questions to me really meant: What idiot would decide of her own free will to share our existence?

I spoke sincerely when I replied that I thought ordinary people got a far better deal under socialism than in a capitalist society. They did not argue with me. But a lift of the eyebrows or a twist of the lips showed that they thought me a liar or a hopeless idealist.

Missing my mother, I said goodbye to Vasili and took a train to Migayevo, the site of the Lenin Commune with its two contingents from Canada.

Not one of the repatriates, least of all my mother, had been prepared for the hardships that confronted them. Families were lodged in sheds with no running water, no toilets. True, the commune was one of the fortunate farming enterprises to have electricity. Indeed, by the standards of the times—the very early thirties, the time of the Volga and Ukraine famines—it prospered, providing three good meals a day in the canteen for all members. Perhaps the commune owed its well-being to the astute management of Chairman Melnik, a red-headed giant who spoke to me in the broken English he had retained from his Canadian days; no doubt the tractors and harvesters brought over by the resettlers helped as well. Some time afterwards the commune was disbanded. What became of its hardworking chairman and other members I do not know; I can only guess the worst.

There was little for my mother to do at an agricultural commune. However, since educated people were in demand everywhere, the local board of education was only too happy to place her in charge of the village school, where she became the principal and taught many of the subjects.

The brief feeling of comfort and security I experienced in my mother's presence was soon replaced by a growing restlessness. The bleak village scene, especially in winter, was more than I could bear. I had to get away, out into the big world again. My mother was sympathetic.

She quickly arranged for me to stay with a family she knew in Odessa. In exchange for their hospitality, she managed to scrape together a little parcel of farm products for me to take them. It was greatly appreciated at a time when food was scarce.

II A dissident of the thirties

Gales swept the streets, snow turned momentarily into slush. A bluish gray mist hovered over the maritime city. I had been told that Odessa had the most beautiful women in all of Russia, heavy-browed, dark-eyed—*eti chorniye glaza . . . oni sveli menya s uma,* "those dark eyes are driving me crazy," ran a popular song. I now came face to face with them in Richelieu Street, huddled in fur coats that had seen better days, and later in restaurants and at the opera, wearing low necklines that revealed tempting white flesh. It was the first time I became aware of the difference between real sex and the spurious commodity purveyed in the movies and magazines of my Montreal girlhood. Chill gusts rising from the Black Sea almost blew me off my feet, they penetrated right through the flimsy Canadian windbreaker I wore. The sting of frost. I loved it. I felt exhilarated, as though riding a chariot, fleeing from the cares and uncertainties of my chaotic youth.

But I had to get down back to earth and face reality, for I was very much at loose ends. My mother had hoped I would go on with my education. She had no idea of the regulation that made enrollment at schools of higher learning practically impossible for the sons and daughters of non-working class or non-peasant parents.

I would take any job and go to evening school, I decided, but first I was determined to get a transfer, through the Youth International in Moscow, from the Canadian to the Soviet Young Communist League. To drop out of the movement was inconceivable to me. I hoped the Odessa League could help.

Morning after morning I kept returning to the building on the Black Sea esplanade where the league had its headquarters. I would pause across the street from it, turning over in my mind what to say. Finally, I plucked up my courage and made my way towards the entrance, almost bumping into a young man in his late twenties who was also going into the building.

He smiled a broad smile. "I've seen you across the street three days in a row . . . hardly a place for a date," he teased.

Tall, lithe, with his head proudly thrown back and slightly inclined to one side, his hat worn at a tilt and back from the forehead, revealing a mass of auburn curls, he was not a man to escape notice. Besides, he radiated an infectious warmth and lightheartedness. I took to him at once.

"I want to speak to the Secretary," I said trustingly. "Do I need an appointment?"

"I can introduce you, if you wish."

Once in the office I hastily stated my case.

"This comrade can do more for you than I can." The secretary pointed to my companion. "He is deputy General Secretary of the Ukrainian Young Communist League."

A few minutes later the young man who held this exalted post was walking with me up and down the Embankment, high above the

Black Sea, and chatting excitedly. When he saw me home, we continued talking indoors for a while, then went out for another stroll.

My new acquaintance, who introduced himself as Ivan Stepanovich Frolov, was staying at Odessa's exclusive Londonskaya Hotel, which overlooked the harbor. He invited me in for dinner.

We lounged against the red plush of the chairs in a cozy nook of the hotel restaurant, away from the cold nip of the Black Sea wind. Cognac and wine were served with the meal. His tongue loosened by the drinks, Ivan Stepanovich spoke about himself. He was twenty-seven, had a degree in engineering, held a high position in the government as well as in the Communist League. There were many privileges attached to his posts, but he did not give a hoot for them. After a pause, he moved his chair closer to mine, cast a glance around, and, inclining his tousled head, told me he was going to Moscow on an important mission. He would be leaving in a few days.

The minute the words "important mission" were out of his mouth, he sat up with a jerk, very sober. It was as if he had blurted out a piece of intelligence. He bit his lips and peered into my eyes without blinking, a peculiar trick he had when he was upset about something.

I noticed that he had on the same khaki tunic, breeches and calf-hugging boots that Vasili had worn, except that they were of superior quality and sat better on his tall athletic figure. I wondered why all party, Komsomol, government, and trade-union officials in the early thirties affected that military look, carried over through the twenties from the time of the Civil War. Perhaps what accounted for it was the scarcity of any but army cloth.

There was a quickness of mind and an urbanity about Ivan Stepanovich that I found quite irresistible. Every night we went to the opera. The Odessa opera house, a replica of Vienna's, was one of the most charming structures in the city. All my friend had to do was produce a card, showing the high post he held, for us to be ushered into the government box. Much as I enjoyed the company of Vanya, as I now came to call him, and was flattered by his attentions, my mind was set on one thing: getting my transfer, joining the Soviet Komsomol, and plunging into work for socialism. A romantic entanglement was the last thing I desired, and I said so to Vanya. With a violent toss of his curls he replied: "As you wish."

"But you want the transfer, I take it?" He paused. "That means we travel to Moscow together."

In Moscow Vanya's good friends, the Ukrainian poet Samborsky and his wife, put me up in their apartment in Karetny Ryad. There were many visitors, to whom Samborsky would read his poetry.

Sometimes the conversation that went on in that home, in hushed tones, puzzled me; my Russian was still faulty. I could only surmise that a common topic was the future of the Ukraine.

When I look back at that period of the early thirties, I realize that there must have been groups hoping to remove Stalin from his post or curb his lust for power. Possibly most active among them were the Trotskyites. They had little to lose, especially those whose earlier association with Trotsky was known.

I had noticed that Vanya carried about with him an attaché case crammed with papers and booklets. One evening when we were alone in the Samborsky dining-room he dug his hand into it and from the very bottom produced a book with white and gray binding.

He handed it to me. "Care to read it?" he asked casually. When I took it from him I could not believe my eyes. It was a Paris edition of Leon Trotsky's *My Life*.

Even to handle a book like that I knew to be dangerous. It could bring reprisals beyond one's wildest imaginings.

I returned it to him immediately. Apart from being frightened, I believed it wrong for a loyal communist to be carrying and handing out a book openly maligning Soviet policies. Vanya was now a greater enigma to me than ever. Why did he walk about with the banned Trotsky literature in his attaché case, something for which he could easily be stripped of his posts and jailed? Quite often now I was stunned by things Vanya said and did. The conviction grew in my mind that he was playing some dangerous game.

The mystery around Vanya deepened even more when he started to take me to visit friends of his at the Select Hotel. In frosty weather, on slippery ground, we walked down from Karetny Ryad on the Outer Boulevard, later uprooted and turned into the wide Sadovaya thoroughfare, to Petrovsky Gates, an intersection of the Inner Boulevard. There we boarded the Annyshka streetcar, which took us to Stretensky Gates. On the right-hand side of Stretenka Street were the hotel's matt glass doors, almost on a level with the sidewalk, the word "Select" traced in barely visible lettering across them. This hotel, about a quarter of an hour's walk from the main Lubyanka building, catered exclusively to the big shots in Soviet intelligence and the security apparatus. Here they stayed for weeks and sometimes months, waiting for new postings, attending refresher courses, or getting established in the expanding Moscow secret directorates.

Interrogators came here from Lubyanka for a short fling before their nightly questionings. The evenings were spent drinking vodka and dancing to the banned music and songs of the émigrés Leshchenko and Vertinsky. Anti-Soviet jokes, forbidden to be told in ordinary Soviet homes, were freely swapped. Indeed, nowhere did I run into such censure of the Soviet system and such open cynicism as among the high OGPU* officials at the Select Hotel. Vanya joined in the conversation and the laughter. He seemed to be taking a macabre delight in the double-facedness of these "guardians of the revolutionary gains," as the security officers were sometimes called.

One could not help being struck by the resemblance between Vanya and the Ukrainian anarchist Batka—Makhno, as he was known. It occurred to me that he was proud of this likeness, for he seemed to cultivate it in the way he wore his hair, in long tangled ringlets, his brisk gait, and his habit of abruptly tossing his head. He also had a way of biting his lips and dropping into a chair, seeming moody and crest-fallen, as though some plan he was hatching had fallen through, and these habits too were strongly reminiscent of Makhno. One would think that there the resemblance ceased between the cruel Makhno, chieftain of one of the worst gangs of marauders the Civil War had produced, and the chivalrous, urbane Ivan Stepanovich. Yet they shared as well a love of adventure and a readiness to gamble away human lives, including their own.

At the time of my friendship with Vanya and acquaintance with the Samborskys I was only seventeen, hardly capable of understanding what was happening around me. Later I wondered: If these opponents of Stalin had succeeded, would there have been less misery and annihilation of human life than under his rule?

Vanya had finally arranged for me to meet with Deniman of the English-speaking section of the Communist Youth International. I saw him at the Luxe Hotel in Gorky Street, where most of the Comintern members resided almost permanently. He turned out to be a short, glum person. He spoke strange words, their gist sinking into my mind only after I left the hotel: Get married, raise a family, and stay out of trouble. In a way he echoed my own growing conviction that I no longer had any heart for politics.

Once again I felt the need to be close to my mother, and I travelled back to the Ukraine. On finding myself in the peaceful little Ukrainian village where my mother taught school, I was no longer as bored and restless as I had been the year before. I had had enough adventure. But I kept my thoughts to myself. Clearly there were communists in key positions who were not at all what they seemed to be; I had seen them in those rare moments when they shed their pretence.

* United State Political Administration (1923–1934).

The mind's departure from set ideas is slow, and it is usually preceded by a period of befuddlement. It was this phase that I had now reached.

Still viewing my surroundings with bubbling enthusiasm, I found an outlet in writing long letters to Mr. Eld, a Montreal *Star* reporter whom I had once tried to convert to communism during a walk along the moonlit paths of Mount Royal. With a picture in my mind of the thousands of unemployed I had seen in the streets of Montreal, lined up for their bowl of soup, I wrote of how everybody I met had a good job. In letters almost thirty pages long I related my impressions of the Migayevo commune; I wrote of the bumper harvest, which after deliveries to the state was evenly divided among all the commune members; about the hardworking Chairman Melnik, who took no greater share than the rest.

When the commune could not find a second bookkeeper I recalled the petite, golden-haired daughter of a neighbor of ours in Drolet Street, a bookkeeper, whose fruitless job hunting I had followed sadly in the spring of 1931.

I perceived no incompatibility between the communist and humanitarian ideals and vowed to cling to both. These feelings were tied up with sadness and regret when my gaze travelled around the room my mother and brother occupied. How shabby and uninviting it looked—grubbier than any place we had lived in in Montreal. My mother had aged greatly in the short time since we left Canada. Her hair had thinned and was streaked with gray, her eyes had a strained look, and shadows nestled in the hollows of her cheeks.

There was a demand for trained specialists in all fields, and after some persuasion I convinced my mother to apply for a job in Moscow.

III We settle in Moscow

With little trouble my mother obtained a post at the Commissariat for Railways. So acute was the housing shortage that when she received an offer of a five-by-three-meter room in a communal flat she ought to have jumped at it. However, she turned it down in favor of two tiny rooms in a distant Moscow suburb, in a shanty with no washroom or running water. My impractical mother! I was dismayed, but powerless to change her mind. Two rooms, my mother argued, were better than one.

In spring and autumn we squelched through mud to reach our quarters, in winter walked in almost knee-deep snow. We had no money for furniture, but even with it, no furniture was available unless you had good contacts. We slept on beds knocked together from boards. My mother worked, designing stations for the North Railway Line, with her customary zeal and spent from two to three hours commuting in a crowded train. The money she earned barely kept us from starving.

I took a proofreader's job at a publishing house that was putting out foreign dictionaries, started a night course in typography, and began making friends. One of them was Vera Schwartz, a fellow proofreader. Fluent in English and French, she had majored in Persian linguistics at the oriental languages department of Tashkent University. Both of us found proofreading dull. Luckily, in 1935 Intourist, a new travel organization set up to attract tourists from abroad, was advertising for guides. We applied and were accepted.

The guides were regarded as propagandists for the Soviet system, and during the slack winter season time and money to advance their education were not spared.

Most of the girls I worked with were college graduates, cultivated and well-read, for whom work as a guide was not much more than an interim period for training in language skills. I was learning a great deal about art galleries, museums, and theaters. Suddenly I realized that I was much happier talking about drama, painting, and new books than about social and political affairs.

Vera and I shared these interests, and we saw a good deal of one another. Graceful, enchanting, with her elongated eyes, oval face, and exquisite small mouth, Vera looked like a figure in one of the Persian miniatures she had collected since her student days. Men were always hovering around her, and it amused me to watch her lead them on; I may have been a little envious of her popularity. Her buoyant spirits had a wholesome effect on me. She took every day as it came.

The atmosphere in her home was cozy and relaxing. Her mother was an excellent cook who managed to produce delicious meals at a time of constant food shortages. I would sit back on their sofa and enjoy the warmth of these two women, the mother looking almost as young as the daughter and just as attractive, though very different in appearance—short, blonde, blue-eyed. Vera's mother was a Russian, and it was from her late Jewish father that Vera must have inherited her dark oriental beauty and zest for life.

Vera had many suitors, but she chose to become the mistress of a Frenchman more than twice her age, the portly Havas Agency correspondent in Moscow. It was just what her mother wanted for her—

an easy life, fashionable clothes, living it up in the "high society" of the foreign press and embassies. Her lover managed to get a large apartment for Vera and some beautiful furniture. She put in much effort to introduce a "Russian" atmosphere with a samovar, embroidered towels, and corner ikons. When she showed off her new home to me I stayed for as short a time as decency permitted and was happy that the man of the house was out. To see or be seen with aliens was to court danger. We knew our friendship was over.

Then the worst happened. The Havas Agency correspondent was ordered out of the country for "immoral conduct": he had a wife in Paris. The apartment was confiscated and Vera was arrested for her liaison with a "spy." I learned from her mother that she had received the fairly mild sentence of five years in prison camp and five years' exile in Siberia. Also, it was clear that she would not be able to live in Moscow after the two terms expired. Her mother was beside herself with grief.

At about the same time, many of the women who hung around the Intourist bars—secret police informants, assigned to flirt and go to bed with tourists or embassy people and then make full reports— were also apprehended. Among them were some of Moscow's most beautiful women, also the few who wore elegant Western clothes. Their glory was short-lived. They had served their purpose. What followed was back-breaking work in labor camps and their end.

Poor Vera! It was the first time, though certainly not the last, when a close friend whom I knew to be utterly non-political was to suffer the horrors of Lubyanka, incarceration, and camp. Strangely enough, fifteen years later Vera's love life would ricochet upon me, helping to substantiate another crazy charge against me.

My work as a guide was bringing me in contact with people from all over the world. Ocean liners on world cruises docked at Leningrad for two days, after which the passengers took an overnight train to spend a short time in Moscow. For these vacationers, mostly wealthy Americans, Intourist arranged gala concerts with top performers in music, ballet, and folk dancing. The concerts were held at the marble-columned hall of the old Red Army Theater. Intourist Lincoln cars would glide to the theater entrance. From them would step out well-groomed gentlemen and expensively coiffured, bejewelled ladies. Passers-by gazed at them in disbelief and wonder, as though they had landed from another planet. (Since that day things have changed greatly: millionaire ladies dress more casually and many young Moscow girls look like fashion plates as they arrogantly pass through the widened modern streets or in their turn alight from small sedan cars.)

At these concerts I was the English announcer. Standing in the middle of the stage one night in the summer of 1935, I felt a thrill on suddenly noticing a familiar face in one of the front rows. The long jaw, the trim moustache, the high brow—at once I recognized H.G. Wells.

During the intermission there was a commotion in the audience: people were rising form their seats and hurrying towards somebody in the aisle. Elegant little books fluttered, and I assumed that everyone was seeking Wells' autograph. Happy that I had seen the writer I so greatly admired, I smiled to myself.

But the smile vanished when I walked into a side foyer and saw standing in a far corner, very much by themselves, the short, stocky Wells and a younger, lankier replica of himself, his son. Curious as to who had caused the flurry of excitement among the wealthy Americans, I stepped down into the auditorium. The center of attention were two popular American variety stars.

Tourists visiting the Soviet Union could not understand why travel was so restricted. Often the explanation was simple: the absence of transportation and the poor sanitary conditions in many cities of historical interest. I remember how exasperated the American writer Richard Haliburton was when Intourist failed to arrange a trip to Samarkand. (He was writing a book about Tamerlane; Samarkand had been the capital of his empire, and his famous tomb was there). The writer was nervously pacing the lobby of the Metropole Hotel when I had the unpleasant task of telling him that Samarkand did not come on any tourist itinerary and that no exception could be made for him.

Haliburton was having his bit of friction with Intourist when Clement Attlee, leader of the opposition and head of the British Labour Party, was also visiting Moscow. His request to see a small town outside the capital was gratified without delay. Attlee came to Moscow with his secretary, an easygoing, sprightly man of thirty-five, with a teasing ironic manner, and the secretary's courteous mother. They were three of the most pleasant and undemanding tourists I ever worked with.

The day I took Clement Attlee on a tour of Gorky Park was torrid, the air laden with gritty dust. We dropped in for lunch at one of the open-air restaurants on the Moscow River Embankment. The whole idea, I must say, was Major Attlee's. I would have suggested going back for his meal to the National Hotel, where he and his companions were staying, but one does not do too much suggesting to a future prime minister. Attlee wished to have something Russian, and because it was so very hot we ordered *okroshka*, an ice-cold soup made of *kvass*, greens, boiled eggs, and meat.

The meal unfortunately resulted in an upset stomach. Instead of seeing Moscow's façade, Attlee got more than a full view of the back yard—that is, the toilets, not easy to find in those days, most of them just holes in the ground with raised platforms and foot treads.

I found the situation mortifying and later, with tears in my eyes, complained to my fellow guides how dirty the public toilets in Moscow were. I sincerely wanted Attlee to see the best side of Soviet life. That these efforts of mine should be thwarted by the silly *okroshka* and the toilets upset me.

Fortunately the visit to Podolsk went off without misadventure. The road to the city was mostly rubble, so we kept the windows of the Lincoln shut to avoid the churning dust, and our driver steered carefully around the bumpy sections. Podolsk, the closest small town to Moscow, was the center of a fertile farming area, and it also had a number of developing industries. Attlee, who had himself been mayor of Tupney, wished to get some idea of the problems and growth of a similar Soviet area. Podolsk was the answer.

After taking us around one of the big outlying farms, the mayor had a huge lunch served in the open air, answering there and then Attlee's questions concerning the municipal management and history of Podolsk.

I was not with Attlee when he was received by Stalin or Kalinin, but I did go with him to the city hall, a red brick building on Gorky Street, where his host was Nikolai Bulganin, then chairman of the Moscow Soviet, or mayor of the capital. It is interesting now to think that both Attlee and Bulganin, each in his own time, were to be prime ministers, Attlee to retire with honor, Bulganin to be booted from his post and blotted out of the public memory.

IV Omens of the times

Forgotten foods were at last appearing in Moscow stores. Tverskaya, renamed Gorky Street after the writer's death, was being widened. Muscovites gasped at the skill with which the massive buildings were being moved back from the sidewalk. The architect Shchusev, of pre-revolutionary renown, still wearing a glittering gold and diamond tiepin, and Chechulin and Mordvinov, of the new Soviet crop, were designing the first modern hotels and apartment buildings. The palatial, marble-lined metro stations were a powerful argument for the contributions a socialist state can make towards urban beauty and the convenience of its citizens.

After a visit to the United States, Anastas Mikoyan, Commissar for the Food Industry, introduced such novelties as fruit juices and freshly canned strawberries, which graced the counters of a newly opened Dietetic Store in Arbat Street. This was the neighborhood where I lived, and with its old mansions of the Moscow gentry, among them the poet Pushkin's home, it seemed to have escaped any imprint of the new regime. Oranges, another novelty, were sold on Moscow street corners—delicious, juicy oranges with which Republican Spain paid for the arms the Soviet Union shipped to her.

Pianist Robert Casadesus played Debussy and Werner Klemperer conducted at the Conservatory on Hertzen Street before audiences better fed and dressed than they had been in twenty years. Moscow became a mecca of the world theater.

It was the year 1936, remembered by Muscovites of my generation for the sudden availability of food after the hungry years of the early thirties, for the flowering of the arts, and for its more optimistic outlook. The blood baths of 1937 and 1938 were still ahead of us, and although in 1936 too there were trials, among them the big Zinoviev and Kamenev case, the defendants in the dock were known for their deviations from the Party line, and there was still some plausibility to the charges.

The security apparatus, through its expanding spy network, had not yet achieved total control of the people's minds, and fear had not yet silenced all tongues. Perhaps this explains the candid outbursts I heard from A.G., the new chief of the Intourist guide department, who took over after the arrest of the former head.

He was so gentlemanly and attractive that many of our guides fancied themselves in love with him, myself among them. A.G. was of slight build, agile of mind and body, his dark eyes, the yellow tinge of his skin, and his lank jet-black hair revealing him to be a member of the small Chuvash nationality. One afternoon in early spring he invited me to join him for a stroll after office hours. We directed our steps towards the nearby Alexandrovsky Garden under the Kremlin wall. The garden was full of promenading couples and we were soon lost in the crowd.

A.G. began by telling me that he was happily married and had two small daughters he adored. Then, to my astonishment, he switched to political topics, speaking with a bitterness I had never encountered before.

"I'm a long-standing Party member," he began. "The principles of communism are dear to me. But what I see happening today makes my stomach turn. The worst part of it is that I can do nothing about it. I dare not even speak up. Everything seems to have gone wrong. Take the plight of the peasantry. My own parents are collective farmers. And to think that they are no better off than were the serfs. For their work they are paid in kind. They are denied identification papers, are restricted in their movements—in fact all of them are tied to the farm, just as the bondsmen were tied to the property of the landlords."

I listened with mounting fear and said nothing.

"We are supposed to be a workers' state. But who runs the state? The workers? Most assuredly not! A bunch of unscrupulous bureaucrats who will stop at nothing to stay in office."

On and on he continued in the same vein. There were always food shortages, the women were doing the hardest work, the Party was becoming corrupt with more opportunists and careerists than honest communists in its ranks.

His caustic words made me think of Vanya, who also could be very outspoken in his own sardonic way. But unlike Vanya, A.G. was not reckless, not flippant about his own and other people's lives. He would not *act*. His protest would go no further than confidences to harmless non-political persons like myself. He dared not confide in his wife for fear of bringing misfortune upon his family.

There were many more walks in the Alexandrovsky Garden. He went on talking about the seedy aspects of Soviet society, vehemently condemning the purges and trials; yet at meetings he approved these same purges and denounced the "enemies of the people."

On the ability to play a double-faced role the life and liberty of everyone now depended. It was becoming a way of survival, taking deep root in the Soviet consciousness. This make-believe was repugnant to men like A.G., and for all that it did not save him. His turn came in 1947; from my interrogator I was to learn that he was a "British agent" and received a sentence of twenty-five years.

Cold weather set in early in the autumn of 1936, with snow flurries following rain. On a blustery morning in October I boarded a train to Kislovodsk for a month's vacation. I slept through the long journey, awaking refreshed to the golden sunshine, blue sky, and healthy mountain air for which this resort in the Caucasus is famous. An Intourist hotel was being built on a hillside terrace, and I had the good luck, as a work bonus, to be accommodated in a finished wing.

Feeling on top of the world, inhaling the aroma of rose bushes, I made my way briskly down to the tiny plaza at the foot of the mountains towards which holiday-makers converged at all hours of the day. There I ran into Jessica, a free-lance journalist writing for the Intourist press center. Jessica introduced me to Victor, who stopped to speak to her, casting a few quizzical glances in my direction. Jessica knew him from the *Moscow News*, a Soviet English newspaper of which he had some years before been the editor.

We stood for a while exchanging generalities. I felt immediately attracted to Victor. He was a forceful man, with a gaze that was disturbingly assessing. It could be, I felt, very friendly or openly hostile; in the present instance, as he looked at me, it was definitely friendly.

That very afternoon he turned up at our hotel with a friend, a sandy-haired doctor as flamboyant as Victor himself. The friend became infatuated with Jessica, and over the entire month that followed we hardly saw them at all; they spent most of their time behind the closed door of Jessica's hotel room.

Victor, on the other hand, showed no ardor. I saw him every day, but always in the company of friends or work associates who, like himself, were on vacation. From what he told me, and from anecdotes about him related by friends, I was able to piece together a little of his background. He came of a middle-class family, had studied languages with tutors, completed an automobile engineering course, joined the Red Army, distinguished himself in the battles of the Civil War. In the late twenties the Party sent him on a mission to China. He was among Chiang Kai-Shek's Russian advisers, escaping prison by a hair's breadth when the Kuomintang turned against communism. I also knew that he had had talks with Stalin and admired Bukharin. At the time I met him, he had long been director of NATI, the Soviet Union's first and most important automobile- and tractor-designing center.

Sometimes I saw a frown settle on Victor's handsome face. He crinkled his forehead and narrowed his eyes, which were small compared with his powerful jowl and straight nose. I imagined—wrongly perhaps—that he was preoccupied with some problem of automobile production.

I was twenty-one and Victor was thirty-nine. Perhaps in some way he was a father figure to me, embodying the most admirable qualities of manhood, just as I believe the mother figure does of womanhood; it seems to me that these two figures, projected on our minds in our most impressionable years, help us to seek in our sex partners the human traits most familiar and dear to us. As our relationship developed, Victor came to sum up everything I valued in a man and a human being.

Limpid air, warm sunshine, the Caucasus mountains with their silvery peaks, wooded flanks, and mauve shadows, gave me a sense of timelessness. I longed to cry out: May this moment never fade! I felt Victor's nearness. His every gesture, every remark, penetrated into my being. Giddy, I seemed to be soaring in mid-air. I smiled. My eyes must have betrayed my happiness. My cheeks flamed. Our love still lay ahead of us! We wished to prolong the gentle and gradual exploration of our two personalities.

Victor was unmercenary, undemanding, dedicated to his work. He had no bank account, no dacha, no free cash, he took no bonuses for himself. He was quite content with the Party maximum of 275 roubles a month. The new acquisitive instincts, the philistinism and vulgarities that later became so prevalent were still in their embryonic stage. Whenever Victor ran across them, he could be devastatingly sarcastic.

Victor worked under Ordzhonikidze, the Commissar for Heavy Industry. Every day at the same hour we saw Ordzhonikidze on the serpentine. Like many Georgians in their middle years, he had a proud, eagle-like countenance, the long nose resembling a beak. Flanking him were his body guards, and at his side walked his wife Zinaida, more thick-set than he and perhaps slightly taller. Both husband and wife had a forthright gaze that was rare in those days.

In less than a year this "eagle" would put a bullet through his head, either to avoid arrest or because so many of the people he had worked with, and with whom he had built up the machine construction and other heavy industries, among them his own brother, were incarcerated, and many executed. Stalin shed crocodile tears over him.

Another person enjoying the mountain air of Kislovodsk was Genrikh Yagoda, the most feared man in the land, for many years head of state security and the secret police, who was later charged with the poisoning of Maxim Gorky and other black deeds. Since at the time there was no Karlovy Vary, no golden beach of Bulgaria, not even the Baltic Sea coast, at the disposal of the Party élite, it was at the sumptuous newly built villas in Kislovodsk and Sochi that the top Party and government bosses spent their vacations. Unlike the "eagle," Yagoda was never seen on the main promenade.

A few times it gave me a start to catch sight of his hatchet face, with the black dots of eyes, suddenly appear from the tall, lush grass on the side of the mountain track. Fascinated, I watched the long, thin form slink away with a faint rustling of the leaves. The reptile who devoured others was soon to be devoured himself. Yagoda's days were numbered. But so were those of most people I met on the smooth, sunlit mountain paths of Kislovodsk; it was their last vacation, their last months of freedom.

A few weeks later, back in Moscow, Victor and I went to see a movie that was the great hit of the time. It was then that I had a glimpse of the disenchantment that must have been settling in him and that prompted many of his pointed and acrid remarks. The film was *Peter I*, the first of a series extolling the strong rulers of the past.

Peter the Great was portrayed as a wise empire-builder. Simonov, Leningrad's tallest actor, had an especially strong face, and he was chosen for the part. He did his best to persuade viewers that, owing to his powerful physique, superior intelligence, and statesmanship, Peter had no match among the monarchs and politicians of Europe.

This superman treatment was repugnant to me. I was also greatly puzzled, for there were always hidden reasons for every new approach and interpretation in the arts, the ideological weaponry of the Party. Scene after scene of the glorification of Peter elicited applause from the audience. Did it touch some deep chord in the Russian heart? The longing for a strong and good tsar?

Peter's known brutality, his boorishness, the terror of his reign, were deliberately played down. Peter had ordered the death of his son Alexei, incarcerated his half-sister Sophia, banished the Old Believers, executed the Streltsi. A different Peter appears in the famous painting "Morning of the Execution of the Streltsi" by Surikov: the monarch is portrayed as small, petty, vindictive. But that picture was painted under a tsar—not under Stalin.

I asked Victor what he thought of the film.

He replied: "No tsar has ever been a hero of mine."

When Victor drove me home I did not ask him in. Neither of us was in the mood for lovemaking; an emotion more powerful than desire had been released in us. I walked into my room torn apart by what I had seen on the screen, fearful of its implications. The sad part of it was that Victor and I could not discuss the film frankly. We dared not trust one another with our thoughts, lest at some future date, perhaps under torture, they might be wrested from us as "evidence."

Yet, though we did not say it aloud, we both knew what was behind the film and why it had shocked us.

It contained the virus of a contagion that would spread and have far-reaching effects. Its purpose was to project a certain image, inculcate a precise idea for Soviet viewers, twist their mentality and turn them away from communism to nationalism, from democracy to dictatorship. Stalin was now to be identified with the great rulers of Russia. His brand of nationalism was to replace Marxist-Leninist internationalism. Patriotism and loyalty were to be the great catchwords.

In the forties I watched with even more troubled thoughts two other films, Sergei Eisenstein's *Alexander Nevsky* and *Ivan the Terrible*. They contained the same underlying message as *Peter I*. It may be argued that artistically they were notable creations. But they had a nefarious purpose that I believed should be condemned: to make audiences see Peter the Great, Ivan the Terrible, and Alexander Nevsky as the precursors of the great Stalin and also to justify the need to rule with an iron hand, to treat dissenters ruthlessly.

It puzzled and pained me that a movie director like Eisenstein, who in his *Battleship Potemkin* had focussed attention on the masses, showing sympathy for their plight and aspirations, should have veered from that humanitarian approach to glorify the Novgorod Prince Alexander Nevsky and the half-demented Ivan the Terrible. I discovered in myself a mounting contempt for artists who had not shrunk from employing their art to deify a bloody dictator like Stalin. None of the fine artistic points of *Ivan the Terrible*—not even the perpetually lauded drawings, by Eisenstein himself, of the costumes for Ivan and the boyars used in the picture—could redeem him in my eyes.

V A reprieve

Victor had many fascinating friends, to whose homes he took me. Among them was Lunacharsky's widow, Natalya Alexandrovna Rosenel. Worldly, literary, a little aloof, with luminous blue eyes, delicate features, and impeccable taste in clothes, she was an actress with the company of the Maly Drama Theater which, like the Bolshoi, overlooks the Theater (now Sverdlov) Square.

Her home on Starokonyusheny Lane, off Arbat Street, remained, as it had been in Lunacharsky's time, one of Moscow's literary salons. Natalya Alexandrovna would draw Victor away from the company for long private chats. I watched them with a jealous pang; her delicate skin glowed and silvery notes tinkled in her voice. She was a far more interesting person than I, but with youth on my side I felt secure in Victor's love.

Among Victor's most trusted friends were the sculptor Sergei Dmitrievich Merkurov and his wife Asta. They lived on the very fringe of Izmailovo Park, in the east of Moscow. Former hunting grounds of the early Romanoffs, the park was visible from the windows of the small timber cottage given to Merkurov, along with a sizeable plot of land, on Lenin's orders. This was after Lenin had signed a decree containing a long list of monuments to be erected in Moscow and other cities. The old statues of tsars and national heroes were to be torn down and replaced with new monuments of revolutionaries and revolutionary events—a true blessing for the country's sculptors.

Part of the Merkurovs' estate was taken up with an apple orchard, a vegetable garden, and a shed for animals; the family kept cows, pigs, and poultry, which made life easier—less hungry—for themselves and their friends. In addition to an indoor studio adjoining the house, there stood apart on the grounds a tall makeshift structure with a detachable roof designed for monumental works. Inside one could see apprentices perched on ladders or scaffolding, putting the finishing touches on an enormous head of Lenin or Stalin.

Of towering height, dark and bearded, Merkurov was half Armenian and half Greek, with the noble profile one sees on old Assyrian coins behind glass museum cases. His reputation as a sculptor was made before the revolution. He had studied at the Munich Academy of Arts and travelled a great deal; he loved to tell the story of how, practically penniless, he had cycled through Europe. At the time when we became friends Sergei Dmitrievich was one of Moscow's wealthiest men, owing largely to the great number of Lenin and Stalin statues he had produced, which stood in city squares all over the land.

Few places I had ever been to had the magic of the Merkurov home. Victor would heave himself out of the driver's seat of his sparkling aquamarine Graham Paige, a gift from an American car manufacturer during a trip to the United States, and ring the electric bell on the left side of the green timber gates. On a mild winter's night, with the feathery snow softly dropping in huge flakes, the car glided down the path leading to the back of the cottage. The odd assortment of statuary gave me a strange thrill. On our left, gleaming in the light of the lamp post, stood the haughty snow-mantled figure of Catherine the Great, the crown knocked off her head, while a few steps away, sprawling in the snow, lay a statue of Alexander III, divested of all symbols of power. (He was one of the few monarchs of Russia to die a natural death.) Looming directly in front was an unfinished monument to the twenty-six Baku commissars executed by the British during the Civil War; the figures were portrayed in standing and falling positions at the moment of shooting.

There was both an unreality and a sense of historical tragicomedy about the scene. I felt as though I were being torn away from the present and transported into a fabled world. From this dreamy state I was returned to reality by the barking of the dogs and the squealing of the pigs that contributed greatly to the lavish meals the Merkurovs served to their guests.

As 1936 drew to a close, the Merkurovs invited Victor and me to see in the New Year at their home. I was enjoying the luxury of a tiny room at the Novomoskovskaya Hotel, which took up a small block on the Moscow River Embankment and had a roof restaurant famous for its view of the Kremlin. A section of the ground floor was set aside for Intourist employees with no place to live.

Meeting an acquaintance in the hotel lobby, Victor introduced him to me as George M., a Comintern comrade. Pudgy, unprepossessing George had an egg-shaped head far too large for his body, but a kind twinkle in his eyes, and were he an ordinary Soviet citizen I would have responded to his friendliness. But because George was an American I gave him a wide berth. By this time I avoided tourists staying at the hotel and had also stopped corresponding with Canadian friends.

When New Year's Eve approached, George complained to Victor that he had nowhere to go. Victor suggested that he accompany us to the Merkurovs. This he did, making a perfect nuisance of himself the entire evening. Finally Victor drove him back to the hotel and returned to the party as we ushered in the first dawn of 1937 with hopes for better and less fearful days in the coming year.

One of the guests asked, "Who is that crazy American? Giving me a wink, Victor lied: "He's an agent of an American firm."

Obviously he did not want it known that the drunken and boorish George had any connection with the Comintern.

One of the counts on which my charge of espionage rested read: "Had a meeting with Boris Victorov, agent of an American firm."

A muddled informer's report handed in fourteen years prior to my arrest must have named George as Victorov—possibly confusing him with Victor—and linked him with me. This is the sole explanation I can offer for the mysterious Victorov who figured in the warrant for my arrest, unless, in his haste to concoct a charge against me, the interrogator had confused the names himself.

I was so wrapped up in my personal affairs and ambitions that I paid only rare visits to Losinostrovskoe, the suburb of Moscow where my mother and brother lived. On the Sundays I did visit, I would find them both engrossed in some mathematical problem. Although happy to see me, they could not tear themselves away from their mathematics. They covered sheet upon sheet of paper with formulas, and when they ran out of paper, which they often did, they proceeded to put down their symbols and figures on the log walls of the room. Ashtrays were always spilling over with cigarette stubs and the small kitchen table would be piled with several days of dirty plates.

My visits began with a clean-up job. The worst part was the battle with the bedbugs. The more I fought them, mostly with kerosene, the more they multiplied and the fatter they grew. If I managed to get them out of the interstices between the log walls, they crawled to the ceiling and from there dropped in a bee-line on the beds, chairs, and table.

Returning from one such visit, I found the newspapers full of the Zinoviev and Kamenov trial and the conviction of two eminent Moscow medical men, Levin and Pletnev.

Frequent guests at Merkurov's gatherings were Pletnev's assistant, Dr. Mikhailov, and his beautiful violet-eyed wife, an actress at the Maly Theater. Like Pletnev, Mikhailov was one of Moscow's leading specialists in gastric disease. He was a well-built, elegantly dressed man, his long square chin giving him a noble equine look. We knew him as a lover of English poetry, especially Byron, and an admirer of the British parliamentary tradition. His conversation flowed with easy grace, steering clear of polemical topics, his gaze often wandering in his wife's direction as though longing above all to catch her attention; his great affection and admiration for her were apparent to us all. At the time in Moscow's theater world she was greatly lauded for her portrayal of Mary, Queen of Scots, in Scribe's play *A Glass of Water*.

We feared for the life of the pleasant, loving couple because of the doctor's connection with the convicted Pletnev. And our fears were well founded: the two were arrested.

We were not unprepared for such disposal of lives. All along there had been "cases" of so-called wreckers, foreign spies and doctor poisoners. They had not yet assumed the proportions of a mass onslaught on the population, the wholesale shootings and arrests that shortly awaited us.

All the same, it amazed me how coolly we were taking these events, how Communist Party members inside the Soviet Union and in the world at large accepted them without a word of protest, a word of commiseration for the victims. The silence and acceptance were contemptible. It was like crushing beneath our own boots good and innocent human lives.

Clearly we were undergoing a deep change of personality. Soon some, though fortunately not all, proud members of the intelligentsia would turn into Stalin's apologists and obedient executors of his man-hating policies. Moscow, the entire country, was being transformed into an ugly jungle; each beast for himself, each saving his skin according to his own lights.

But hope had not yet been completely abandoned. We prayed with all our hearts that the blood baths would come to an end. And indeed the trials would be followed by a brief breathing-space, a lull and even recantations from those on high, as later happened in the case of security chief Yezhov, removed from his post for his "excesses."

There were people who tried convincing themselves that the repressive measures were justified and, most important, foolishly believed that they themselves might be allowed to go on unharassed with their own lives. Some indeed were being rewarded by stepping into the shoes of their convicted superiors.

When Bukharin was kept on as editor of *Izvestia*, the guests at the Merkurov home said it was a good omen. Victor too was reassured by this piece of news. Optimism surged. Victor went to see Bukharin and speedily wrote a lengthy article for the paper on problems in the automobile and tractor industry.

The article appeared in record time. How like Bukharin, everybody said. Bukharin, called by Lenin the Party's favorite, might yet be spared.

"If no action is taken against Bukharin," Victor proclaimed, "there will be a reprieve."

How wrong he was. How wrong we all were in thinking that silence and acquiescence would save our skins. It did not. Instead it created an atmosphere in which it was possible to bring millions to a death all the more cruel because so many of the victims were loyal supporters and dedicated builders of the Soviet system. If a firmer stand had been taken at this early stage, the entire course of history might have been less brutal. Stalin and his great admirers the world over paved the way for this great treachery and annihilation of human life.

VI The "traitors" of 1937 and 1938

The year whose coming we had welcomed with hope at the Merkurovs' was shedding its benign mask. Once it was off, 1937, and later 1938, struck out with enormous force, the blows rendered so suddenly that shock, bewilderment, and confusion gave way to naked, animal fear for one's life and the lives of one's closest and dearest.

Besides the big trials, spectacles that glued the eyes of the world to the Soviet Union, small fry by the thousands and hundreds of thousands were also being caught in the net. For the new victims, who were not top Party members, not internationally known figures, there would be no trials, no judges, only torture, death, or deportation to places where they would perish unknown and unmourned, for even to mourn them was forbidden.

When you arrived at your job you never knew who would be missing next. Department heads went as fast as the big bosses. You found their offices locked or sealed. Presently replacements were brought in. A new brand of executives! Some were recruited from the provinces and judged to be more reliable. The new bosses were hard, suspicious, and surly. Manners were brusque; beneath the high-handedness there was often a hidden insecurity and incompetence. These newcomers went about with a doglike, homeless look. Little attention was paid to them, for we were not at all certain what their fate would be. Many of them, indeed, followed their predecessors down into the overcrowded prison dungeons. Before work started there would be meetings with readings from *Pravda* or *Izvestia* about the crimes of the arrested, their involvement in plots to overthrow the government, undermine the system, restore capitalism, and other nonsense. Somebody with whom you had shaken hands just a few days before was now branded an enemy and a traitor. The "disclosures" were met with applause and votes of approval. If you did not join in the farce, you jeopardized your own safety and that of your dear ones. It was always the same vision I had at these meetings: cannibals dancing to the tom-tom of drums, clapping their hands in glee, as one after another the victims, often their own blood brothers and sisters, even their parents, were hurled into the flames.

Most people at these meetings knew the charges to be fabrications. Yet with a few exceptions—these courageous people suffered for it and were in their turn thrown into jail—all of us endorsed the resolutions condemning the "traitors."

When Stalin's name was mentioned people applauded, at first mostly out of fear, later as if in a hypnotic trance, and still later with a convenient conviction that he was the great father in whom people must put all their trust.

I hated Stalin and refused to find excuses, as other people tell me they did, for the glorification of the "leader," the need for arrests and executions. Some thought: Perhaps the trials are necessary, perhaps the defendants in the dock and those hundreds of thousands of others, declared "enemies," are in fact responsible for the ills, the backwardness, the dangers facing the country. ("The Soviet Union has wiped out its fifth column!" world communists, to their eternal shame, shouted in unison.)

Others adopted a different way of thinking: The Party is obviously doing something crazy, cruel and irrational, but one has to live with it, better still, accept it as the correct way. Such thinking was essential for those who wished to get ahead with their careers, realize their ambitions, and who craved high posts.

Later, in self-justification, these people would say that they had no idea the millions sentenced to die or rot in the prison camps were innocent. Was it possible that they really thought that? Or did they persuade themselves to think it for their own comfort?

For me to forget the people I knew in 1936, 1937, and 1938 who were shot outright, or condemned to a slow death in the camps, is equivalent to cutting out a part of my heart and brain. But even this feeling, throughout my life, I was compelled to keep to myself because it was shared only by a small minority.

Most of the people whose arrests shocked me so deeply were communist zealots, uncynical, idealistic. Their doom was sealed, for if the system was to pursue its devious course of survival, they had to make way for a new breed, the Stalin breed, power-lusting, treacherous, venal, unscrupulous.

One of the first among those I worked with to be mown down by the Lubyanka machine was the high-spirited Kurtz, a descendant of the Germans who had settled on the banks of the Volga at the time of Catherine the Great. He was a brisk, open-hearted, trustful man, bubbling over with energy, remarkably resourceful in grappling with difficulties, responsive to other people's troubles, kind and courteous.

Kurtz was the founder and later chairman of the German Autonomous Republic on the Volga banks, his energy and initiative helping to turn it into one of the most productive areas in the land. After diplomatic relations with the United States were established and the Soviet Union launched into tourism, Kurtz, who spoke German and English, was put in charge of organizing the Intourist travel agency. It was a wise choice, which paid enormous dividends to the state.

A month before his arrest I was sitting in his office adjoining the National Hotel when his plump, rosy-cheeked pregnant wife walked in. They were recently married, and I caught Kurtz's proud and tender glance on her lovely Madonna face. When he was taken away to the Lubyanka prison she, too, was incarcerated. Cruel repressive measures followed against his first wife and their sons. Having devoted his days and nights to his country, devising ways of attracting more tourists and making hard currency available for industrialization, Kurtz was doomed.

Most likely he was accused of becoming a German spy in his swaddling clothes, and later a secret agent of all the imperialists. (Think of the many contacts he could strike up with the "spies" from all over the world, disguised as "tourists," who sneaked into his office!)

A very different man from the robust, buoyant Kurtz was Axelrod, assistant editor of the *Moscow News*. Pensive, preoccupied, he rarely looked up at you when shown an article for the paper, but would poke his bony finger at a line to which he objected. Axelrod was in the last stages of tuberculosis, but he did not miss a day of work. Soon I realized that this frail, cadaverous man in his middle years was one of the most cultured persons I had ever met, simple and lovable. At the office we all knew that he had very few years to live. But even those few years were denied him, for this long-standing and highly respected communist was among the first group of persons arrested at the *Moscow News*.

Joe Zilbert, whom I met through Victor, was a general in the Soviet air force who had fought for a year in Spain. Long before, he had served under General Blücher (a Civil War hero who was later purged) and was with him and Victor in China as an adviser to Chiang Kai-shek. The Soviet advisers' lives were in danger when China broke with the Russian communists.

Joe's wife Katya, a former baroness of German descent, who had become a fervent revolutionary and Communist Party member, employed her feminine charms to persuade the German consul to engineer the Soviet advisers' flight from China. On returning from Spain, Zilbert discovered that Katya had been arrested. With her background it was easy to pin the most fantastic charges on this remarkable woman, who had rejected family and aristocratic origins to devote herself to the noble cause of equality and a good life for all. Katya, as I remember her, was the archetype of the liberated woman of the period, with sleek, dark, short-cropped hair falling in bangs over her broad forehead and a long cigarette-holder poised in her slender fingers as she spoke, intense, passionate in defending her ideas.

A few months after her arrest I met Joe Zilbert near the *Moscow*

News building on Petrovsky Pereulok in downtown Moscow. He had suddenly emerged from behind a house and after we parted hastily slipped into a courtyard, as if he wanted to keep away from exposed sidewalks. Perhaps he had acquired the habit in beleaguered Spain. In his melancholy gray eyes and the pathetic hunch of his shoulders I recognized the feeling of inescapable doom—the look of the hunted animal—that had become so familiar to me. Soon he too disappeared.

The sons and daughters of shot or arrested persons! I have seen so many of them, my own beloved daughter among them. The pain in their eyes is forever. Joe Zilbert was not yet forty when the Lubyanka steamroller passed over his body; his son Lyova was fourteen.

Joe's sister and her husband, who were childless, took in their nephew. (Nine years later, in 1947, both were arrested: they were freed in 1956, exonerated—as were Joe Zilbert and his wife, posthumously.) They dared not speak to Lyova of his parents' fate lest he become embittered and politically indiscreet. To prove that he was a Soviet patriot, he volunteered to fight in the war against Hitler when he was not yet of drafting age. He was killed in his very first battle.

Leonid Petrov was a carefree, lackadaisical kind of person. He held a non-spectacular position in the musical-instruments industry and liked to read English books. Now and then he would drop in to borrow a book from me.

Much as he loved Sima, the woman he had been living with for several years, he could not make up his mind to marry her. His excuse was that Sima, being a true city girl, would not care to live in the country, while he hoped eventually to return to his native village and get together a balalaika orchestra; he would show the world how talented Russian villagers were. "Sima would never follow me there," he claimed fretfully.

A few months went by. He had failed to return two books of mine— a well-illustrated edition of Andersen and Grimm fairy tales and a volume of stories by Edgar Allan Poe. I phoned him. There was no answer. Some time afterwards I met Sima close to the Kropotkinskaya metro station. I was shocked to see how she had aged. She was carrying a huge bundle.

"I'm going to join him," she said.

From the way she spoke and from her appearance, I guessed that she was not going to the countryside, but to quite a different place.

"You are very brave," I told her. "How much did he get?"

"Ten years . . . I'll try for a job near his prison camp. He's all I have in the world and all I care for."

VII Victor

Victor and I now spent as many evenings together as we could. Sometimes he would just drop in for an hour or two and then rush back to the big research center of which he was head. It was the style in those days for high-ranking executives to work through the small hours of the morning—decreed by Stalin.

We deliberately avoided discussion of the arrests. Nor did we talk of a life together as we had during the first months of our love. Often now he sat opposite me at the table in my long narrow hotel room, silent, drained of strength.

At such moments the world took on the quality of a horror film from which I longed to escape, only to find that I was nailed to my seat, kept there at gunpoint by two guards who stood on either side of me. Victor was with me; we were trapped.

We who always talked a great deal seemed to have suddenly lost the power of speech. Arrests, intimidation, the constant sowing of fear, the mushrooming of informers, imposed silence on all of us as a means of survival.

The heavy, oppressive armor of silence stifled, it strangled, and sometimes, if only for an hour, it had to be cast off. One form of relief was the anti-Soviet joke. But there was always sure to be an informer in the company, and some time, perhaps years, afterwards, the person who related the joke would be pulled in and given a sentence of ten years. A life finished—because of a single joke! Yet people risked it.

There were other ways of defying the imposed silence. You could be engulfed by it, yet the human mind, resourceful as it is, enabled you to converse in half-meanings, innuendoes, twisted sentences, and in this way convey your thoughts. Words could be treated in a manner so ingenious that they denoted the opposite of the intended thought, and yet they were understood. When spouted by officials they could be a jumble of meaningless stock phrases, and yet trigger off a stream of indignation, make people strain at the leash. To channel one's speech into restricted patterns of conversation was not easy. But I noticed that gradually people, myself included, were doing just that and getting to be adept at it.

But Victor and I—how could we use that trick language? More often than not we would lapse into silence. Those long, agonizing silences hung heavy in the empty air between us, and perhaps they alone saved my life; for had I been hauled off to Lubyanka in the late thirties and landed in a prison camp, I would not have survived.

A panic I had never known before seized me when for three days

Victor neither came to see me nor phoned. On the fourth night I walked across half of Moscow until I reached the house where he lived. With a pounding heart I paused in front of the entrance. Two men in plain clothes, along with the yardman, whom I recognized at once, and a fourth person I could not place were climbing the stairs, the first two with a firm step, the others trailing along. Four persons late at night, two security men and two "witnesses": an arrest! At one point the two who walked ahead threw a glance behind them. Their faces were a blank. Presently all four stopped on Victor's landing, on the fourth floor.

There were three apartments on that landing.

The men had not noticed me. I dashed down the flights of stairs and reached the yard. It was long past midnight. I stood in the shadows of a row of tall dust-bins. Most of the windows were dark. The people who lived in this newly built apartment house were either asleep or had been dragged from their beds and, after a search of their homes, hauled off to Lubyanka.

Suddenly two windows on the fourth floor came ablaze with light. I tried hard to keep calm. Were they Victor's windows? It took me a long time to figure that out. Finally, with a leap of joy, I realized what a fool I had been. The corner windows belonged to Victor. They were dark: Victor was either asleep or spending the night working at his office, as he often did. Greatly relieved, I trudged back home, arriving around three in the morning. Then from a deep sleep I was awakened by the ringing of the phone.

Victor's tone was level: "Never do that again, never!"

"Do what?"

"I saw you in the court last night . . ." There was a pause. Victor added that he would drive over to the Merkurovs' after work.

He never turned up. I stayed for a few hours and then left. Oddly enough, we who always talked so much about Victor never mentioned his name at all that evening.

Around midnight he knocked on my door. Neither of us dared voice aloud the fear in our hearts. Victor gave me a long, weary stare—devoid of all hope. Like dumb animals we let the eyes convey that all was lost, that the sword would descend. It was our last night together. Victor fell asleep but soon woke with a start and quickly left.

Another two months of freedom. We both knew that he was being shadowed and that it was best for me not to see him. We communicated through Asta, Merkurov's wife.

Victor took turns staying now with one friend, now with another, avoiding his own apartment and spending a few nights at the Mer-kurovs'. Neighbor after neighbor was being hauled away at night from the house on Kaptelsky Street where he lived; most of the ten-ants were top industrial executives. Soon after the men disappeared, the security police came to arrest the wives.

One morning Asta phoned: "Did Victor spend the night at your place?"

"No, he didn't."

My heart stood still. Asta's voice sounded flat, deceptively une-motional: "I have had no word from him for two days."

She replaced the receiver. It was not safe to pursue the conver-sation. We both knew too well what had happened.

A couple of days later Banovich, a friend of Victor's, phoned to say he was coming over right away. They were pals from their teens, when both fought in the Civil War. Banovich, who had lost an arm in that war, also held a post at the Heavy Industry Commissariat under Orzhonikidze, as Director of the Oil Industry Board.

"Victor was arrested a few days ago," were his first words. "I can't believe it. I simply can't believe it. Victor was absolutely trustworthy, a dedicated Bolshevik. He built up the tractor and automobile indus-try—from scratch."

I looked at Banovich. His florid, ugly face showed plainly how per-plexed he was by Victor's arrest. He was a true friend, and yet I dared not bare my sorrow, even utter a single expression of regret. All those who had been intimate with someone arrested now feared for their own safety and that of their relatives. Silence was our sole refuge. We pretended that the arrested person never existed—and in this we became stout allies of the state's repressive apparatus, acquiescing in its policies. Nothing can bring Victor back, I told myself, he is as good as dead already. I must think of myself, my brother and mother. I shall not forgive myself if they come to harm.

Such were my thoughts in the daytime. The nights were harder to endure. I would suddenly wake up with a vision of Victor in a torture cell, pummelled, knocked about, taunted, and humiliated. And it was all the harder for him, I knew, because he was a proud man.

Banovich was pacing up and down my tiny room. I felt numb. Presently I persuaded him to sit down. I made a glass of tea.

"Could there really have been some evidence against him, grounds for his arrest?" he asked suddenly.

How many times I was to hear this same question, even ask it of myself! How could the mind resign itself to the arrest and killing of devoted communists by their own supposed comrades?

"Just listen to what I have to say!" Leaping to his feet, he burst out in staccato tones.

This was a different Banovich from the jovial friend who loved to listen to Victor's funny stories and laughed heartily at them.

"Listen to what I have to say," he repeated. "I'm not a spy, not a saboteur." He laid emphasis on every word. "No imperialist agent. I was never in any opposition, I do not want to see capitalism restored. I am an honest, hard-working communist, ready to die for my ideals. I shall never be arrested."

Wasted breath, poor Banovich.

Not having heard from him for a few days, I phoned his wife.

"Yes, it has happened," she said and hung up.

FIVE

I *Attitudes among the intelligentsia*

A few weeks after Victor's arrest, on a Saturday night, I went to see the Merkurovs. Some fifteen persons sat around the tea table in the spacious living room next to the sculptor's studio. There was the usual lively chat and laughter.

Clouds of steam rose from the big-bellied brass samovar, topped by a brightly coloured porcelain teapot. A hush settled around the table when I entered. The guests raised their heads from the cake plates and eyed me as though I were a ghost. One of the men, known for his biting remarks and the pleasure he took in shocking people, blurted out with a wry smile: "Well, well, what a surprise to see you, we were sure you would follow . . ." He did not finish the sentence, but the company knew well enough what he meant: I would share Victor's fate.

I do not think he was a vindictive person. He spoke out of a general bitterness. But I was stunned by his words and utterly at a loss for an answer.

Rising from her seat at the head of the table, Asta walked up to me, threw an arm around my shoulders, and guided me to a seat next to her husband. As though nothing painful had been said, the conversation interrupted by my arrival was resumed. The talk was perhaps typical of the period—veiled, noncommittal. I caught the name of the journalist Mikhail Koltsov.

"Nobody's reportage about Spain was so vivid . . ."

"Vanished as soon as he came back from the Spanish Civil War."

"And Kirshon?"

"His plays were staged across the country. Great hits . . . and then banned overnight."

"One of the first to drop out of the scene was Pilnyak, wasn't he? Just when everybody was reading his book *O'Key*, about the United States, and then those intriguing stories about Japan."

It may have been only the year before that I had seen Pilnyak in a little Caucasian restaurant in Gorky Street, a favorite haunt of Moscow writers and artists. He was arguing vociferously, in a haze of tobacco smoke and alcoholic fumes, waving his hands about so violently that they almost slashed into the faces of his two interlocutors.

The people around the table, sipping their tea and treating themselves to Asta's delicious apricot jam, spoke of the writers' arrests as unconcernedly as though these unfortunates had gone away on a holiday to the Mediterranean.

Talk about writers, even in the innocuous form it was taking, was hastily dropped when the next visitor arrived. This was Alexei Tolstoy. Redolent of pre-revolutionary luxury, he wore a loosely wrapped fur-lined *shuba* of excellent cloth, a tall beaver hat in the boyar style, and an expensive scarf. He had just published *Grain*, hailed as a true socialist-realist novel, about the prosperous life of the collective farmers.

He exuded well-being from every pore of his oversized body. So smug and arrogant! Grudging him his happiness and success, I thought of the writers who had been mentioned around the table. They were paying—or had already paid—with their lives to gratify the mad whims of a man who wielded unlimited power and in whose good graces Alexei Tolstoy had always been. His position with the Great One was secure. Even the most feeble gesture from him in defense of the persecuted writers would have been a ray of hope in the dark.

There were other towering figures in literature and the arts who could have raised their voices. But they did not. They owed too much to the new regime to imperil their positions. They had been allowed to keep the mansions in which they lived before the revolution, been given sizeable grants and subsidies to carry out grand projects in the arts, so that they were in many ways better off than under the tsar. Why jeopardize all these favors to save the lives of a few thousand of their associates?

Honest and moral Soviet writers would have liked to speak up for their confrères. But the price was too high—their own liberty, perhaps life, and retribution falling on their loved ones. What about Western men of letters? They too would pay a price—run the risk of losing their Soviet readership and, worst of all, foregoing invitations from the Soviet Writers' Union. Avowed humanists from the West were in Moscow during the trials and mass arrests. We all saw and heard them. Henri Barbusse published a paean to Stalin, and Lion Feuchtwanger condoned the show trails in his *Moscow 1937*. Romain Rolland and Bernard Shaw made little attempt to speak up against the summary dispatching of thousands of human lives. Shocking numbers of intellectuals accepted or pretended to accept the so-called evidence against the "enemies of the people" as truth. Was it possible for a single country to have bred within its borders such a multitude of traitors, spies, and "agents of imperialism"? They might have asked themselves this question.

At the time I was so deeply disturbed by what I saw happening around me, I had already begun to work in journalism. But my desire to pursue it as a career was dampened by the gross and tragic events of the late thirties. How was one to comprehend and assess such cruelty on the part of the state?

At my job I received encouragement. My senior colleagues wished me well; they edited my writing and gave me assignments that suited my taste and temperament. Journalism had its attractions—it brought you closer to the outside world, broadened your horizons. You could make interesting friends, follow up events and trends more closely. But whatever conclusions you arrived at you had to sublimate, and such compliance to the state was abhorrent to me. My back was up.

You arrived in the morning and carefully perused every line of the *Pravda* editorial. In it were the cues for your topics and how they should be presented to the reader. Whatever you contributed, regardless of your beat, had to be an enlargement and illustration of the Party stand.

I remember interviewing a Ukrainian writer and then attending the premiere of his play at the Moscow Art Theater. The work was a corny piece about a doctor and his architect girlfriend, caught up in the usual predictable situations from which they emerge successful owing to the superiority of the Soviet system over the capitalist. What galled me most, because it was so incompatible with the communist beliefs I held, was that the Soviet heroine's supreme reward was a free trip to the decadent West.

Did my review say what I really thought of the play? Not at all. I wrote what was expected of me and despised myself for it. Translation was my salvation; I switched from original writing to translation.

There were fewer arrests among painters and sculptors than within other artistic groups, perhaps because they were less of a danger to the state, having little direct contact with and influence on the public. Painters could spend years over a picture in their studios without arousing suspicion. They did not appear before audiences, rarely mingled with persons outside their circle, and so were less frequently exposed to informers.

Painting Stalin was the easiest way for the artist to establish himself. Poking his physiognomy into every picture—of women's conferences, parliamentary sessions, children's rallies, sports events, harvest festivals—was a sure ticket to fame.

But by far not every painter or sculptor was willing to peddle his talent in this manner. There was A.L., whom I frequently met at the Merkurovs' and who under one pretext or another avoided all commissions to paint the great leader. Visual artists managed to get away with it, while writers and people in the theater were forced to pay constant homage to Stalin. They could produce pots with flowers, still-lifes that brought practically no remuneration, and earn a living by designing textiles or painting theater backdrops. They had little chance of exhibiting their work and were attacked in the press for "keeping aloof from Soviet reality." Yet they stood their ground.

But the artists pampered by fame, accustomed to a comfortable life and eager for commissions from the state, lent themselves with amazing zest to glorifying Stalin. This was true of Alexander Mikhailovich Gerasimov and also of my friend Sergei Merkurov.

Gerasimov became secretary of the Soviet Artists Union and Merkurov had charge of the Arts Fund. Because of these two influential posts, the sculptor and painter often conferred on matters of Soviet art, mostly at the former's home in Izmailovo. That was where I met Alexander Mikhailovich Gerasimov.

This renowned and talented painter, whose works were on view at the Tretyakov Gallery, was of a totally unartistic appearance—stocky, pot-bellied, with a head that sat like a cannon ball on his powerful shoulders. He had puffed cheeks, shrewd small eyes, and a fleshy spatulate hand with stubby fingers. Like many Russians who knew some English, he was a great fan of Agatha Christie.

I admired his work but could not forgive him his "court portraits." Nor was I alone in this attitude. Boris Ioganson, an artist of equal stature but far less subservient, took revenge on Gerasimov in an interesting way. In his famous painting "In an Old Urals Foundry," which now hangs in the new branch of the Tretyakov Gallery devoted to Soviet art, Ioganson used Gerasimov as the prototype for the villain: the lone figure of the boss, standing apart from the exploited workers who, stripped to the waist, feed coal into the glowing furnace. The likeness was unmistakable—there was the same fleshy face, sly look in the eyes, and chubby form. Moscow painters, many of whom loathed Gerasimov, were delighted with the resemblance. Such veiled forms were not infrequently used by Soviet painters and other artists to express their revulsion for the Stalin personality cult and its zealous perpetuators.

Gerasimov had come to be so closely associated with Stalin and his rigidity towards art that after the 20th and 22nd Party congresses Soviet painters were only too happy to consign the former secretary of their Union to oblivion. Under Stalin's rule Gerasimov was the country's leading painter. His works were widely exhibited and he was held up as an example of socialist realist art.

Painters who did not glorify the great leader and Soviet achievements enjoyed no such privilege. Among them was the master craftsman Alexander Yakovlev; by his own admission he always kept the painting he did "for the soul" separate from that which provided his livelihood. He was one of the few artists in whose studio I saw no portraits of Stalin. Instead, the walls of his big, government-subsidized workshop were hung with paintings of voluptuous nudes in the Rubens manner.

At the time I knew him, Yakovlev was working on a wall-sized canvas of figures in the most startling dramatic poses. He called it "Gorky's Den of Iniquity," because the characters were inspired by the outcasts of society described in many of Gorky's writings. The canvas was half-finished when I saw it. The central figure and focal point of the entire composition was a wanton creature with titian hair; because of my own wealth of reddish auburn hair, he asked me to pose for the head, something I had neither the inclination nor the time to do.

While he painted, Yakovlev kept up a run of chatter with visitors who kept dropping in and out of his studio, and with them he emptied one bottle of red port after another. The passion he had for life showed in his lush palette. His themes and manner invariably fell out with socialist realism; it was mostly by supervising the public decoration of Moscow for holidays that he supported himself and his family.

He possessed a phenomenal memory. I saw him open a book, pass his eyes over a printed page, lay the volume aside, and reproduce word for word from memory what he had read only once. He also contrived to do exactly the same thing with the paintings of great masters. This talent had led to his involvement in a sensational court case, in the twenties, in which the defendants were charged with smuggling art treasures out of the Soviet Union and disposing of them to Western dealers. The treasures, it was revealed, were not the genuine paintings but frauds—copies made by Yakovlev, from memory, of Rubens and Snyders, which even the most astute art connoisseurs failed to distinguish from the originals.

A man who chose a different road from Gerasimov and Yakovlev was A.L. He belonged to a younger generation and sat with a melancholy detachment while the venerable painters around Merkurov's table reminisced. They were splendid raconteurs, men of great foibles, who had been members of the famous "World of Art" and "Knave of Diamonds" groups, siring trends in painting that were to be taken up thirty or fifty years later and carried forward in the West.

Never having joined the ranks of socialist realist art, A.L. barely made a living. He was representative of a group of painters and sculptors who formed a silent opposition to the regimentation of art by the state. He did not adjust, and went on painting work quite different from that demanded of him. Life was not easy for such artists, either materially or intellectually, for they were cut off from the viewing public.

II The sculptor Merkurov

Like so many Russian artists, Merkurov had passed through a phase of deep devotion to the Tolstoyan philosophy. Having in his youth visited Tolstoy at Yasnaya Polyana, he later tried to model his own home and life style on those of the renowned writer. He put into his dining-room a huge unvarnished table with long benches on either side of it, turning his home into a gathering place for the most curious characters from all walks of life, especially the arts. Although inordinate amounts of vodka, along with Georgian and other wines, were consumed by his guests, Merkurov never touched alcohol.

More than anything else, the sculptor delighted in human companionship, always picking up new friends and wrapping them in the warmth of his heart, happy to have an audience for his stories, his wit, his antics. He was a prolific sculptor, a true master—but I often wondered how much more he could have produced, with his team of apprentices, if he had given less of his time to his friends.

In his home people, their souls, their woes and idiosyncracies were accorded undisputed priority, obscuring even his sculptures, the splendid paintings that hung often askew on the walls, the antiques and bric à brac. The expensive and beautiful furniture that came from his wife's once extremely wealthy home, like a bedroom suite of Karelian birchwood encrusted with mother-of-pearl, was always in need of polish, and the costly tapestries revealed greasy stains. This indifference to things made all human beings feel at ease in the Merkurov home. As unrestrainedly as the times permitted, they could bare their souls, unleash their emotions, as Russians have always been wont to do.

And no human being was more worthy to grace that home than Asta Grigoryevna, at the time one of the few women graduates of Moscow University. Her father had owned the big drugstore on Trubnaya Square and therefore, though a Jew, was permitted to reside in Moscow. Using the screen name of Asta Grey, she had appeared in some of the very early Russian silent movies, scripted by Mayakovsky and directed by Nemirovich-Danchenko.

Merkurov was fond of telling the story of how he first saw her. He was then a widower with two young daughters.

"I was standing in the lobby of the Actors Club, chatting with friends, when I looked up. There, at the top of the staircase leading down into the lobby, stood the Juno of my imagination—a statue I had long wished to chisel in white marble. What my hands had itched to mold appeared in the flesh.

"'A Juno come to life!' I exclaimed. Like myself, my friends gasped at the perfection of form and features they beheld.

" 'This woman will be my wife,' I said to myself."

Quite a few Russians I knew claimed to have chosen their wives in this manner. Possibly Merkurov's exclamation could be traced to that passage in Tolstoy's *War and Peace* in which Andrei, lost in admiration of Natasha, promises to himself: "If she first approaches her cousin and then . . . she will be my wife." But my dear friend had not said "if"; he was an Armenian, and Russian fatalism was not to his taste.

With her crown of soft curly hair, her aquiline nose, ivory skin and slightly protruding lids—perfect for a sculptor to mold—Asta had the kind of beauty that went beyond sexual attraction. She was truly adored by both men and women.

I remember seeing Asta once in the lobby of the Bolshoi Theater talking to two younger women also renowned for their beauty. One was the famous Art Theater actress Alla Tarasova; the other was Lyudmila Tolstoya, recently married to Alexei Tolstoy. Just then the actor Maxim Shtraukh walked up to me and said, "There stands the most beautiful woman in Moscow." I looked at the three beauties and asked, "Which one?"

"Can you doubt it?" he replied. "Asta Merkurova, of course!"

When a son was born to the Merkurovs so much wine was drunk that a deep trench was dug behind the vegetable patches to bury the champagne bottles alone. A great lover of women, soon after the birth of this son Merkurov went back to his accustomed way of living, moving from one mistress to another. When I met him he was fifty-five, and his mistress, to whom I believe he remained attached to the end of his days, was twenty-six.

This mistress, who later became Merkurov's wife, was very different from Asta. For one thing, she was unattached to bourgeois morality or values; in fact she was blissfully ignorant of both. She was, however, far from a simple and straightforward Soviet "new" woman. At a time when Dostoevsky was a forbidden author she steeped herself in his work. She had a typically Russian, almost morbid, love of torturing others and herself by dramatizing the most trivial situation to the extreme.

She wielded an intense sexual power over Merkurov. A clever and intuitive person, he was aware of the symbolic implication of his choice; he was trying to come to terms with the new life and the rigid "proletarian type," as opposed to his liberal-minded, cosmopolitan wife.

He saw himself that this new love was a break with the old life and a step forward in his understanding and acceptance of the new society. He had a purely artistic explanation, too: "She is my finest sculpture. Her contours unfold from the world around me. They reverberate in every stroke of my chisel."

There was nothing new or odd about older men falling in love with younger women, setting up new homes, plunging into new marriages. But as I witnessed the new unions formed by many artists of Merkurov's stature, they seemed to fall into a recognizable pattern, created not so much by nature as by social exigencies. They reflected the conflict in the hearts and minds of men who had their roots in the old pre-revolutionary Russian culture, and the Western culture as well, yet found the communist ideals alluring. To them these ideals represented equality, brotherhood, jobs for all, government by the people: "Every cook will run the state," Lenin had said.

Merkurov and many others like him took no issue with the new order. They complied. They did not flee abroad. Indeed, they embraced communism in the way Lenin had admonished: "You cannot become a communist unless you have learned and assimilated all the culture of the world." They had gone to schools and universities where they had sought Truth, where they had themselves participated in demonstrations against tsarism. They dreamed of a new kind of human society, of happiness for all people.

Gradually, however, it had become obvious how far removed from their dream was the daily activity of Soviet society. Men like Merkurov must have seen that—but there was nothing they could do, except stop posing moral problems, cast away their doubts, and above all disentangle themselves from the burden of the old values. And who was it who shared these doubts and confusion, who held them back from wholeheartedly accepting the new order? In a good many cases it was their wives. What a relief it was, therefore, to be united with the new proletarian-thinking partner, the new wife who "looked only ahead and never back," as one friend had said to me.

I could see the struggle that went on in the heart and mind of Merkurov who, much as he may have desired it, never became totally integrated into the new establishment. He continued to harbor under his roof the children of arrested friends; he also befriended members of the Russian clergy who had served their prison terms and returned to no home, no church—most of them to be hounded, blacklisted, and later rearrested.

His guests would often be startled by the appearance of a timorous black-garbed nun at the head of the stairs leading into the dining-room. Lightly, on tip-toe, she would come down, only to hastily withdraw at the sight of people she knew she must avoid, like the gross Alexander Shcherbakov, Secretary of the Moscow Communist Party City Committee, visiting Merkurov on some matter of the arts, or the puffed-up Marshal Choybalsan, newly arrived from Mongolia to sit for his bust.

A priest would leave his hiding-place and diffidently join the company if the faces were familiar, but even so he would rarely converse, sitting in a far corner by himself. Merkurov tried to find work for these unfortunates, often paying the wages out of his own pocket. Luckily his statues of Lenin, Stalin, and other great ones brought in large sums of money.

Merkurov liked to talk about his work to anyone who was ready to listen, and I was no exception. His features lit up as he dissected a new work for me, going back many centuries into the history of sculpture to explain a fold or a curve, or revealed the secret of his own foreshortening technique in the huge monuments he was designing.

His statue of Timiryazev overlooks Nikitskiye Gates, a busy intersection at Moscow's inner boulevard; this figure of the father of Russian agricultural science is one of the early Soviet modernist sculptures. In 1941, at the outset of the war on Soviet territory, it was knocked off its pedestal by a bomb blast, the head rolling away from the torso. Along with a few helpers, Merkurov worked through the morning hours after the all-clear signal to get it back in place.

"Timiryazev is up again," he told me. "Damn the Nazis! Whatever they blast will rise again like the phoenix from the ashes."

It was in 1941, too, at a very crucial time for his country, that Merkurov further proved his loyalty to the socialist regime. At the age of almost sixty he joined the Communist Party.

Most of Merkurov's statues of Stalin showed him draped in a long army coat, which served well to give the illusion of height and dignity to the puny figure. When he began work on the colossal monuments of Lenin and Stalin commanding the entrance to the Moskva-Volga Canal, Merkurov wrote a letter to Stalin, asking him if he wished to be portrayed with or without his many regalia.

He showed me the brief reply: "Better without." I made no comment. Merkurov's face, too, was inscrutable. To talk about Stalin was to paddle in dangerous waters; Merkurov apparently felt a need for some sort of communication with the man of whom he made so many statues—mostly from photographs—and perhaps the letter helped.

Despite his numerous portrayals of Stalin, Merkurov did not enjoy the trust of the powers he courted, a trust he tried to gain at no small price to his individuality as an artist and as a human being. This I was to realize when my interrogator plied me with questions, the object of which was to extract politically defamatory information against the sculptor.

III Mikhail, 1939

Fear being my counsellor, I decided I would never marry a man as conspicuous in public life as Victor had been. I was working at the *Moscow News* when I met Mikhail, an unassuming, benevolent person to whom people in our office were in the habit of pouring out their hard-luck stories. It might have been this humane quality of empathy that first attracted me to him.

In every way he was the opposite of Victor. Overpowering physically and mentally, with high animal spirits and scathing wit, Victor had a sense of his own worth and superiority that he never bothered to conceal. Mikhail was subdued, willowy, devoid of all vanity. Where Victor was every inch a fighter for what he thought was right, Mikhail was tolerant, forgiving, and fatalistic. Possessing none of the bitterness of A.G., nor the adventurism of Vanya, Mikhail was a realist, loyally serving the socialist society. Neither did he have Victor's ambitious drive—perhaps because he was wise enough to realize the price one paid in journalism to rise to a top position.

We embarked on a long, old-fashioned courtship, untypical of the times—with the traditional flowers, evenings spent together, visits to friends and relatives. He did not rush me; I needed time to get over my feelings for Victor.

When we started our life together—with no wedding, without registering the marriage—like many other couples we had no home of our own. We could only snatch brief moments of privacy and, as during our courtship, spent our evenings out. We would sit for hours at the National Café, talking, dancing, and drinking coffee out of a tall, spindle-legged nickel urn, kept hot with a bluish-pink flame.

Sustenance for our spirit we often derived from the theater, lovingly called by the Russians "a shrine of art." Censorship was stiff and there were unequivocal directives on what to stage and what to ban. But the artistry of the productions, the acting or dancing skill—and, moreover, the possibility of reading our own significant messages into what was presented on the stage— made a theater performance an uplifting experience. Muscovites still flock to the theater with something like the fervor and hope with which Roman Catholics go to church.

When Stalin gave the Art Theater the green light to stage Bulgakov's *The Days of the Turbins*, a tremor of delight passed through Moscow's play-going public. At last a shred of political truth had seeped through to the stage, we told ourselves. For once the White Guards were portrayed as human beings. Stalin's magnanimity was lauded, and people foolishly hoped for a little more leeway. The slavish mentality had become so ingrained that nobody questioned the imposition of such interference and censorship from the top.

Few people can boast of never having had any superstitious fears. At this time in my life, in the early summer of 1939, I became prey to a recurring nightmare; I always woke with the certainty that it was an omen of some disaster to come.

I was traversing a green pasture, fresh with morning dew. On the fringe of the pasture cows and horses grazed, enjoying the luscious grass. The cows flapped their long red tongues and the horses tossed their manes. The serenity of the scene, the happy animals, and the bluest of skies filled me with a pleasant sensation, but it soon melted away. The atmosphere abruptly changed from peace to evil foreboding. The animals now fidgeted nervously. Somber shadows blotted out the sky. Gray turmoil replaced the vibrant, cheerful hues.

Before my gaze the shadows took the shape of monstrous grizzly bears drifting low overhead. They came swooping down on me and the frightened animals. I tried running away but seemed to be chained to the spot by some supernatural force. In the end I got away. Escape filled me with relief. (Nightmares I had in subsequent years brought no such relief; there was no escape.)

The year 1939, a crucial year for all Europe, brought fundamental change in the Soviet Union's international policies. It was a time of territorial expansion and concern for the safety of the country's borders. That summer, the non-aggression pact with Nazi Germany was a hard pill to swallow for all Soviet people. Political passions surfaced and clashed. Piercing the silence, some spoke their despair; a few gloated. One man I met at the Merkurovs' condemned the pact openly while another was in raptures revealing, to our horror, his adulation of Hitler.

The first was the director of a big Moscow industrial plant—work-worn, harried, obsessed, like most Soviet executives, by a fear of not meeting the exaggerated targets of the Five Year Plan: "to rival and outstrip America." He was uncynical, dedicated, harping forever on what measures must be taken to improve the living standards of the proletariat. Certain of the imminence of war, he gave much time to the organization of civil defense, boasting what good marksmen his workers were and how well they could handle a gas attack.

His opinion of the pact he repeated without end: "It is plain foolishness. Hitler *will* strike! Are we prepared? No! My plant isn't! I keep saying it needs to be re-equipped to meet war needs. Do I get support from the top people? Again no!" He was panic-stricken when the war broke out and Hitler's armies were blitzing farther and farther into Soviet territory. His "defeatist talk" earned him a prison sentence. But men as good at their jobs as he was were so badly needed that, to our great amazement, he was released.

The second man whose reaction to the pact was extreme, though not so unusual, was Vsevolod Blumenthal-Tamarin, a magic name throughout the Soviet land. In Moscow he ran an extremely popular state-subsidized one-actor theater, and there was no honor, no privilege the Soviet state did not shower on him.

On that August day of pale sunlight, when the newspapers were full of the pact and the visit of the German foreign minister, von Ribbentrop, to Moscow, my husband and I went to see actor friends of ours at their dacha. The table was set for tea in the garden. Shortly after we arrived a car pulled up and Vsevolod Blumenthal-Tamarin alighted from it; his chauffeur followed behind, lugging a crate of champagne, which he dropped on the grass close to the table.

Swiftly, with an elegant gesture, Vsevolod drew two bottles from the crate and set them down on the table. He was a pampered man: the one wine he drank was champagne, sometimes emptying bottle after bottle with no visible effects. Glasses were filled and passed around. Vsevolod raised his glass, a jubilant light in his eyes. The rest of the company lifted theirs half-heartedly, wondering what the toast would be.

It was indeed unexpected.

"Let us drink to the noble alliance of the Soviet Union and Hitler Germany, and that Britain may be wiped off the face of the earth."

He pronounced the toast in the mellow voice beloved by millions of fans, who would listen entranced to his recitals of Hamlet's and other monologues.

Scandalized, I glanced at the faces around me. They were expressionless.

"I will drink no such toast." I tossed the contents of my glass into the withered grass. Pretending not to hear me, the rest of the company swallowed the champagne at almost a single gulp, as though it were vodka.

Two years later, in 1941, the Germans reached the banks of the Istra, a picturesque hilly area close to Moscow, where many actors had their private dachas. It was here that Blumenthal-Tamarin welcomed them with bread and salt, in the tradition of Russian hospitality. The Germans, in their turn, recruited him as a radio announcer. On behalf of the Nazi command he made countless appeals to the Russian troops to surrender to the Wehrmacht. In 1945 he fell into the hands of the Soviet fighting men, and rumor had it that he was strung up there and then.

Now that I was married I spent less time with my friends and more with my husband. I would look across the table at Mikhail and watch him fill the usual four or five pages of an article for the newspaper with his distinct neat handwriting, each written page the exact equivalent of a typed sheet. I was glad he did not possess Victor's hauteur and qualities of leadership. He would remain a competent rank-and-file journalist. I would be safe with him. So I thought.

Among my friends Mikhail came to be known as the ideal husband. I hoped that if I had a daughter she might inherit his blond coloring, blue eyes, and long, slender fingers.

SIX

I War! German tanks advance on Moscow

It was a cool and cloudless Sunday—June 22, 1941. We slept late, and it was not until noon that Mikhail plugged in the loudspeaker on the wall across from our bed. Molotov was on the air: Hitler's armies had crossed the Soviet border in the small hours of the morning.

"We do not claim another nation's territory, nor shall we cede an inch of our own." These words of Defense Minister Klim Voroshilov had been repeated so often over the past few years that the Soviet people knew them by heart and drew comfort from them.

But that very day, in a matter of hours, great hunks of territory had been sliced off by the enemy. Mikhail and I dressed hurriedly and walked out into the street. Knots of bewildered people, many with tears in their eyes, crowded desolately around the black disks of loudspeakers attached to street poles to hear the news. Horror, disbelief, and puzzlement glared from their faces. Men, young and old, some in uniform, others in ordinary suits with haversacks slung across their shoulders, were hurrying to the drafting stations, accompanied by weeping relatives.

I listened to Churchill's speech at the home of friends who owned a radio set. The news that Britain was our ally, that we did not confront the Nazi war machine single-handed, was reassuring. With his penchant for vivid language, Churchill was saying that he could see Russians everywhere, in the farm fields, in the cities, framing their lips in prayer. Addressed to atheistic Russia, these words rang strange. And since the speech was censored, they never reached the ears they were meant for. Two months later I was amazed to find how true they were.

I was standing on a station platform, from which one troop train after another was departing for the front. Nadezhda, a doctor friend of mine, was leaving with the Army Medical Corps, and I had come to see her off. As she was boarding the train her mother, a shrivelled woman, old before her years, raised herself on tiptoe and made the sign of the cross over her. Glancing around, I noticed that a few other women too were crossing themselves and mumbling prayers.

Air raids started in late July. Moscow skies rocked with the sinister shapes of enemy bombers, reminding me of my nightmare. Cool weather had given way to a torrid spell abetting the outbreak and spread of fires from the numberless incendiary bombs that descended upon the city. Buildings crumbled from the direct hits of demolition bombs. That very day a bomb had barely missed the Central Committee, burying in the rubble of a nearby house Afinogenov, a playwright I very much admired.

A turquoise sky shimmered in the fiery glow of the setting sun. For a moment I was entranced by its beauty. War, danger at every step, sharpened the senses, made life more precious. It puzzled me that I should feel so light-hearted—the frivolity and buoyancy of young womanhood, dismissing all thought of misfortune, anticipating only the good things of life for oneself.

I quickened my step, eager to get home in time to cook some supper for my husband and have him eat it before he took up his nightly duty on the roof of our building, along with the other fire wardens.

A hand was laid on my shoulder. I had to throw my head far backwards to look into the eyes of the man who towered above me. It was a friend from the days I had spent with Victor in Kislovodsk. We had kept in touch. A few years earlier he had graduated from the Zhukovsky Aviation Academy and become one of Moscow's best test pilots. He was in uniform, sunbeams glancing off the blue tabs on his sleeves and collar tips.

His usual jaunty air was replaced by a morose look. He scowled as he spoke, his voice shaking: "Look, I'm an expert navigator and I walk idly about the streets of Moscow. The Germans have put most of our air force out of commission right at the outset of their attack. Many of my best comrades have come down in flames."

He clenched his big fists: "God, oh God Almighty how I itch to put my hands on the controls of a fighter or bomber. And I can do nothing about it. The situation is unbearable."

How costly in human lives, both of fighting men and of civilians, were the early months of the war. It was numbers, a human avalanche, that in the end, after months and months of severe combat, held back the German advance. Then followed the miracle of regearing all industries, the home-front directing all its effort to supply the armed forces with materiel.

Silently, perhaps thinking the same thoughts, we reached the entrance of my home and I invited my friend in to share our supper. But there was no time even to drink a glass of tea. The siren wailed. My husband rushed off to the roof, while the flyer and I, along with all the tenants, made our way into the basement, which had been hastily converted into a shelter. The building above us heaved and shook. It seemed now that at any moment we would be blown to pieces. With every blast my friend's face turned darker. How crushed he must have felt, sitting among mostly old men, women, and children, when he should have been hitting back at the enemy behind the controls of a Soviet plane. Those were bitter days.

Many years after the war my friend and I once again met by chance. I caught sight of him as I was passing through Nogin Square in Moscow. He was one of many war veterans who had come here on the celebration of Victory Day. He wore an aviation colonel's uniform, his entire chest covered with medals and other decorations. But his hair was white, his handsome face deeply furrowed, and he limped.

"Nothing ages like the years," he said, smiling.

"Like a war," I corrected him. "So you got your planes after all?"

"My plane! Just one bomber all through the war, and I cherished it more than life."

There was hardly a night now when the city was not bombed. But, apparently not having achieved the desired effect, the air raids were discontinued after a few weeks.

The Merkurovs had dug trenches in their backyard. There Mikhail and I took cover when we visited them during the early heavy bombing of the city.

Asta had greatly changed; she was no longer her usual serene self. I realized it was one thing to face a calamity for the first time, another when you had been through the experience before.

This was true of Asta. She talked on and on about World War I. Beautiful Asta had become careless about her appearance. When two journalists called to interview her husband on his proposed 100–metre statue of Lenin, which was to top the Palace of Soviets—an ambitious project, eventually dropped—Asta was wearing a soiled dressing-gown. She hurried into the bedroom to change, only to reappear in front of the callers without a skirt, attired in a silk blouse over her faded blue bloomers. Nor did the general embarrassment bother her.

Asta's mind was preoccupied with fear for her son, who was near-ing drafting age. He was her only child. One member of the family, her step-daughter's husband, a man in his thirties, had already fallen in battle.

Just as Asta had her unpatriotic thoughts, I had mine. My brother Shurri, nineteen years old at the time, was a student of mathematics. Any day now, I knew, he could be drafted. In the early battles of the war, casualties were enormous, especially among the youngest of the fighting men. Many perished in their very first encounter with the enemy. Shurri had his haversack ready. He was going to enlist even before he was called up. After some arguing, I persuaded him that, with his perfect knowledge of English, he could be of greater service in the war if he trained as an army interpreter.

He enrolled as a cadet in the Army Institute of Foreign Languages, where I was now teaching. For a while he was in my class. Every time our eyes momentarily locked in a loving gaze, or I watched his tall, slightly hunched figure lose itself in the crowd of cadets as they filed out of the classroom, I felt immensely relieved. A few months later the Institute was evacuated to a city far removed from the fight-ing. I did not go along with the rest of the faculty but stayed behind with my husband, who was then working for the newspaper *Trud*. It was not until the end of the war that I saw my brother again.

Soviet soldiers were now marching into battle with the rallying cry "For the Motherland! For Stalin!"

Only substitute "Tsar" for "Stalin," and it was the same battle cry that had spurred the soldiers and officers of the tsarist army in the First World War. At the beginning of the war the army was still called the Red Army, presently to be renamed the Soviet Army, with the old pre-revolutionary ranks restored.

Nor was the war referred to as the Second World War, but the Great Patriotic War. There was logic behind that. First, the name indicated that it was a war against an enemy's incursion, as had been the Patriotic War against Napoleon. Second, a different name implied disassociation from the goals and aims of the allies. Both the name of the war and the battle cry were carry-overs from the tsarist regime. It was a new and unexpected tactic, very different from the Leninist ideal of international fraternization of the workers versus nationalism and patriotism.

However, in 1941, when the Soviet fighting men marched into com-bat with the same cries as their fathers had in 1914, they felt the warmth of their native soil and new hope sprang in the hearts of those who dared think for themselves. Surely, they thought, after the war is over, after with our blood and our dead we win victory, there will be more freedom and less repression. The people around me, still apprehensive of speaking up, exchanged hopes and little confidences, *tête à tête*, like the Jesuits of old, avoiding a third person's presence, lest he bear witness to their heretical words at some later date.

"We'll breathe freely after the war is over," my husband said to me.

''Things are bound to be different after the war,'' Merkurov repeated with assurance.

Leaving with a field hospital for the battlefront, my dear friend Nadezhda took me aside and, dropping her voice to a half-whisper, said: "There will be great changes, mark my words."

So intimidated had we all become that we dared not utter the words that were really on the tip of our tongue, such as individual freedom and democracy.

The war had a cathartic effect. It overshadowed the tragedies of 1937, 1938, and earlier years. The rancor and pain for loved ones, the innocents so needlessly sacrificed, were for a while cast out of the mind.

Yet right at the outset many cruel measures were carried out: shootings, arrests, resettlings, deportations, sometimes of whole nationalities, like the Kalmyks or the Crimean Tartars. The results were often more deaths than on the battlefield, thousands of broken homes, divided families, parentless children. Rigid labor laws were enforced and even more stringent ones were to follow, when people were jailed for one year if they were twenty minutes late for work.

War, people thought, justified everything. And how we toiled for victory! The more anguished we were by reports of the retreat of our troops, by the capture of one city after another, the more fiercely we threw ourselves into our tasks.

In mid-October of 1941 we witnessed a frantic exodus from Moscow, reminiscent of the way Muscovites abandoned their homes and all their worldly possessions before Napoleon's rape of the city. By that time, Moscow was already half-deserted. Mothers and children had been evacuated even before the air-raids started. Factories, government offices, and educational institutions were relocated eastward too.

Muscovites were hoarding groceries. By the time I got to the hoarding stage, foods everywhere had been swept off the counters as though by a whirlwind. Nothing was to be had except chocolate bars, almonds, and dried apricots. Soon these too vanished. I managed to store about fifty chocolate bars and two bags of nuts and dried fruits.

Asta Merkurova had been safely evacuated to Sverdlovsk, where her son was a student at an exclusive diplomatic college. On October 14, when German tanks had advanced to within thirty kilometers of the heart of the city, Merkurov arrived in his car, urging and arguing that my husband and I leave Moscow with him. He was not going to stay and wait for the Germans to march into Moscow, he declared, as they had into Paris more than a year before. His black eyes, usually twinkling with merriment, showed the strain and alarm of all eyes in those days. There was no transport to take his work out; he would go without it. He was ready to start that very night.

Mikhail was at the office and we waited for him, hoping that he might bring reassuring news. He had different news when he arrived. Next morning, he said, there would be massive evacuation from Moscow. We took counsel and decided it would be best for us to leave in organized fashion. We hoped that there would be some means of taking Merkurov's sculptures to a place of safety.

We remained in the city for yet another two days. On October 16 the news was more alarming than ever. I had never loved a city as I loved Moscow. And now I was to abandon her in her hour of need! I packed one suitcase with warm clothes and another with eatables. Mikhail and I set out on foot to the Kursk Railway Station, quite a long way from where we lived. When we reached the square in front of the station, it was teeming with people.

Mikhail rushed back to the city to fetch our two mothers, hoping that there would be room for them in the train carriage that had been reserved for the newspaper *Trud*.

II We flee to Sverdlovsk

On that bitterly cold October day, after sitting on their belongings in the open square for twelve hours, my mother and mother-in-law were convinced of the hopelessness of their situation.

"At a time like this, old people don't count," my mother said. "Come what may, we shall remain in our homes in Moscow. It is you who are most in danger. You must go."

It proved a wise decision. Even if we had succeeded in squeezing them into the train, these elderly women might not have survived the tough and perilous journey to Sverdlovsk in the Urals, which was our destination.

So crammed with evacuees was the train that we spent the first twenty-four hours standing on the wind-swept platform between the carriages. Later we took brief turns sitting down on the benches inside.

Our journey lasted nineteen days: normally it took forty-six or fifty hours. We learned to sleep standing up, like horses, to do without water and with little food for whole days. The German Messerschmitts were on our trail. Hearing their approach we would jump off the train, tumbling over one another, and scurry off in all directions. If there were woods we made a dash for their cover; if not, we fled into the open fields and stretched out in the frozen grass, faces buried in the icy ground.

We could count on no food except bread. When we had moved far enough inland for the enemy planes to stop their pursuit, our bread rations were delivered regularly at the stations on our way. Thus we did not starve, and for that we were thankful to the organizers of this last-minute evacuation from Moscow.

At the same time, along with people everywhere, we were experiencing our first pangs of wartime hunger, a foretaste of the deprivation we would suffer throughout the war and for several years after.

Food was on the minds of the men I travelled with and, being literary persons, they vied with one another in describing succulent roasts, shashlik, sturgeon baked in dough and served with piquant sauce. Their imaginations oozed with savory dishes, quite different from my dried fruits and bland chocolates, which nonetheless were speedily devoured.

Bleak, overpopulated Sverdlovsk greeted us with icy blasts and the sullen faces of the local inhabitants forced to share their homes, often just a single room, with us. That first night, when at long last we were able to lie down on the floor of an office building, I found two overfed white lice on my lace nightgown.

All available trains were engaged in transporting civilians away from the fighting zones and enlisted men and arms to the battlefields. The movement of food supplies was greatly delayed. Bloated with refugees, Sverdlovsk had nothing but bread rations to offer them.

On our very first night I saw tremendous queues outside the few central grocery stores. Bundled up, only their eyes exposed, thousands of people stood in gray clouds of vapor rising from their frozen breath. The next morning they were still there, having spent the night in the bitter frost. Large-sized tins of black caviar, the sole product in stock, were their reward. But these too were soon sold out. From then on, there were lines for hastily baked black bread tasting and looking as though it were half mixed with sawdust. I went to the farmers' market. The stalls were empty except for a few women sell-ing milk in frozen disks. One of these I bought at an exorbitant price.

It was a very hungry New Year's Eve for us in Sverdlovsk; the spread consisted of nothing but rye bread cut in tiny elegant squares, which had been sprinkled with salt and dried in the oven. These we drank down with vodka and champagne. Among the guests with whom we saw in the year 1942, a year of agonizing defeats, were the Bolshoi opera singer Kruglikova, whose husband, a general, was fighting Hitler; the painters Ryazhsky and Ioganson; and the movie actress Valentina Serova, sex bomb of her day, who at the time was in love with General Rokossovsky, dragged from prison to a leading position in the army. This was a New Year's party at which we neither smiled nor laughed. And, like Chekhov's three sisters, the one desire and thought we all shared was to return to our beloved Moscow.

With a large sprinkling of Moscow's scientists and artistic person-alities in its midst, grim, dour Sverdlovsk, was acquiring a cosmo-politan air. In all fairness it should be said that before the war, too, it boasted a musical culture of some refinement; the opera house, with its blue-gray columns, did much to relieve the monotony of the tenement-like buildings on either side of Lenin Street.

It was at the Urals Hotel on Lenin Street that many Muscovites lived or congregated. The rooms and lobby swam in a haze of cig-arette smoke and alcohol. Men reeled and staggered out to return shortly with more bottles of vodka. Some of them were the brave, reckless flyers, like the Pokryshkin brothers, soon to become heroes whose very names spelled out the glory of Soviet arms. There was no denying that war had its romance and appeal: you could reach dazzling heights without the plodding that leads to accomplishment in peacetime. These thoughts ran through my mind as I watched the flyers swill their liquor, knowing that the next day or the one after they would be off on their perilous missions. The men designing and testing new weapons also lived at the Urals Hotel, but kept aloof from their dashing and carousing comrades—understandably, because they guarded some of the major secrets of the war.

On nights when my husband did not work late we went to the theater, mostly the opera. There were many patriotic productions, among them the opera *Mademoiselle Fifi*, its anti-Prussian fervor ech-oing our own hatred for the German invaders. Asked to write a review of the production, I called next day on Reinhold Glière, its elderly composer, who lived only a few blocks away from me on Lenin Street. He could hardly speak of his work, so dismayed was he by the Red Army defeats.

"If only I were able to do more than just write music," he said. I comforted him by describing how deeply moved the audience was by his work. Many of the spectators, I told him, were young men, who would be carrying away their impressions to the battlefront. But the composer's patriotic outburst reverberated in my own heart: "If only I could work day and night to help win the war."

The four half-idle months I spent in Sverdlovsk were a painful waste of time to me. In early March, after the Germans had suffered a major defeat at the gates of the city, my husband returned with his newspaper staff to Moscow. Soon I was able to leave Sverdlovsk. That spring the trains were almost as crowded with joyful Muscovites going back to their homes and jobs as they had been with evacuees in the autumn of 1941. It was by a miracle that I squeezed into a carriage after being pushed in from behind by two Sverdlovsk friends. The sleeve of my coat was ripped out of its armhole and all the buttons wrenched from my blouse.

III Back in Moscow

Moscow was unbelievably deserted, but a work-worn Mikhail met me at the Yaroslavsky Station in the spring of 1942. A translator's job awaited me at the Soviet Information Bureau (a kind of propaganda ministry). The head of the translation department was Alexander Antonovich Troyanovsky, one-time ambassador to Japan and also to the United States. He was immensely liked by our staff because he was so open and friendly, with nothing of the tight-laced diplomat about him.

The long-vacant office of vice-chairman of the Sovinformburo was filled by Kondakov, a man very unlike the amiable and well-wishing Troyanovsky. He came to us from a top post in the propaganda department of the Central Committee and turned out to be a conceited bully, perpetually aggrandizing himself and demeaning people on his staff. Kondakov demanded the signs of homage that an inferior was expected to pay a princely personage.

A natty, short-legged, impatient man in his late thirties, Kondakov was shockingly uncivil and had a way of unexpectedly popping out from behind a door or a corner in the hallway, his shrunken form expanding into menacing dimensions. Never on his life would he greet you first. Emitting an offensive cockiness, he waited for an obsequious bow, which he acknowledged with a tilt of his head.

I remember how disgusted I was by the imperious manner in which he conducted our weekly briefings; it clashed so with his ridiculously short figure and his flat, snubby face. The briefings were held in a luxurious, high-ceilinged hall, with wainscotted walls, crystal chandeliers, a long oak table, and red plush chairs. Before the outbreak of the war the building had belonged to the German embassy. Most of its furniture, rugs, and expensive plateware had been left behind by the hastily departing diplomats.

After everybody was assembled, Kondakov burst into the conference hall. With a sharp glance around, his jaws working in disapproval, he barked sharply: "Each be seated according to rank of office. Department heads up in front, closer to me, deputy heads in the next row, editors behind them, translator-editors at the back wall."

I would sit down on the very edge of a chair "at the back wall" as ordered, actually glad to be as far away as possible from the Caesar personage that Kondakov imagined himself to be. I stole glances at the others, watching for a sign of shock or resentment at this overt command to observe the hierarchy of rank. But the eyes of everyone I could see were blank and the faces bore that craven look of servitude which I came to recognize so well—my own too, I am certain. The late thirties had taught us a good lesson.

One morning Kondakov swept into Troyanovsky's office. A meeting of the translators was called. Castigated for our work, we in turn blamed the poor editing of the Russian articles. (Translated into English, French, and Spanish, they described the Soviet people's war effort and were designed to win friends for the Soviet Union, which they did.)

Kondakov said, "Come straight to me if you find errors. That is the way to improve our work."

His instructions seemed sensible to me. But for the moment I had forgotten the nature of the man. I have done things in my life of which afterwards I was very much ashamed. One of these things I associate with the effect Kondakov's speech had on me.

The next day, finding on my desk an article containing a few examples of what I thought was slipshod editing, I felt justified in bringing it to Kondakov. It's good for our work, I told myself. Kondakov was pleased. Nor did I have any uneasy feelings about what I did.

Not until the following day, when in the corridor I ran into Shpigel, the editor of the article. He stopped me and with his habitual doleful look—none of us looked cheerful in the war years—said, "Why didn't you come directly to *me* with your criticism? Surely we could have thrashed the matter out between ourselves."

There was no hint of accusation or animosity in his pleasant, cultured voice. But before I could reply he turned on his heel, leaving me with a sense of self-disgust.

A moment later I visualized the whole scene: I could see dignified, embarrassed Shpigel standing (Kondakov, I was certain, did not offer him a seat) before the ideology boss like a naughty boy in front of a particularly sadistic schoolmaster. I swore to myself that if ever again I had any criticism to make, or was asked to review another person's work, I would do it to his face. I hardly saw Shpigel after that—I believe he managed to get himself transferred to another job—but I was grateful to him for the lesson he taught me.

Kondakov had not held his high post for as long as a year when we were informed of his downfall. It seemed he had been caught negotiating shady deals, including the sale of coupons for Persian lamb coats and valuable property left behind by the German embassy. He was not prosecuted, merely dismissed from his post.

Many people I knew starved during the war and many died of hunger. As always, Moscow was in a privileged position. But in Moscow too quite a few did not live to see the day of victory because their bread rations were so meager

Our room on Bolshaya Bronnaya Street, close to Pushkin Square, was unheated; the basin of water I prepared before bed to wash myself in the morning froze overnight. Quite often I did not return home at all but slept at the office on a long, hard table. However, I did not go hungry. The Soviet Information Bureau being part of the Central Committee ideology apparatus, its translators enjoyed food denied to ordinary Soviet people even in peacetime. Indeed, I was astounded at the enormous rations issued in wartime to Central Committee employees.

In 1942, when I began work as a translator, in the morning and evening we were served snacks of two sandwiches, one of caviar, the other of cheese or salami, and a glass of delicious tea with a sweet roll. In the afternoon we went for our mid-day meal to the Central Committee canteen in a green building on Staraya Ploshchad. I do not want to sound noble, but I was happier when the translators, as inferior employees, were cut off from these lavish meals several months later. Even so, we were issued far bigger rations of groceries than, for example, workers in the munitions plants.

Before the war I often ate in Moscow's finest restaurants, either with tourists, when I was a guide, or as the guest of friends. I enjoyed the cuisine, the warmth, and the pre-revolutionary splendor of the Metropole and the Savoy, but never in these internationally known restaurants was I served the exquisitely prepared dishes I ate at the

Central Committee dining-room in 1942, one of the hungriest years of the war. I couldn't believe my eyes when I saw the mountain of white bread in the middle of the table, the pitcher of rich sour cream served with a borshch so full of nutrients that it alone sufficed for a meal. There was a wide choice of dishes on the menu: goose stuffed with apples, tender pork chops, beef Stroganoff, stewed fruit, ice-cream.

One day I ordered chicken croquettes, prepared by an excellent chef. After eating one, I looked around for paper napkins to wrap the other two and take them home: there were none, only snow-white linen serviettes. From then on I came to the dining-room with two glass jars, which I filled with more than half my meal to feed hungry friends.

That same year a free-lance translator, denied a ration card for herself and her small daughter, because for some bureaucratic reason her Moscow residency permit could not be renewed, died of hunger.

Engrossed in my work, worried about the news from the battle-fronts, as we all were, I hardly noticed that summer had slipped into autumn and the raw, cold weather was back.

The Germans had launched another attack on Moscow. More and more men were now being drafted and sent into the thick of the fighting. On returning home late one day, I discovered that my husband had been called up. I could bid him only a brief goodbye. Learning next morning that Mikhail was at a drilling ground near Moscow, I hurried there to have a little more time with him. There was a pinched look about him that wrung my heart. Tears filled my eyes.

"Don't cry," Mikhail said brusquely. "War is war!" After a pause he added more gently, "Compose yourself. You have your work!"

"But your knee?" My husband had a stiff knee, the result of a fall.

"The Examining Board passed me. Besides, I'm a fatalist. Whatever must, will happen."

It was the worst thing he could have said, for I abhorred a fatalistic attitude. I bit my lips, making no retort. Mikhail looked so fragile. But as I waved to him in parting and stared at the other freshly drafted men, I noticed that they had the same unmilitary appearance. They were indeed the *Opolchenye*, or People's Guard, among them quite a few middle-aged professors, some wearing the Moscow University badge. Could these men, so puny, so unwarlike, push back the "invincible" Wehrmacht?

I was soon to learn how few of them returned alive from the battlefront. My husband was among the lucky ones; after eleven months' fighting not far from Moscow, he was wounded in his bad leg, brought to the Bodkin Hospital, and operated on. And yet these men did stem the German offensive. Perhaps valor is not in the way you look but in the way you feel. And their feelings? They knew they were fighting for a just cause.

IV Involvement with the secret police

A day or two after my husband departed for the front I was called to the office phone. The peace of mind I hoped to gain by immersing myself in translation was shattered by the voice at the other end of the line. From the tone and very first words I knew I was talking to an NKVD secret-police officer.

It was in 1935, when I was twenty years old and working for Intourist, that I had first become involved with the Secret Department of the NKVD (People's Commissariat for the Interior, now KGB).

A patient, good-tempered man named Meyerovich was at the time in charge of assigning guides to individual tourists and groups. At about ten o'clock one morning he called me into his office, shut the door, and, lowering his voice, told me I was expected at Lubyanka headquarters. A pass in my name would be waiting for me at an entrance on the left side of the building.

That warm late-summer day I walked into the Lubyanka on Dzerzhinsky Square of my own free will, tingling with a foretaste of adventure, quite certain that no harm would befall me, giddy with romantic visions of being commissioned with important secret work, for I knew English like a native—an obvious asset.

After a twenty-minute wait on a polished bench of solid oak my name was called out. I approached a wicket and was handed a pass. A sentry at a massive door leading from the lobby into the main building scrutinized it along with my internal passport, and looked closely at my features to make sure they matched the passport photo.

Arriving on the floor indicated on my pass, I went down a long panelled corridor.

Young men carrying bulky folders hurried past me, almost bumping into one another. They kept their eyes averted, as I did mine; their very movements suggested a compulsion to secrecy.

I soon found myself in a spacious office with a few desks, only one of which was occupied. Behind it sat a man in his middle years with a large, heavily blotched face. The blotches flamed purple as he eyed me through the thick lenses of his glasses. How different he looked from the dashing secret-police officers I danced with at the Select

Hotel! His wispy, faded blond hair and pale face gave him an anemic look.

It seemed an effort for him to break the ice between us. He was like an actor who, out of charity, had been assigned a few lines in the prelude of a play that augured no good for anybody, including himself. He was acting out his part mechanically, with no bluff or histrionics, as later I saw others do.

"You are working with foreign tourists." He came to the point at once when he at last addressed me. "It is imperative that we know what these tourists think and what they say. Put down your impressions of them, what they tell you about themselves, and what their comments on Soviet life are. Above all we want to know their political views. Compose a report and hand it to Meyerovich, your boss."

Years later, on going over this interview in my mind, I concluded that because the reports were submitted to an official at my job, and not to an undercover man, the section for which I was asked to work was different from the network controlling those who informed on their fellow citizens.

With a fatherly air he continued: "Your assistance is going to be of great value. It is an honor to cooperate with us."

My response was enthusiastic, earnest. What would I not do to maintain the socialist country's security? I replied I was ready to perform the tasks required of me.

He slipped a sheet of paper across the desk.

"Sign this after you've chosen a code name for yourself."

The paper clinched the deal. It also contained a non-disclosure vow. Searching my mind for an appropriate sobriquet, one that would reflect my idealism, I chose the initials I.S.T., The first initial stood for "international"; what the other two represented I cannot recall— the words are buried in some deep recess of my mind. At the time I signed up I had the conviction that I was doing the correct and noble thing; to say no seemed inconceivable to me.

The man behind the desk looked abashed and so uncomfortable that throughout the conversation I was somehow aware of the incongruity of such a person within the walls of the powerful Lubyanka. Events were brewing in the mid-thirties, soon to come to a head, that were far beyond my comprehension. Later, looking back, I could see that there were still decent communists in the Lubyanka security service, who longed for an escape; and some did indeed break away, finding employment elsewhere. If they had stayed on they would have become the cold-blooded executioners of the late thirties.

What choice the man in front of me made I do not know. Meye-

rovich was arrested along with hosts of other Intourist employees.
A few months later I quit my own job, thus dropping out of the
Lubyanka picture—but not forever as I had hoped. The purges so
darkened the horizons everywhere that my attitude to secret work
changed radically.

The first attempt to renew contact with me dated to the end of 1939
when, after two years of free-lance journalism, I took a teaching position. Walking down the mazy corridors of the First Moscow Institute
of Foreign Languages, where I taught, I was stopped by a man in a
crumpled tunic worn over a pair of faded khaki breeches. In the dim
light of the dilapidated building, made even dimmer by the grimy
windows, I could hardly make out his features, except for a general
hard and tense look.

"Keep in step with me. I have a few things to say to you."

I complied without answering.

"Write down an address, quick!"

He stated the day and hour on which we were to meet. "You realize
you are not to mention this or future meetings to anyone?"

"Yes."

Only vaguely do I recollect what the rendezvous was about. My
tasks were to be specified at the following meeting, which I skipped.
The war broke out; it was natural for contacts to scatter and be lost
track of.

Moreover, luckily, I had no permanent residency registration in
Moscow because, after quitting my job at Intourist, I was forced to
move out of the Novomoskovskaya Hotel. I was roomless, like thousands of other Muscovites, renting privately now a "corner," now a
room or even an apartment for brief spells. I had been living that
way during the closing arrests of 1938, too, and this may well explain
how I escaped the fate that befell so many of my friends and co-
workers of those days. A similar situation had saved other would-
be victims of the persecution, especially those who had relatives
abroad or had frequented the homes of arrested persons.

The man now phoning me in the war year of 1942 had a gruff,
commanding voice that fully accorded with the power the secret
police wielded over the citizenry. He would brook no refusal from
me. But if he was different from the official who recruited me in 1935,
I too was a changed person, with the searing memories of those who
perished in 1937 and 1938 alive in my mind. The secret police,
Lubyanka, NKVD! I wanted nothing to do with their prying and surveillance. Somehow I must shrug them off.

"I work twelve hours a day and more. I haven't time for anything else."

"Never mind your work. We meet tomorrow at seven."

Again I jotted down an address—a private place for a rendezvous.

With a choking resentment I returned to my typewriter in the cigarette-smoke-filled room at the Sovinformburo headquarters. My mind was made up: by hook or by crook I must find a way to sever all ties with the secret police.

I knew it would be hard to stand up against their pressure and possible threats, but I felt that no personal peril would be involved: it was not a time of persecution and arrests. Besides, translators were badly needed. These considerations made it easier to stick to my decision.

The address took me to a downstairs apartment in a small street behind the TASS building, about fifteen minutes' walk from where I worked. I rang the bell. A shabbily dressed, unshaven man with bloodshot cobalt eyes answered. He led me through a small shadowy hall into a musty room with a few rickety pieces of furniture, among them a round table covered with a soiled, ink-stained plush tablecloth. The man's own seedy looks fitted the surroundings. Bracing myself for what I knew would not be an easy conversation, I sat down across the table from him. I did not look my best either; I had lost about twenty pounds and my prewar clothes were anything but chic. The whole atmosphere was one of strain and gloom. The strain and gloom of war.

"You have a wide circle of acquaintances," he began. "People take you into their confidence . . . We need your services."

How to slip out of the net? "That's where you're wrong. I see nobody, lead no social life."

"You visit the homes of painters and writers . . ."

"Not any more."

"All we require is brief reports of what people say."

Damn him! "I have a poor memory . . ."

"Don't hand me that crap! There's a war on. We protect the Soviet country's security. We don't want people to wag their tongues. And if they do, we must know what they're saying. You've got to help expose the harmful elements in our society."

"I do not know any harmful elements."

"Okay, what about the people in your office?"

He was beginning to show his impatience. I knew I must alter my tactics.

"I'll think it over." I wanted to gain time.

We agreed that he would phone me in a couple of days. But it was not until a couple of weeks later that I heard from him. I pleaded illness. Soon there was another call. A new voice, more airy and casual. Again I gave the excuse of not being well. He insisted on an appointment. I did not show up. More phone calls.

The last call. Would I persist in breaking appointments and wasting the precious time of security agents? Yes, I longed to be released. The voice was insistent, truculent. I was given a new address. The man appealed to my duty as a citizen in wartime. It was no use, I mumbled, they must not count on me. There was a pause. What accent did the man have? An Odessa accent, of course. And the phrase he used—*Tak ne fontan?* ("So, no fountain?"—actually meaning "No go?") was unmistakably Odessan. He was telling me to go to hell. I was relieved. I had done it! They would strike me off their lists, leave me alone.

V *We survive the war*

Twice a week I was on night duty at the Yauza Hospital, a big, sprawling building of solid gray masonry overlooking the small Yauza River, which runs through one of Moscow's oldest quarters.

The chill nights, filled with moans and the sight of mangled bodies, brought me as close to the tragedy of war as I ever got. Every ward and corridor was crammed with wounded men, mostly young amputees, delivered here from the battlelines. The hospital reeked of pus and rotting flesh. The men ran us off our feet with their feeble and at times hysterical cries: "Bring the pan, Sister! Quick!" "Water, a drink of water!" "Get the doctor, I'm dying!"

Exhausted by lack of sleep, longing for the briefest of catnaps, there were nights when I performed my duties as volunteer nurse halfheartedly. I chided myself, yet could not help feeling relieved and happy when morning came at last, bringing me escape from the hospital's tomb-like atmosphere, and I could emerge into the daylight. The attitude of a co-worker of mine, who lost her only son, aged nineteen, in the war, was different. Although considerably older than myself and much weaker, she did not rest for a single minute during the long cold nights, ministering patiently to the needs of the wounded and dying. We all knew how deep was her own grief.

There were other voluntary jobs. One of them was unloading freight trains, which we did either early in the morning or sometimes late at night. The lifting of heavy crates had disastrous effects on many women. I suffered a miscarriage.

True, I had had no idea I was pregnant, as I had stopped having my period soon after the beginning of the war. All the women of my acquaintance shared that experience during the war. This was also true of prison and prison camp, with rare exceptions.

Nor when I was pregnant the second time, towards the end of the war, did I suspect it.

"You look pregnant even from the back," one of the women at the office told me then.

I have always been a great vegetable eater. Practically the only vegetable besides potatoes available in wartime was sauerkraut sold at the private market, and I had indeed been buying and consuming a good deal of it.

Therefore I replied, "Nonsense, it's the sauerkraut—it bloats you so!"

When my daughter was born, she was jokingly christened "the sauerkraut baby."

Mikhail and I had to find new living quarters but there was a permanent housing shortage. For years Moscow families waited in vain to have a room or "living space" of their own. New houses were built, but at a slow pace, and were occupied mostly by government officials and important people in the sciences and the arts. There were the fine modern apartment buildings in Gorky Street, designed by the architect Mordvinov—whom I often saw standing outside the National Café, thoughtfully surveying his own work—but they too were for the élite, or their protégés and mistresses.

An elderly friend of ours, a widow with a very small pension, offered to sell us one of her two rooms. Originally it had been one big room; a partition of thin wood now converted it into two. We jumped at the offer. Buying or selling "living space" was illegal, since all property belonged to the state. But between close friends it could be arranged.

Mikhail and I worked hard to pay off the debt, which I finally did shortly before my arrest. It was in this room that my only child was born, in August, 1945, and from this room, with a period of ten months between the two arrests, that my husband and I were dragged away by night to the Lubyanka Prison.

The house stood on the Moscow River Embankment, and we had only to cross the Moskvoretsky Bridge to find ourselves in Red Square. Visible from the Embankment where we lived were the Kremlin walls and the dizzy, flaming cupolas of St. Basil's Cathedral. The house itself was a curiously designed structure, amazing in many ways. It was built of such solid masonry that it had survived the

Moscow fire during the Napoleonic invasion, when the Kremlin palace itself, across the river, was in flames. It also escaped destruction
from the direct hit of a German demolition bomb during the massive
air raids in the summer of 1941. Before the Revolution it had been a
cheap rooming house.

It stood next door to the Novomoskovskaya Hotel, associated with
the happy days of my love for Victor. Just as it must have been in
pre-revolutionary times, it remained a foul-smelling, dilapidated,
bug-infested building. And it had the oddest assortment of tenants.
Among them was a quixotic revolutionary who at the end of the Civil
War had brought Lenin a carload of gold, American dollars, and other
valuables; he handed it all over to the new Soviet Treasury, without
leaving himself the money to buy a meal. There lived also, on the
second and third floors, a couple of pimps who provided visitors at
the hotel with prostitutes; two highly intellectual lesbians; a police-
man noted for his black-market deals during the war; a famous architect; and a popular film and stage actress.

The rooms were laid out along a maze of corridors, winding and
twisting in a figure eight. Families lived in single rooms, sharing
washrooms and latrines that were in a frightful state of disrepair. It
took several weeks of living in the house before I could find my way
through its labyrinths. It struck me what a marvelous setting the
place would make for detective stories, with all the innumerable little
niches and dark nooks behind small staircases to stack away dead
bodies. But instead of corpses, I would often come upon drunken
men in these hideaway places. Snoring noisily or lying in a stupor,
they presented such a common sight that people rarely took notice
of them.

In the late summer of 1943 the hope of victory dawned. The bedraggled remains of von Paulus's army were tramping through the streets
of Moscow. We rushed out of the office and made our way to Gorky
Street to watch them pass. The German war prisoners, the men who
had brought such suffering and death to the people of the Soviet
Union and Europe, were a sorry sight. I looked away. I did not want
to see them, and quickly returned to my work.

My husband, who had joined the Party in 1941 at the front, in the
darkest days of the war, now walked about with a bright sparkle in
his pale blue eyes. The battle of Stalingrad was won.

He phoned me at the office: "Do try to get home earlier tonight.
I have a bottle of vodka and have brought over a few friends. We
are going to celebrate the good news from the front."

I told him to start without me. With what elation we all worked in those days! We were translating more and more stories about the heroic performance of the Soviet army. It was a time when the attitude of the allies was amicable towards the Soviet Union, a state of affairs not destined to last long.

When I finally arrived home all the vodka was drunk and all the food consumed, along with the bread ration for the following day. Fortunately my husband and I were used to the most meager fare. There was an asceticism ingrained in both of us, perhaps stemming from the hardships we had known. When I opened the cupboard it was empty as though a hurricane had swept through it. My husband grinned drunkenly and blamed everything on the victory at Stalingrad.

There was a flow of refugees from Central Asia and Siberia back to Poland at the end of the war. Among them was a Jewish Polish sculptor whom I had met at Merkurov's and who had become a dear friend.

Passing through Moscow on his way to Poland, he dropped in to see me. He had a lean Christ-like face and a melancholy gaze. He never smiled; his young wife and three small children had been shot dead against a house wall by the German soldiers when they marched into Warsaw. His own escape from the Nazis, along with a large group of painters and sculptors, many of them Jewish, was carried out with the assistance of the Soviet government.

And now, as he sat at the table of my scantily furnished room, he looked more emaciated than ever. I guessed that he must have starved all through the war. The worst of it was that I did not have a crumb of food in the house. I felt so guilty at not being able to offer him even a cup of tea that the joy of his unexpected visit dissolved into a gnawing embarrassment.

I could only listen with half an ear to what he was saying, his pallor and sunken cheeks tugging at my heart. Most likely sensing the reason for my discomfort, he muttered casually and quite beside the point, "I'm used to going without food for days. What I eat, a stale heel or fancy pastry, doesn't matter to me." (Nobody I knew ate pastry during the war, and many people starved to death.) I remember him vividly for those words, as well as one other remark: "If the Soviet Union had not given asylum to so many Polish refugees when the Germans captured Warsaw, I would not be sitting here talking to you."

This was true. It was later that with his help my mother learned of the tragedy of her Warsaw family, of relatives in Paris who had not fled when the city fell into German hands. All her sisters, along with their children and grandchildren, had perished in the Nazi gas chambers.

My mother echoed the Polish sculptor's words: "How fortunate we are to be living in the Soviet Union. We enjoy the protection of the Soviet government. We owe it to its humane policies that we have not been made victims of anti-Semitism."

We all came out alive from the war. It was a miracle: on Victory Day my husband and brother were with me, and many friends too, army surgeon Nadezhda among them. In her low, throaty voice she said, "Our hospital train was bombed over and over again, yet I escaped without a scratch."

In May, 1945, visible from our windows, Red Square was a sea of rejoicing crowds. We feasted on American luncheon meat from tins my brother had saved out of his army ration, washing down the meat and other *zakuski* with tumbler after tumbler of vodka. We poured champagne and clinked glasses. We sang patriotic songs and went to sleep ecstatic with joy. The war was over. The war was over. We knew we had helped win it.

The author's mother, Helen Eve Halbère, before her second marriage, c. 1910.

The author's father, Benjamin Rosenberg, c. 1915.

Helen Eve Rosenberg, c. 1914.

In the late 1920s.

Sergei Dmitrievich Merkurov at his studio in Moscow talking to art students, February 1936. Note Lenin's death mask on the wall, first on the left.

The author's first husband, Mikhail Zinde, with family friend in woods near Moscow, 1939.

In 1942.

On the left is the old house in Moscow where the author lived from 1943 until 1962. Next to it is the Novomoskovskya Hotel (today the Bucharest Hotel). The photograph was taken in September 1987.

Shurri Rosenberg, the author's brother,
on the Island of Sakhalin, 1947.

With daughter Vicky in Moscow, 1946.

In 1948.

Vicky Zinde, aged seven, then in the first grade, with Georgi Mikhailov. The photograph was taken in Moscow during September 1952, a year before the author's release from the Gulag.

Kislovodsk revisited, 1954.

Vicky, 1973.

In Leningrad, visiting with Georgi and his family.

A Saturday-night party at the author's home in Moscow.

SEVEN

I A toast to the Russians

All through the war years we worked without a single day off, no summer vacation, no winter holiday. At the close of the war it was the men who had been wounded in battle who received the first vouchers. Rather reluctantly, because he knew he would miss his newborn daughter terribly, Mikhail went off to the Crimea, to a holiday home for war veterans.

Influenced by newfangled ideas on the parent-child relationship, I imagined that to tie my little daughter emotionally to myself was wrong. I tried not to be overaffectionate with her. Mikhail, on the other hand, who doted on her, practiced no such restraint. Indeed he loved her as only a father can his firstborn, when after years of war and hardship raising a family was in itself no common thing. So strong was their attachment that when my daughter remained parentless she dreamed about her father and longed for him more than for me. (My daughter never talks of her father to anyone but me. It is too painful. I do not think she can forget or forgive his cruel death.)

With my husband away I was seeing more of my mother, who helped me look after Vicky. It seemed to me that she still believed every word she read in *Pravda*, but I was not at all certain. It had become too troublesome, too disturbing, and moreover too dangerous to utter one's thoughts.

What went on in the minds of those I loved—my mother, brother, and husband—remained a sealed book to me. Nor did I much care to read it. I was too busy working—and work was a panacea; too busy trying to make life liveable. Whenever bitter thoughts stole into my mind I tried to brush them off, persuading myself that I must see the good sides of the socialist society: the total employment, the free education, the zest for reconstructing the ravaged economy, the imaginative flair of the artistic intelligentsia, struggling desperately, as always, to get around the rigid censorship. I still hoped that the socialist society would fulfill its goals. I closed my eyes to the ugly manifestations and implored my dear ones to do likewise.

My brother arrived from South-Sakhalinsk in the northeast for a brief vacation. It was good to have him with us; the gleam in his velvety eyes brought new warmth to our one-room home, where we had to put him up to sleep on the floor. He looked manly in his army lieutenant's uniform, but the vulnerability I remembered from his childhood glimpsed at me from the soft contours of his swarthy face and the tenuous smile in the corners of his mouth. He was now married with a daughter of his own.

We talked on general subjects in a loving and bantering way. Shurri, who had a wry sense of humor, thought it rather amusing to tell a dream he had about Stalin; for some reason he related it several times, even when we had company. As it was Stalin's custom to summon his acolytes in the middle of the night, he ordered my brother, too, to appear before him at a nocturnal hour. Clutching his pipe in his stubby fingers and waving it as he spoke, he said to him affably: "See how I toil for the people's sake. I burn the midnight oil. This is what I expect all my subjects to do. Get that? Now back to your job!" The account elicited no comment, only a polite and indulgent smile.

During the postwar years, when he was staying at our home, daily life meant experiencing one shortage or inconvenience after another. Almost every night the electricity failed or was cut off. Electric appliances were unavailable. The one-burner electric cooker we had was falling apart; an electric tea kettle refused to serve; the alarm clock kept erratic time; the furniture legs splintered.

Every time I came home from work I would find my husband and brother in the middle of a repair job; one blond and one dark curly head bent over a table littered with the parts of some household object. The two men were marvelously adept at taking things apart, but somehow never managed to put them together again. Impatiently I would scoop up all the tiny screws, electric coils, springs, and chair legs, desperately looking for a place to stow them away in our cramped quarters.

When the dismantled object was something we could not do without, I would quickly fetch Ivan Mikhailovich, our janitor and odd-job man. He would arrive groggy, reeking of alcohol, a glazed look in his eyes, but it took him no more than a minute to pinpoint the damage. And—wonder of wonders!—he was able, unsteady as he was on his feet, to fit the minutest screw into the padlock or alarm clock, to connect the coil in the cooker. To our joy the clock ticked, the padlock clicked open and shut, and the coil of the electric cooker blazed red. Ivan Mikhailovich was worth his weight in gold—in vodka rather, which he was only too pleased to receive in return for his services.

My brother left. I missed him but I knew he was planning to return to Moscow after his discharge from the army. I loved him dearly, and the thought that he would soon be living close to me with his wife and little daughter was a happy one.

I could not keep the resolution I had made to lose myself so completely in my work as to drive away all troubled thoughts, for it was clear, especially to the intelligentsia, that dark clouds were once again gathering around us.

From the loudspeaker came the thickly accented voice we knew so well. In the stumbling Russian spoken by uneducated Georgians, Stalin began his postwar address with a toast "to the Russian people." Perplexed, I wondered what effect his words would have on our life. Why had he not said "to the Soviet people"? Why was he setting the Russians above others, playing them against other nationalities of the land, as on previous occasions he had played the other nationalities against the Russians?

But the wily dictator knew what he was doing. He needed to oppose Russian identity not so much to other nationalities as to the concept of internationalism. He was paving the way for isolation from the West, for persecution of all who had the least sympathy or even tolerance for Western ideals, and finally for a vicious anti-Semitism and attack on intellectuals.

After Stalin had delivered his speech with its toast to the Russians a tremendous snowballing process was set in motion, ostensibly to boost and flatter the Russian ego.

Were this process not to have the gravest consequences for thousands of persons, it could have been put down as one more great lunacy.

Most of us chuckled when, in doing our shopping, we discovered that the names of many groceries had been "Russified." A French roll was no longer French; it was a Moscow roll. My favorite chocolate's label was changed from American Nut to Southern Nut. Swiss cheese was christened Soviet cheese.

Streets with foreign names were rebaptized. Every significant discovery and invention was claimed for Russia. Thus the wireless was invented by Popov. Architecture and sculpture owed their glory to Russians alone, as though Versailles were a copy of Peterhof, rather than the other way around. Russians were proclaimed the pioneers of aviation and the earliest discoverers of the American continent's northern territories. Priority in every field. No one would deny that the Russians are a talented people. But traditionally they had never been averse to learning a great deal from their European neighbors.

"The first elephant, too, was born in Russia," the Russians themselves joked. But the whole situation was far from funny; it assumed the gross proportions of a smoldering hatred for all that was non-Russian.

Freud's writings were not to be had for love or money. New sciences, such as cybernetics, and whole schools of learning were dismissed by Stalin as "quasi-scientific." At that time I was teaching English, which had fallen into understandable disfavor—foreign languages being so very "un-Russian."

Great minds were set to the task of devising ways of teaching these languages by Russian. They indeed came up with a solution: why bother with the spoken language and vocabulary, when you can teach the grammar rules in Russian and let it rest at that? Fortunately, as I have sometimes seen it work out to the general benefit, the Russians were not as methodical as the Germans, and the grand scheme of teaching English by Russian was not followed through to the end. The students kept complaining in hushed tones. The teachers circumvented the instructions of their superiors and somehow managed to convey a minimum of knowledge. "What madness!" we sometimes whispered to one another.

But there was method to the madness. The whipping-up of this insane xenophobia was essential in the new campaign against the intellectuals, and the "foreign" religious sects like the Baptists, Seventh Day Adventists, and other believers I would later meet in the Siberian taiga, as well as to enforce the law forbidding marriage between a Soviet citizen and an alien. Marriages contracted before the new law were declared null and void; Moscow girls who had married Britishers or Americans during the war were convicted of espionage. (One of these women, married to a Mr. Squire, was to be a cellmate of mine. She was sentenced to fifteen years and stripped of her married name.)

It was on the morning of a clear summer day in 1946 that a bombshell was delivered to us which blasted all hope for a relaxation of repressive measures after the war. This was the notorious Zhdanov decree. We picked up *Pravda* and there was the wisdom of the Party staring at us from half of the front page. Worded in the usual bullying jargon, the decree attacked the poet Akhmatova and the satirist Zoshchenko, both Leningraders.

Stalin was a champion hater. Of all cities he hated Leningrad most. It was the cradle of the revolution he betrayed. He hated Leningraders because they retained more of their idealism and integrity than did the motley, kowtowing Muscovites he surrounded himself with. In his insidious way he belittled and humiliated the city, tempting away its outstanding figures with higher salaries and better working conditions, gradually forcing it to sink from its former grandeur and importance to a gray provincialism. He did away with Kirov, head of the Leningrad party organization and a dangerous rival. He concocted the infamous "Leningrad case," killing off all of the city's leading men.

Without finishing his breakfast, my husband jumped up from his seat at the table and strode off into the garden of the tiny dacha we had rented for the summer.

Akhmatova's refined, ascetic face rose before my eyes. How it contrasted with Zhdanov's small "little fat boy" face, the features buried in rolls of flesh, and the eyes bloodshot from a surfeit of alcohol. I hardly knew Akhmatova's poetry because it rarely appeared in print, but I did know something of her fate. Her first husband, the poet Gumilev, had been shot, her second or third husband had fallen a victim of the purges, and her son was serving his third term for a "political" crime.

Mikhail returned to the porch, the pain caused by the Zhdanov decree showed on his face. I refilled his glass with steaming tea. He drank it absent-mindedly. Unable to repress my own emotions but fearful of voicing my thoughts, I scribbled a few words on a piece of paper and passed it across the table to Mikhail. I cannot now recall what comments I had made, but his face turned white. He shot me a reproving glance and tore the note into shreds. Lighting his pipe, he brought each scrap to the flame of the match and watched it burn.

Soon we were back in our Moscow home. There was more shrapnel in *Pravda*, this time against Shostakovich and other composers, to be followed by virulent outbursts against scholars and scientists.

My husband was nervously pacing the room.

"We started out with a noble idea," he muttered to himself. "But the deed rarely fits the word."

It was the nearest to censure of the system that Mikhail had ever got. I think both of us were frightened and believed it best not to discuss politics.

II Anna Louise Strong, American spy

When a newspaper item of no more than two or three lines appeared inconspicuously on the back page of *Pravda*, few readers, I am sure, took any notice of it. What it said would have been quite astonishing if people had not long ago become inured to the bizarre actions of their government. Thus it appeared that the American journalist Anna Louise Strong, who had lived for long periods in the Soviet Union, was an American spy, and had been ordered out of the country.

I did not for a moment believe the accusation. Most people who knew of her long-time loyalty to the Soviet regime, and her admiration of Stalin, must have thought it preposterous. What had she done to incur the wrath of the Great One, I wondered. But I had other matters on my mind, and soon forgot about Anna Louise Strong.

That very day, as I dropped into the office of my department chairman at the Army Institute of Foreign Languages, I was reminded of her.

"Did you know Anna Louise Strong?" asked Major Tomilin, the department chairman, who was an old friend from the days when I worked for Intourist, where he held a managerial position.

His question seemed innocent enough, and I replied offhandedly, "Yes, of course I did."

I merely meant that I knew her as a public figure. Indeed, most of the English-speaking people in Moscow had heard about or run into her at one time or another.

Major Tomilin was a man of disarming candor and charm, liked by the women and for some reason heartily disliked by the men of our faculty. He took a personal interest in other people's affairs and was always sympathetic if someone was in trouble; cordial and hospitable, he was eager for people to visit his home. It was these qualities that I admired in him. But, perhaps unwittingly on his part, he was slated to play a sinister role in my life. My charge of espionage hinged on the supposition that I had been acquainted with Anna Louise Strong, and Major Tomilin happened to be the only person with whom I had ever talked about her. I therefore assume that he was an informer—most people who had at one time or another worked for Intourist were—whose report provided the "legal" grounds for my charge. (Even so, were there no such report some other pretext would surely have been found to apprehend me.)

"Have you read the item about her in *Pravda*?" Major Tomilin inquired after a pause.

"Oh, yes," I replied as I left his office—the bell had rung for my class. I had not the slightest inclination to pursue the topic. Anna Louise Strong's expulsion from the Soviet Union was merely one of the innumerable crazy things that were happening around me, and I was not going to bother about it.

This was in the late forties. But earlier, at different periods in my life, Anna Louise Strong had claimed my attention as a journalist. I first read her in 1928, when I was thirteen; her articles on Lenin fell into my hands and I was quite carried away by her own enthusiasm for him. Later, at the *Moscow News*, I had worked for the arts and literature department under Shubin, a reticent but pleasant scholarly man who was recently married to Anna Louise Strong. Whenever I saw her heading for his office I would hastily slip out, finding anything but attractive the cold look of her aquamarine eyes.

I had often seen her, too, going in and out of the office of Mikhail Markovich Borodin, the paper's editor and a legendary figure in the early days of Soviet Russia's foreign affairs. We who worked under him knew him as a gentle, worldly-wise man. With his walrus moustache and warm brown eyes, he retained a chivalrous air even in his advanced years. Eventually he who had miraculously survived the purges of the thirties was also caught in the enormous net of people in some way connected with the "American spy."

Miss Strong's expulsion from the Soviet Union triggered off a long chain of arrests of people who either had worked with her at one time or another and knew her intimately, or who merely recognized her as a journalist and public figure and had no personal connection whatever.

Anna Louise Strong was only one of a thousand and more pretexts to nab people from all sections of the population. Branding her an American spy was an accusation that did not need to be substantiated by a single shred of evidence. It was sufficient to state it, and if Stalin saw fit to have it stated, how could it be a falsehood? This was the logic that nobody dared even question. If Anna Louise Strong was a spy, it followed that all persons who had the remotest association with her were spies too.

III The new terror

The section commander made his usual report: so many present, so many absent. I began with translation from Russian into English of newspaper material, all the time puzzling over the commander's report. Why had he cited two cadets absent when three were not in attendance? And who was the third? Yes, of course, I remembered now; it was Zhukov, who for some reason had not turned in his term paper. It would have been quite simple to inquire about him from the section commander, but some inner voice cautioned me against it.

"Zhukov has been missing my classes—does he attend yours?" I asked a teaching colleague. With a glance around the hall where we were standing, she blurted out, "No, he's been arrested." Some time later I learned about the jailing of other students.

Among the translators I knew were many people of English, American, and Spanish extraction. I had quit my job at the Soviet Information Buro a year after my daughter was born, but had remained friends with many of the translators. I was now horrified to learn of the large number of arrests in the translation department. Some of the best translators were jailed as early as 1947: Talmi, George Hanna, Julius Katser, and Hilda Kazanina, all well known for their English translations of Russian classics and Soviet fiction. The same was happening among the faculty of the Moscow Institute of Foreign Languages.

Suddenly we were reliving the agonies and fears of 1937 and 1938. The atmosphere in Moscow had become unbearably oppressive. Close to a corner column of the Bolshoi Theater I was stopped by a friend, a successful painter. I was shocked by his appearance. From a picture of elegance, a buoyant, self-confident, flirtatious man, he had turned into a ghost; he looked as if he had lost all substance and would collapse any moment at the slightest whiff of air. He could talk of nothing but the new arrests, especially the vicious attacks against Jewish intellectuals and professional people.

"I never imagined I would see it happen again. It's madness!" Greatly agitated, he enumerated the individuals who had recently been arrested. I listened but said nothing. Then suddenly I caught the name of my dear friend Nadezhda. This painter had once been in love with her and hoped to make her his wife. But instead she had married a colonel in the Red Army and had accompanied him to the front at the time of the Russo-Finnish war of 1939–1940. It was just after she had graduated from medical school, and for her gallant work as a surgeon she was decorated with the Order of the Red Star. She had come back from that war, as I well remembered, greatly chagrined by the way things were organized, resulting in the needless death of thousands of fighting men.

Nor, as I also remembered well, did she keep quiet about what she saw. Her charge—I learned from her husband—was "anti-Soviet agitation." She received a ten-year sentence. Nadezhda died in camp after having survived two wars. She left two children.

The new terror and mass arrests that started in 1947 were not a clean-up of the Party apparatus as had been largely the case in 1937 and 1938, but a form of still further intimidation of an already utterly intimidated population. This time the main targets were professional and other groups. Arrest thirty or a hundred doctors, thirty or more translators, fifty leading writers, sixty Jewish intellectuals, and you will strike fear into each of these sections of the population.

In 1938, after Yezhov was booted out of office and disappeared into the unknown, a few cases were reviewed. Some lucky individuals, after a year's interrogation, were unexpectedly released and exonerated. "Sorry we've tortured you for a year, made your family tremble with fear and disown you. You're innocent, you're free to go home and resume normal life."

Stunned, hardly believing their good fortune, these people— among them Joe F., a translator I had worked with, and a young neighbor of ours—were so scared that they never uttered a word about their prison experiences. The look of abject terror in their eyes forbade anyone to ask questions. What went on in the dungeons of the security police remained a secret. Every released prisoner had signed a pledge of non-disclosure.

To prevent the truth about the prisons and forced-labor camps from leaking out to the outside world, nobody that I knew among the victims of the 1947–1953 period was released under Stalin. The majority, if they survived, waited until 1956 for their cases to be reviewed.

The trials and purges of the late thirties, it will be remembered, received some publicity and were partially reported in the Soviet and world press. Between 1947 and 1953 there were no open trials. All the arrests and executions proceeded in an atmosphere of silence and secrecy. Every little fact, every arrest, every death sentence, was carefully concealed from the public, at home and abroad.

It is apparently to the advantage of the Party to keep silent about the mass arrests and shootings that swept the country in the late forties and early fifties, to ascribe most of the "mistakes" and "illegalities" to the late thirties in order to make it appear that there had been at the time a kind of Party strife or struggle for power. This would give the whole nightmare of terror and shootings a semblance of normality and thus indirectly minimize the guilt of the Party.

As for the 1947–1953 period, people today are expected to pretend it never happened, to bear no ill will to the security apparatus and the Party chiefs who condoned the crimes, who signed papers of executions and lists of arrested persons—"to forget." Moreover, it is permissible to strike out major events, personalities, and whole periods from the history books. Historical events are being craftily distorted. When tributes are printed in the newspapers or books written about outstanding revolutionaries and public figures who disappeared during the purges, there is usually a gap of many years in the middle of their lives, or at the end.

The utmost care is taken to hush up the fact that these persons were victims of terror, whether in the purges of 1937 and 1938 or in the new mass repressions that began in 1947. The years spent in prison and camp are omitted from accounts of their lives. If the personalities now honored were shot or died in camp, that abrupt end is never specified; the reader is free to interpret in his own way. He can indeed imagine that they were carried off by an avalanche or other natural disaster. If, however, they survived, what happened during the ten or twenty years excised from their lives? Are we to suppose that they dwelt in an enchanted wood, like Sleeping Beauty, until they were awakened by a kiss from Prince Charming—Khrushchev—and then returned to their jobs?

IV Cosmopolitanism

There are good and bad words in the Soviet lexicon, catch phrases and slogans that have a mesmeric effect. "To beat America" was a longtime slogan that summed up the economic targets of the five-year plans. (A good Party slogan.) As for "liberal" and "liberalization," they have always been dirty words—ever since Lenin spoke so contemptuously of the liberal bourgeoisie, the same liberals among the Russian capitalists who donated large sums of money to the Bolsheviks in their struggle to overthrow the monarchy and establish a Soviet regime. To this day "liberalization" is so reprehensible that no leader dares utter the word; a liberal is seen as a shilly-shallying, insecure person who can be expected to defect to the enemy at any moment.

In the late forties the words "cosmopolite" and "cosmopolitanism" were suddenly sprung upon us. They carried the same portent as "enemy of the people" in 1937 and 1938. Venom and abuse were hailed upon the "rootless cosmopolites." The Party denounced them in every newspaper as persons "without a homeland," "without kith or kin," tribeless. It was a campaign directed mostly against Jewish professionals and intellectuals. Most vociferous in this chorus was Mikhail Sholokhov, who in his articles "exposed" the Semitic origin of popular Russian writers by citing their long-abandoned Yiddish names.

One day, after work, I dropped in to see the Merkurovs. The door of the sculptor's studio was open; I entered but remained on the threshold to get a better view of his work, familiar and new. In the middle of the studio was a lifesize bust draped in wet muslin. It revealed only the bare outlines of the head; and the head seemed familiar.

A number of death masks had been added to the collection I already knew so well. This was an art at which Merkurov was extremely adept. No sooner did some important Party leader, writer, or actor pass away than the sculptor was called in to make a last imprint of the lifeless features, as he had done of Leo Tolstoy, and many years later of Lenin. I paused, as I often did, to gaze at these faces, preserved at almost the moment of death, when someone gently took me by the elbow and steered me deeper into the studio.

I turned my head and found myself looking into a face so ugly that its very ugliness was a magnet of attraction. Merkurov lumbered in through the open door. He was a burly man, nearly two heads taller than the person who was still clutching my elbow and to whom I needed no introduction, for I immediately recognized him as Solomon Mikhoels, founder and zealous architect of the famous Moscow Jewish Theater. Now I realized why the head of the bust looked familiar to me.

Throwing back the wet cloth from his work, Merkurov said pleasantly: "Sit down and keep us company. Watch me sculpt the head of a Socrates." Merkurov was not exaggerating. I often heard the Jewish actor called the "philosopher of Moscow's art world," and the "wisest, most humane person," by his Russian colleagues.

He was one of the first casualties of the cosmopolitan campaign. In the late forties his popularity, as both artist and man, cost him his life. Perhaps the reason he was not shot outright, as many of his colleagues were, can be attributed to the world homage he won as a Soviet good-will ambassador in wartime. He therefore met with a road accident, engineered by the great Stalin himself. Stalin needed to get the internationally acclaimed actor off the stage before he enacted his own gory drama of hatred and death against the Jews and other intellectuals.

"Cosmopolite" was a foreign word, new to Russian ears. The man in the street had not the vaguest notion of its meaning. However, it was a well-tried practice to replace ordinary, comprehensible words with veiled expressions and niceties of language. "Cosmopolite" became a euphemism for "Jew."

At the start of this campaign against them the "cosmopolites" were more flabbergasted than anybody else. Why were they branded "rootless" and "without a homeland," when this very homeland, the Soviet Union, had been brought into existence through the dedication and efforts of a proportionately larger number of Jews than persons of any other nationality?

Soviet Jews had long ceased to think of themselves as Jews; in any event this was true of most Jews I met in Moscow. They identified themselves with the culture of the Russians and in their internal passports, which all Soviet people carry, they would have gladly put down "Russian" or any other nationality—Eskimo, Chuvash, Unti, any of them was better than "Jewish."

If such accusations as "rootless" and "without a homeland" were utterly unfounded, especially in a state that proclaimed communist society to be its ultimate goal, the stigma of being tribeless was quite justified. There was no tribal feeling among Soviet Jews. They did not live in segregated communities, as they had before the revolution and as they do at present in some cities of the world. They mingled as freely with the Russians and Ukrainians as they did among themselves.

Sadly, in 1948, 1949, and right until Stalin's death, Jews were being made aware that they belonged to a national minority open to insult and persecution. This was a period during which in the press and at meetings there was undisguised talk of excluding Jews from certain professions.

One Saturday night, at a get-together in my house, the husband of a friend of mine, a colonel who had commanded a regiment in the battle for Moscow against the invading Germans, delivered himself of the current Party line. He was not in the least anti-Semitic, but merely accepted Party policy as the gospel truth.

"In Russian schools Jews should not be allowed to teach such subjects as Russian or Russian literature," he proclaimed.

Half of the guests, including his own clever, pretty wife, were Jewish. Too fearful to start an argument, we let his remark slip by.

On Pyatnitskaya Street, close to my house on Rauzhskaya Embankment, I ran into the plump, pink-cheeked wife of a newspaperman who had worked with my husband for many years. Her pretty Slavic face lit up with a smile whenever we met. This time it was contorted with pain.

She came to the point at once: "My husband's editor told him to hand in his resignation. He said there were Central Committee orders to bar Jews from the literary field."

The same Damocles' sword that now hung over every Jew working in journalism threatened to descend on my husband's head. He knew he could be fired any day and stood little chance of getting work elsewhere.

Ostrich-like, I refused to face up to reality. "You could free-lance and make out just as well," I would say encouragingly. "Above all forget you are a Jew. We must live through it. We can! By ignoring this madness."

Krasny Flot was the newspaper for which my husband had now been working for a few years. It was published in Moscow, had a wide circulation, and was designated for the men and officers of the Soviet Navy, an arm of the service with a larger proportion of Jews than any other. It was quite likely that anti-Semitism was less popular in the navy than in the army and air force. The editor of *Krasny Flot* was an admiral in his mid-fifties whose wife—so rumor had it—was Jewish.

The campaign against "cosmopolites" was not to his liking. Possibly he was nauseated by it, as were many communists I knew. Therefore, instead of following Central Committee orders to sack the Jews on his staff, he decided to put up a fight. When pressure was exerted, he tried to offer objections, tried refusing point-blank to fire the Jewish journalists, tried stalling.

Editors all over the country had long since carried out their purges of Jewish personnel. He held out. We could pay tribute to him as a good and upright communist who stuck to his principles. Unfortunately, in the long run, his stubbornness turned out to be a greater disaster for the Jews on his staff, my husband among them, than the readiness of other editors-in-chief to abide by Party directives.

A couple of ideologues were sent down from the Central Committee to look into the situation. A Party meeting was called at which they laid down the law, making no bones about how "cosmopolites" should be treated. They warned the editor to show no leniency to the "agents of international Jewry." Ludicrous as it may seem, half of the Party members present at this meeting, and listening to these vicious attacks, were Jews themselves.

Mikhail returned around midnight. I woke up and switched on the bedside lamp. His face was ashen. He was coming apart right before my eyes. His lips moved to say something, but no sound came. Dropping into a chair, he stared past me as though I were not there at all.

Alarmed, I almost shouted at him: "Tell me what happened at the meeting."

He did not seem to hear.

I got out of bed and sat down on a chair opposite him.

"Pull yourself together, darling, or we'll all pay dearly . . ." When I pronounced these words, I did not know how prophetic they were. "Forget you are a Jew!" I repeated my pet admonition.

"How can I forget something I'm being constantly reminded of?" he answered. "You can't imagine what the meeting was like. The speeches made by the Central Committee representatives smacked of the old tsarist pogrom battle cry: 'Kill the Jews and save Russia!'"

"We must not let them hurt us!" I argued. " Don't you see that this virulence is artificially whipped up? It rebounds on the hater, turns him into a brute. Forget your nationality!"

"I can't and I refuse," he retorted.

The admiral needed no further proof than the meeting to realize he had lost his battle. I can only surmise that, after being questioned by security-police officials, it became clear to him that charges were being framed against the Jewish journalists he had refused to fire. By sticking to his guns he had rendered them a disservice; he was now well aware that their liberty and very lives were in jeopardy. Hastily he ordered their dismissal, hoping, perhaps, that he might divert attention from them, save them from their doom.

Alas, he was mistaken. A "group" case had already been fabricated against them. A few months later the very people whose interests he had defended were arrested and charged with organized anti-Soviet and Zionist propaganda.

More Jewish journalists of the Krasny Flot staff were arrested and killed than those working for other newspapers, where the editors-in-chief had complied with Party directives. Why did that happen? What was the logic of it? For a long time I pondered these questions, until finally I arrived at the answer.

The reason was obvious: the Party brooked no resistance to its policies; the admiral had to be punished for his disobedience. The best way to punish him was to destroy human life, destroy the very persons whose rights he dared to protect. This would no doubt teach other champions of the Jews a good lesson.

I had no way of knowing how the admiral, a man of integrity, reacted to this manner of punishment. But I know that very often such retribution added to the Party member's ideological confusion, turning brave and humane persons into cowards or making them go to pieces. The Party "logic" was to achieve just that, so that people like the admiral would think twice before embarking on a quixotic course of action.

To get our little daughter away from our hot, poorly aired room, we spent the summer of 1949 in Bykovo, a pinewood recreation spot near Moscow. Early on the morning of September 7, 1949, I was expecting Mikhail, who had spent the night in the city, to arrive with a truck to move our belongings back to Moscow.

Two men in the gray suits worn by many government officials, including the MGB, strode through the garden gate down the path towards me. With no greeting or preliminary introductions, one of them said: "Last night we arrested your husband."

I became wooden, numb. The sparkling day darkened. I knew I must show no emotion. Every word, every tear, if I dared shed it, could be interpreted as censure of the state. The men's eyes peered, searching for a sign of weakness. I tightened.

"Open your bags!"

I did as I was told, wondering if they could hear the loud beating of my heart.

They rummaged through everything. No search warrant had been produced. I dared not ask for one.

Among my papers was a manuscript of about fifty pages, which I was translating for an arts publishing house. It had to do with the restoration of old churches. One of the men picked it up.

"This we're going to confiscate," he said as he leafed through it.

"Please don't, it's only a translation I'm doing." I now spoke with emotion for the first time.

How indeed, I thought, would I explain the absence of the manuscript? I plainly visualized the fear in the eyes of the editor who gave me the translation, the horror of being mixed up with anyone who had an arrested husband.

"Okay, we won't confiscate it," said the MGB man with a magnanimous air.

Later, I concluded that the search was a put-on act, a bit of strategy on the part of my future interrogator to test my reaction to my husband's arrest. If I reacted with strong emotion and let slip some uncautious remark, I could easily be charged with lack of confidence in the security organs.

There was no greater calamity in the Stalin era than arrest. The arrested person would be struck off the list of the living, his family knowing for certain that they would never set eyes on him again. There would be no trial, no defense lawyer, no semblance of justice; communication with the prisoner during the interrogation period was forbidden, and never a clue given as to what the charges were. After conviction it could be either no exchange of letters--if the sentence, as I believe it did in my husband's case, stated "Without the right to correspond"—or only a few a year.

The family of the arrested person was at once under a cloud of suspicion. Every member was compelled to state at his office or factory that he had an arrested relative, which immediately put him in danger of losing his job. And in the end, quite often, the worst happened: other members of the family were jailed and deported to camps.

My mother was so stricken by Mikhail's arrest that she came down with a high fever. Mikhail had always been a thoughtful son-in-law, showing her the same compassion he did most human beings. She now lay in bed, her deeply creased cheeks flushed, tears trickling from her eyes onto the pillow.

Now and again she dozed off, only to wake with a moan and a shiver. I wanted to call a doctor.

"Don't," she admonished. "I'll get over it soon, the fever comes from the visions I have of Mikhail in prison. You don't know what prison is like, but I do from my own experience in tsarist times."

My mother had often described tsarist prisons to me. But what my imagination had conjured up—prisoners allowed to meet at mealtimes, given books to read, paper and pen to write, treated like human beings, often even with respect, by the warders—was a far cry from what I was to encounter at Lubyanka, Lefortovo, and Butyrki prisons in Moscow.

A few days after Mikhail's arrest Lenya Ivich, a friend of my husband's and a fellow journalist at *Krasny Flot*, came to see me. I knew him from the time he had been a war correspondent reporting on the fighting in the Crimea and the seige of Sevastopol. There was about Lenya, as about my husband, an air of chivalry; a deep-seated humaneness marked both men. It was a brave action on Lenya's part to risk a visit to the wife of an arrested comrade at the height of the cosmopolitan campaign of which Mikhail was now a victim.

He kept repeating: "Mikhail never said a word against the system. His loyalty was beyond reproach."

I thanked Lenya for his visit. He could say nothing to comfort me. We both knew that Mikhail was lost to the world. But what neither of us could guess, at the moment, was that Lenya's own days of liberty were running out. Shortly after this visit he was arrested as a co-defendant in the group case under which Mikhail came, on the same charge of anti-Soviet agitation and sympathy for Zionism. Both men were dead long before the "breaches of legality" were condemned and both were posthumously exonerated.

V "Nowhere!"

With my husband's arrest a dark chasm opened up before me. I teetered on the edge, trying hard to keep my balance, to muster the moral strength needed to go on living, working, remaining a normal person and not letting bitterness overcome me. Overnight I became a pariah. I could not blame the colleagues, friends, and neighbors who now avoided me for their own safety; on the whole, however, people proved to be more fearless and kinder than I expected. My job hung on a thread. The MGB redoubled their vigilance.

Could one blame the wives and husbands who shortly after the arrest of their spouses filed for divorce? There was my gifted friend Tina, an exquisite woman who was courted by some of Moscow's most brilliant men: she ended up with a fifth marriage, to her third husband, Nikolai. Tina had divorced Nikolai shortly after he was apprehended in 1947, and married Leonid, a journalist. Upon Nikolai's release in 1956, during the Khrushchev thaw, she remarried him. There was an element of the absurd in it. Yet was it not absurd that one never dared to question the actions of the state, but was at all times expected to laud them, no matter how erratic and criminal they were?

Political prisoners were the only persons not subject to the rigid divorce laws introduced immediately after the war to strengthen the marriage tie. A man could be callously told that his marriage had been dissolved and that his wife and children, his only link with the outside world, had disowned him. Nothing was easier for an arrested man's wife than to get a divorce by proxy—no taking of the case to court as the law required, no notifying of the other party about the pending of divorce.

A brief written statement—"My husband was arrested by the state security organs and I request a divorce"—did the trick. You were no longer an outcast, no longer bound to a "traitor," "spy," or "Zionist." You could revert to your maiden name, update the long, recurring questionnaire forms at your job, making it clear that you have severed all connections with your spouse. You were applauded for your loyalty to the regime.

This was the official stand. In fact the people around you knew that you had been forced to abandon a family member in misfortune because you hoped you and your children could go on with your lives without being harassed, without the fear of sharing the fate of your loved one.

For all that, it was not easy to extinguish the spark of goodness in human beings. Tina and Leonid kept sending Nikolai parcels and letters. A well-known stage and film actor, B.Ch., mailed packages of food to his mistress, who lived in the same hut with me and sixty other women prisoners at a Taishet camp. And in the Butyrki Prison I became friendly with the young wife of a high-ranking naval officer who intervened on her behalf—to no avail, of course, but at great risk to his own position and liberty.

During the recess periods between my classes I would retire into some inconspicuous corner of the common room. But even there the compassionate eyes of my colleagues would seek me out. There was Captain B.R., the dashing, chivalrous vice-chairman of the department, and Professor R., who taught English literature; in their long stares I read a whole gamut of emotions, which in our fearful times they dared not put into words. Could they have spoken up, they would have told me how sincerely sorry they were for me, what an outrage the mass arrests were, and how they deplored their powerlessness to help people like myself. Such messages I read not only in the eyes of my colleagues, but also in the glances of neighbors and friends.

Two or three evenings a week of that bleak, hapless winter of 1949 and 1950 I spent where most wives of arrested men went in hope of receiving the barest information about their husbands: at the Lubyanka Inquiry Office. This office was situated in a small house some five or seven minutes' walk from the Lubyanka building.

The house overlooked the narrow, busy Kuznetsky Most Street, in an old quarter of the city. A few doors down the street was Moscow's well-known bookshop selling publications in foreign languages, which tourists frequented. In my carefree days I had loved sauntering through this part of the city to pick up a dictionary or a Soviet edition of an English novel. Kuznetsky Most, meaning Blacksmith Bridge, had indeed been a bridge several hundred years ago, spanning the small Neglinka River, which was later locked into pipes.

The street itself was humped and reminiscent of a bridge. As I walked along it to the Inquiry Office I wondered if, as some claimed, deep beneath its surface the Neglinka River was making a sorry bid for freedom, gurgling and swirling in its futile struggle to break through its iron casing. I felt a little like that tiny streamlet, except that there was no fighting spirit in me and I was condemned to inaction. Meekly, like everyone else, in our common tragedy hardly even speaking to one another, I would go up to the little wicket window at the Inquiry Office, show my identity passport, give my husband's name, and each time receive the curt reply: "Under interrogation."

What we all waited to hear was "Bring a small amount of money," or "Warm clothing allowed." The former usually signified that the interrogation was going well and that the prisoner, having made it easy for the MGB, could be rewarded with the privilege of ordering cigarettes or groceries from the prison commissary. A request of warm clothing meant that the prisoner had been sentenced. It was important for the wife, husband, or other relative to call regularly at the Inquiry Office in order to get the message in time—before the convicted person was railroaded to camp.

In my case, finally, it was "Warm clothing." I was not told what my husband's sentence was or where he would serve it. Years later, when Mikhail was exonerated, I learned—or rather was able to deduce from the brief conversation I had with a KGB officer when his case was being reviewed—that he was sentenced *in camera* by a tribunal to ten years' prison, a more severe penalty than camp and a sure road to death, as indeed it was for my husband. Since neither I nor his mother, nor his sisters or brothers, ever received a single letter from him, I could well conclude that his sentence read: "Without the right to correspond."

Hastily I packed a bundle of warm clothing. We were all so very poor in those days that a warm sweater was a luxury Mikhail did not possess. My neighbor Georgi kindly gave me his. I dashed off to the Inquiry Office. The man at the wicket opened the door leading from his room into the big waiting hall and took the bundle from me. I have no idea whether he received it or not, because I never heard from him. I did not discontinue my visits to the Inquiry Office, not until rudely and impatiently the officer at the wicket said: "You're wasting my time. Your husband is no longer on my lists."

"Where can I inquire about him?"

"Nowhere!"

Waiting for two or three hours, evening after evening, at the jammed Lubyanka Inquiry Office, I would see troubled faces of all ages, old and young, including teenagers whose parents had both, apparently, been arrested. It disturbed me greatly. Everybody stood or sat in silence. It was an unwritten law not to ply one another with questions, often not even to address anyone; each carried a big enough load not to be burdened by other people's woes.

The mental anguish I was suffering manifested itself in physical symptoms. One morning in early February, shortly after I had been turned away by the officer at the wicket, my fever was so high that I had no strength to get out of bed and go to work. To obtain a sick-leave certificate my mother called a doctor from the local clinic.

It was not until evening that the doctor, a woman in her thirties, arrived. I remember her bending over me, flipping a thermometer, and hastily slipping it under my armpit; no word or question escaped from her. I noticed that she was good-looking, with an oval face, hazel eyes, and dark glossy hair visible from under her white doctor's cap.

With one hand she now held the stethoscope as with the other she threw back the covers. The moment she saw I was bleeding and wearing a pad, she covered me up roughly and quickly thrust the stethoscope back into the pocket of her smock.

"You've had an abortion," she snapped angrily. "I'll send an ambulance to take you to the hospital at once."

At that time abortion was illegal and punishable by several years of prison.

"This is February, doctor . . ." Instinctively I dropped my voice to a whisper, as one always did when speaking of an arrest. "My husband was arrested by the security organs at the beginning of September. I've had no sex since. This is just my period."

A cold look was her answer. She drew on her coat. "The ambulance will be here in less than an hour," she flung from the door. Turning to my mother, she added, "Pack her things."

The doctor's bluster woke up my little daughter, whose crib was only three or four feet from my bed. She lay awake, fear in her dark brown eyes, as though she sensed the trouble we were all in.

Why in an unpunctual land was evil so punctual? Before we could gather our wits and think how to deal with this new insane problem, the ambulance arrived. The gynecologist was a large flabby blonde approaching middle age, with a much less rigid face than the first doctor. I gave her the same explanation. She knew I spoke the truth but submitted me to a thorough examination—before my daughter's startled eyes.

After the second doctor departed, I fell into a deep, fitful slumber. I awoke feeling better, but with a smoldering hatred for all doctors. I dragged myself to work. That afternoon I was called to the personnel department and told I was fired. In later years, when I recalled the manner and hostile tone of the young man behind the desk who spoke to me, I knew I should have realized that my days of freedom were numbered.

VI My brother Shurri

A few months before I lost my job, Shurri lost his. Communication between secret sections of the army and the secret departments that exist in every office, factory, and university is rapid and efficient. My brother was regarded with suspicion; after my husband's arrest, he fell into the category of family members of arrested persons. He was hastily discharged from army service in South-Sakhalinsk, thousands of miles from Moscow, and deprived of his post as language instructor.

He returned to Moscow. His job hunt in the winter and spring of 1950 made it quite plain that there was no hope of getting any position. Every person applying for a job had to be cleared by the secret section of the personnel department. And there was one crucial question, dreaded by all who had arrested relatives, in every job application: "State if a member of your family or your spouse's family has ever been repressed."

It was recorded in the great Stalinist constitution, as it is in the current one, that all Soviet citizens have the right to a job. But this ruling did not apply to you if one of your family was or had been in the past a political prisoner. You were then blacklisted and, as in my brother's case, could not even count on an unskilled laborer's job, for labor legislation banned the employment of anyone with a college degree in a menial capacity.

My brother was jobless for eighteen months, right to the day of his death. No unemployment relief, no welfare, nothing as demeaning as charity, can exist in a socialist society. Full employment was and is the boast of socialism. But in that fearsome Stalin era, no matter how hard he tried, how humbly he begged, there was no job for Shurri. Needless to say, matters became a thousand times worse for him when my mother and I were arrested.

I saw a good deal of my brother in the months preceding my arrest. Shurri did his best to distract me from my troubles, engaging me in long discourses on linguistic themes. He had in fact used his enforced leisure to write a thesis, inspired by Marxist views, on the class essence of English idiomatic phrases.

The snows of the long winter of 1950 suddenly melted away. Spring set in with a flourish of brilliant sunshine, as Moscow spring has a way of doing. The tawny little buds swelled fast and sturdy on oak and birch twigs. Faces that had been surly all winter softened and lit up with new hope. "Look, the trees are in leaf," people said to one another.

These same words dropped from my brother's lips that early spring. I can still hear them. And the thought that he never saw the budding of another spring is all the more painful to me because his death was so purposeless, so devoid of meaning—except that it demonstrated one thing: there was a limit to what the individual was able to endure under the Stalin regime, even when he was at liberty.

What I most feared, in my cell at the Lefortovo Prison, was that my brother too might be jailed. Appalled as I was by my own plight, I found immense relief in believing that I alone was fated to bear the family cross. I was not religious, but every morning, just before reveille, on returning to my cell after the night's interrogation I repeated the prayer: "Let it be me! Oh God, if one member of our family must suffer, let it be me! Spare my mother and brother!"

In October, five months before his death, I signed a long deposition clearing my brother of suspicion. He was not a spy; I never saw him associate with aliens; he never met with foreign intelligence agents when he worked as an army interpreter during the war in the Russian north. It took all night for the interrogator to write down the answers. Gradually, as I signed sheet after sheet, the significance of that night's interrogation dawned on me. Of course, it was all a comedy. My answers could carry no weight because I was miles away from where my brother was in wartime. But they were among the twisted "legalities" that could be used either to imprison an innocent person or to prevent his arrest. Most likely my brother was to be the next culprit in our small family, his name on the dreaded list of arrests. My interrogator, aware of the silly tangle of utterly unsubstantiated charges my own case presented, decided not to get himself involved with my brother. Shurri had had a narrow escape.

In their magnanimity, the Soviet security organs had decreed that this youngest member of our "criminal" family be spared. The MGB made my handsome, upright, sincerely communist brother a gift of his liberty. Shurri, at the time twenty-eight years old, knew nothing of this, of course. He still could not find a job, belonging as he did to a family with three spies in it, and was therefore not to be trusted; indeed, he was to be treated as an outcast from the socialist society.

He was a candidate member of the Communist Party. The time had now arrived for him to be accepted as a full-fledged member. His fate was in the hands of the Communist Party District Committee in Mytishchi, the large industrial district on Moscow's outskirts where he lived. The Committee, composed mostly of industrial workers or former workers who had become Party functionaries, rose to the occasion and lost no time in expelling Shurri from the Party. They performed their duties as Soviet workers always do on orders from the higher-ups.

Nobody with so many spies in the family could be a member of the Party. In early March, 1951, all the dependable, sedate worker communists on the Mytishchi committee raised their hands. For unanimous expulsion. Knowing exactly the consequences, the stigma and ostracism that went with such a decision. My interrogator, Major Porunov, expected Shurri to live. My brother judged differently. The day he was expelled he threw himself under the wheels of a running train.

Shurri was always full of new ideas; he prided himself on his thorough Marxist approach to philosophy, literature, and linguistics, a last passion. On that final meeting of ours in June, a week before my arrest, he was airing some of these ideas. But I was too preoccupied and downcast to take in what he was saying.

VII Strawberries

June was hot and dry. I remember it well for its good harvest of sweet crimson strawberries. Indeed, in Moscow June is the strawberry month, the only time of the year when they are available, usually at high market prices. Rather than serve them to the family, Moscow housewives make the fragrant jam to which guests are treated at tea-time during the cold winter months—a pleasant reminder of warm days, of the beautiful month of June.

My arrest on the last day of June is linked in my mind with crushed strawberries. I had bought a kilo of berries at the farm market not far from my house to take to my mother. Not having a fridge, I kept the berries on a big flat plate on the floor, where it was cooler. The moment the two security men in plain clothes crossed my threshold they accidentally stepped on the plate, their heavy soles reducing most of the delicate berries to a bleeding pulp.

Strawberries. My memories of the Taishet strict-regime camp too bring back to me a little incident that revolves around them. Suddenly, one day, a diminutive patch of wild strawberries appeared on the camp compound. How anything so exotic, fragile, and beautiful as these berries could have burst from the parched earth of the hot

Siberian summer is a mystery to me. To behold in the hell of our camp the tiny red berries peep out from their awning of serrated green leaves was nothing short of a miracle.

It was a situation that did not catch our jailors unawares. They knew exactly how to deal with such emergencies: there were express instructions to dig up any flowers, bushes, plants, and berries on the camp compound that could be a source of pleasure to political prisoners.

Unmindful of our jailors, the wild strawberries had rashly, thoughtlessly, ventured onto territory cut off from the outside world by barbed wire, guarded by armed warders with shepherd dogs straining at the leash and by tommy gunners pacing the small but sturdy watch towers high above the camp, their rifles at the ready.

Those of us who were fortunate enough to stand close to that little green patch could not take our eyes off the berries. We were lined up to be counted, a procedure, if everything went well, lasting for a good part of an hour. A warder who had absented himself soon returned with two rusty spades. He flung them at our ranks, one falling close to where I stood.

Giving me a cold, blank look, he commanded: "Pick it up and get busy."

"You there, too!" he yelled to another prisoner.

I longed not so much to taste the berries as to smell their fragrance. For the briefest moment I closed my eyes and that fragrance suffused me, bringing memories of Moscow, my home, my friends.

"Everybody remains standing until the whole patch is levelled and covered with earth."

I picked up the heavy spade and was soon hacking away at the amazed little berries, bent on doing the job quickly, for I knew how tiring it was for my fellow prisoners to stand in the scorching midday sun, with another eight hours of hard toil ahead of them. Soon we had the little green leaves and berries entombed beneath the crust of dry clay.

June 30 blackened into July 1. After the search many of my belongings lay in a heap on the floor in the middle of the room where they had been cast by the two secret police agents who had come to arrest me.

"Some of your bedding and clothes you can leave for your child with your next-door neighbors," the man in charge of the night's proceedings told me.

One of my most prized possessions was a Latin script typewriter, a German war trophy. There was a Russian typewriter too, borrowed from my neighbor Georgi, who stood outside my open door. I now begged to be allowed to return it to him, adding that he could help carry my things next door.

The typewriter was returned to him. My own was confiscated along with my personal letters and other papers.

"Are there any pets?"

"Yes, a cat and a tortoise."

The tortoise had disappeared under the couch while from atop the wardrobe my sleek jet Cleopatra surveyed the scene with flicking whiskers and a disdainful gleam in her green eyes.

After tying into a bundle the things that lay on the floor, Georgi carried them into the next room. There they were hastily taken in by the kindly widow to whom we owed the possession of our one-room home. It was about two o'clock in the morning. Most of the neighbors were awake, fully aware of what was going on.

"No gaping, go back to your own place," the detective, who had replaced the warrant for my arrest in his breast pocket, told Georgi. "Remove the animals too."

As he was leaving, with the pets tucked under one arm and the typewriter in his other hand, I begged: "Please take the strawberries as well." It was perhaps a crazy request under the circumstances.

Georgi smiled uncertainly, sadly. How dismal the future looked.

EIGHT

I Lefortovo Prison

After spending four days at the Lubyanka Inner Prison on Dzerzhinsky Square, in the heart of Moscow, I was taken to Lefortovo in
the far northeastern section of the city.

Steel and stone replaced the oil paint, wood panelling, and polished parquet of Lubyanka. The door clanged shut. Cold air seeped
through the grimy, ancient stone floor of the cell, nipping viciously
at my ankles. I shivered. The whitewashed walls and ceiling were a
filthy gray. An iron cot stood in the middle of the cell, fettered to the
floor. Across from it, against the wall, was a long, narrow table of
rough boards and a single rickety stool. In full view of the Judas-
hole, drilled in the cell's double-framed door, a tiny rusty sink and
a seatless, badly cracked toilet bowl huddled precariously against the
wall; the stained, dirty bowl was flushed by the water from the tap.

Slimy and falling apart, a sink and toilet were yet unheard-of lux-
uries, never again to be encountered in my wanderings from cell to
cell and prison to prison. I sat down on the narrow cot. The air was
clammy, with mingled odors of disinfectant, rust, and mold. A last
glimmer of the July day shot through the barred window high up at
the ceiling and winked off the steel door.

Barely having had an hour's sleep in the last few days, my head
drooped. I was about to lie down when the hatch in the door shot
open.

"No sleeping until lights out!" the guard barked.

The peep-hole slid up and down. I was watched. Just as I dozed
off in an upright position, the hatch clanged down again: "Keep your
eyes open!"

Mercifully, what seemed an eternity to me, but must have been no more than four hours, came to an end. The siren hissed. With the glare of the bulb in my eyes, I fell into slumber.

This was when I first had my prison dream. It was to recur night after night during the ten to twenty minutes of sleep allowed me before being summoned for interrogation and again in the twenty minutes after I was led back to the cell in the early morning.

In my dream I was cleared of all charges and free to return home. Joy welled in me at the sight of the familiar objects in my room, and I gazed long and fixedly at them. I walked to my desk and switched on the light of the lamp so that it fell on my unfinished translation. I picked up a pen but could not write. After sitting in a kind of trance, I rose from the desk and turned to look at my daughter, peacefully asleep in her cot.

I picked her up lovingly and hugged her. Then I put her down. The room grew dimmer. My daughter's cot was no longer in its customary place, at the wall opposite the bed my husband and I had shared. Suddenly I grew restless and uneasy about something: there was something important I had to do, but I had forgotten what. I made a great effort to remember. I remembered. I knew what I must do: return at once to my cell. The darkness grew dense; I could no longer discern the objects in the room. Nervously I groped my way to the door, slipped out, and broke into a run. I was soon back in my cell. I had returned of my own accord. The real world, as represented by my home, no longer had any meaning for me. I was shut out from it. I now had to grapple with the unreality in which I was trapped and from which I knew full well there was no escape.

A dim, dark, and silent world! Such was the secret Lefortovo Prison. I was being led from my cell to the interrogator's office on the first floor of the prison's Administration Wing. Just a few flights of stairs led down to it, yet we meandered through a warren of endless steel galleries.

"Hands behind your back!" No sooner did I step out of the cell than I linked my hands tightly behind me. "Straight ahead!" It meant I dared not turn my head or look back.

Other than these two commands there was never any verbal communication between prisoner and guard, nor between the guards themselves when they were escorting prisoners. A different language was used: a snap of the fingers and click of the tongue, sounds that rang eerily in the empty prison corridors.

As soon as this warning signal came from a guard passing with another prisoner, my escort shoved me into a niche, my eyes to the wall. A snap and a click; then an answering snap and click to say the coast was clear and we could proceed to the interrogator's office. On my way I had never once come face to face with another prisoner. But one morning, as I was being led back to the cell, a woman's shrieks reached my ears, piercing the musty air: "I am innocent, totally innocent!" she cried hysterically. "Long live Stalin!" I could feel my jailor tense. Quickly he prodded me on, deeper into the silence of the prison.

Major Porunov was sitting at his big birchwood desk when the guard brought me in. A hard stool at the door was the prisoner's place, which I now occupied. The interrogator rose and slowly approached me.

"What intelligence service have you been providing with information about the Soviet Union?" He continued in a more menacing tone: "We know Anna Louise Strong recruited you."

I gave the negative answers I now delivered night after night. After each interrogation he handed me the deposition sheets. I signed them. He wrote down my replies exactly as I worded them. They were denials of the accusations against me, clearly revealing my innocence of the espionage and treason charges. There was nothing to link me to Anna Louise Strong.

Questions concerning Boris Victorov—supposed agent of an American firm with whom, it was alleged, I had some sort of a meeting—led nowhere. Major Porunov was making no headway with my treason charge.

"You wrote letters to Canada maligning the Soviet system."

This was a shot in the dark. Every avenue was to be explored to gain a conviction.

"We have evidence that you were in touch with Mr. Franseez, a Canadian spy."

I was as mystified by this new character as I had been by the reference to Victorov.

On the following night, however, Major Porunov waved his evidence at me.

"I have here a letter sent to you by this spy . . ." I suddenly recalled that I had once received a single letter from a Toronto cousin of mine, many years before my imprisonment. The name of the cousin was Frances.

I couldn't help laughing. I told my interrogator from whom the letter was and explained that "Franseez," as he pronounced it, could be a female as well as a male name.

Major Porunov resumed his questions about my mother. I suspected nothing. I could not believe that my mother had been arrested and was in fact at that very moment in a cell at Lefortovo, not far away from my own. Even when the thought did at times force itself into my mind, I dismissed it as impossible. My mother arrested? To the last she remained loyal to the Soviet system. I thought of her advanced age, of all she had been through—the tsarist prisons, two wars, the struggle to support her children, the tragedy of having left her first two children to fend for themselves from the most tender age.

My mother had three more years to live. Major Porunov was her interrogator as he was mine. He did not spare her. He told her outright that her daughter was a spy. Night after night he plied her with questions about me. She tried her best to see through the subterfuge and lies, fighting a double battle, for herself and for me.

On being driven for interrogation from Lefortovo to Lubyanka one September night, I found a man with a big, menacing head leaning forward over the second, usually unoccupied, desk next to the one behind which sat Major Porunov, my interrogator. Behind these two men was a large window. The drapes were not drawn and I let my gaze settle on the dark glass. I wondered if the window overlooked the big Dzerzhinsky Square or the prison yard of the Lubyanka building. Behind the window was the somber Moscow night; the air circled freely, people slept in their beds, not knowing how lucky they were.

"Your husband is a dangerous criminal," rasped the stranger at the second desk. At once I shifted my attention from the window to him.

It seemed to me for a moment that the fierce black pupils of his eyes had popped out of their sockets and were whirling around the room in a frenzied dance of hatred. What a hideous face, with a twist to the thick, moist lips and a clamminess about the unhealthy skin. I shuddered to think what a man like him could do to his victim— hit out blindly with his strong fists, kick with his feet, hurl himself on the defenseless prisoner.

"Did you know that your husband was unfaithful to you, that he kept a mistress?"

He expected a response from me. I said nothing. Very often during interrogation I found myself utterly at a loss. How could I respond to the sordid lies and insults, the savage attacks and lunatic reasoning with which I was kept awake night after night, straining every nerve to fight off sleep so that I could remain in my seat and not drop on the floor from exhaustion?

That September night, however, I was jolted into full wakefulness.

I knew I was looking into the face of my husband's interrogator. Branding Mikhail a "dangerous" criminal was an ominous sign. It meant that the worst physical torture was justified in the course of the interrogation. Even the weakest of human beings have proved capable of enduring physical torture for a noble cause. But human beings were so debased, so befuddled by the lies and tricks of a Stalinist interrogator that they ceased to feel and think like normal people.

They were lost, cut off from the world, betrayed by their own ideology, crushed in mind and spirit. The big, ruthless security butcher I now saw before me might well have been my husband's murderer. The evil he represented had triumphed—and he never forfeited the protection of the socialist state. He may be living now in respectable retirement in a dacha near Moscow, enjoying a better pension than any Soviet working man, never fearing that he and others like him will be brought to justice.

II Interrogation by a general

Appeals to my interrogator to tell me what would become of my daughter, now that both her parents were imprisoned, fell on deaf ears. In the hope of extracting some information about her, I went on a hunger strike. For three days I refused all food. On the fourth I was taken down to a ward in the prison infirmary. There I was pinned down by two silent husky women and a man. A long crude rubber tube lay on the floor beside me. The very next moment it was forced down my throat.

There is a Soviet film shown frequently on Moscow television. Its heroine is Lenin's mother. When Lenin's older brother Alexander is sentenced to death for an attempt on the tsar's life, his mother has an interview with the chief of police in St. Petersburg. She is permitted to see her son. What struck me in this film was not only that she was able to do things no Soviet person was allowed, but also that wherever she went she was treated like a human being. Even the hated, feared, ruthless tsarist police, responsible for the death and stifling of so many good lives, treated political prisoners and their families like human beings.

In the prison world where I found myself, I was nothing but a captive animal to be kicked about and tormented at the will of whoever were my masters. To be suddenly hurled into an animal jungle and stripped of their humanity was the prisoners' worst horror, one that could be and was for many more fearful than death.

There was yet another horror: the complete dissolution of reality as you knew it. The rational understanding of things, which human beings have always sought, suddenly ceases to exist. You find yourself trapped in the vagueness, the utter nonsense of the accusations against you. Your mind rebels against the absurdity of an innocent person like yourself, uninvolved in politics, never in the Party, hardworking, honest, suddenly becoming the target of a powerful state apparatus.

You refuse to believe it. You try hard to find some plausibility; many prisoners in endeavoring to end the vagueness of the accusations levelled against them had even contrived to provide the so-called evidence to substantiate their conviction. To get at the truth, to perceive the logic of things. Order as opposed to chaos—was this not what the human mind craved from childhood, from the dawn of civilization?

In the avalanche of lies that descended upon me, I was overjoyed when I stumbled upon something that resembled truth. I was sitting at the prisoner's tiny table, far from the interrogator's massive desk, on the right side of the door.

From the way proceedings were going, it was apparent that there did not exist a scrap of evidence that could even remotely be linked with the charges brought against me. I was dumfounded by the utter idiocy of my case, the lack of logic, the confusion. Nothing hung together.

Both Major Porunov, my interrogator, and Lieutenant-Colonel Boyarinov, the prosecutor overseeing my case, were present at the questioning. In front of the Lieutenant-Colonel lay three fat dossiers. Hastily he was leafing through them. The interrogator, I could see, was examining me on the charge of "anti-Soviet conversations" and was getting nowhere.

Suddenly out of the blue came a question that was a ray of truth. It was put by the prosecutor who had picked it out of an informer's report in one of the dossiers. He asked it without taking his eyes off the page in front of him. Unlike Major Porunov, who seemed to enjoy his job, Boyarinov gave the impression that he was eager to get things over with as soon as possible, either because he was so very busy or because he wished to distance himself from the filth he was raking up, and the lies.

"Did you go around saying that Moscow toilets were dirty?"

Here at last was something I did say—a rational seed in the entire weird examination. Relieved, even happy, I replied: "Yes, I did, I certainly did!"

The Moscow visit of Clement Attlee, Britain's future prime minister, and his diarrhea, sprang into my mind. But somehow the
absurdity of bringing toilets into the interrogation must have struck
all of us; we smiled, the smile clearing for a brief moment the animosity that always hung so oppressively in the air between me and
my two persecutors.

But the treason charge? Espionage against the Soviet Union for a
certain state. What state? How was I to know that this was a ster-
eotyped formula used against thousands of prisoners as innocent as
myself?

I was pacing my cell, bewildered, shocked, still endeavoring to pick
up some logical thread, when I recalled an incident that dated way
back to my work as an Intourist guide. Perhaps it had something to
do with the bringing of an espionage charge against me? I'll tell it
and explain . . . For a self-destructive thought like that to have even
entered my mind reveals how distraught and totally lost I must have
felt.

What was this incident, which as things turned out later, helped
to earn me a conviction on a milder charge? It had to do with my
having spent a half hour or so in the American embassy in Moscow,
in either 1935 or 1936—that is, about fifteen years before my arrest.
I was assigned as personal guide to a first-class tourist. He was a
certain Mr. Lush, an American who had written a book called *Six
Roads to Happiness*, a copy of which he presented to me. We were out
sightseeing when he said he had some business at the embassy.
Rather than wait outside and make myself conspicuous, I had gone
in with him. That it should have flashed back into my mind during
the interrogation period was perhaps not so astonishing. What was
astonishing and foolish was that I now of my own accord provided
my interrogator with a "piece of evidence" he had never known
existed.

The moment I related the incident he gloated; exultation twinkled
in his brazen eyes. During the long nightly questionings I had frequently asked him: "How can you bring these wild accusations
against me, when you possess no evidence, no proof of any kind,
can produce no witnesses?"

Once he burst out: "We do not require any evidence. You will provide it yourself."

That was exactly what I had done. To cross the threshold of a foreign embassy, even as part of one's job—what could be greater proof
that you were indeed a spy?

For three weeks now I had had a cellmate. Olga Manina, a Muscovite, told me right away she was a graduate of the Institute of Foreign Languages, where I had taught for a few years. She spoke vaguely of her own charges; all I remember her saying was that she had dated men from foreign embassies.

Olga was extremely vain about her looks; with her green eyes, dark hair, pale skin, and small, well-shaped nose, she was very attractive. She had a regular beauty routine, which she followed religiously. Every morning she did her setting-up exercises and tried hard with her fingertips to smooth away the lines that were settling around her eyes and mouth; in one year of prison or prison camp, as I was soon to observe, women aged ten to fifteen years. Olga would set her hair in paper curlers every night before going to bed, and she was clever at inventing substitutes for cosmetics. As she smoked she dropped the cigarette ash into an empty matchbox. On collecting a fair amount, she mixed the ash with spittle, turning it into a fine mascara that made her sweeping lashes look even longer. Chalk from the whitewashed walls of the cell served as powder, and above all Olga treasured a small red beet, which was her lipstick and rouge.

"How do I look?" Olga would ask me after she had spent about an hour on her grooming. Mirrors and glass objects were proscribed and so there was no way in which she could see the results of her beautifying efforts.

"You look like a movie star!" I told her.

Pleased, she rewarded me with a rare smile.

However, as Olga talked to me about herself, I began to have the strange feeling that she was lying, and that she had been isolated from the normal world for a longer period than she claimed. There were indeed many things about Olga that should have put me on my guard. But I was too naive, too new, to comprehend their significance. For one thing, Olga was never interrogated by night, always in the morning or afternoon—and for long days not at all—so that she was not exhausted as I was by lack of sleep. Moreover, she was allowed parcels from home and had permission to buy food and cigarettes at the prison commissary. Quite often I caught her mocking glance on me. Once or twice, from the questions my interrogator asked me, I realized that Olga had been reporting on my behaviour in the cell.

I now guessed that Olga was a spy brought in from camp to trick me into making some admission that would help my interrogator to convict me. Months later, in prison camp, I met a young woman who told me that Olga had also shared her cell at Lefortovo, watched and spied on her. Olga was a useful informer, and her snooping on others made her own life as a prisoner easier.

At a late hour, after about ten weeks of interrogation, I emerged under guard from the clammy Lefortovo walls into the cobblestoned prison yard. It was a dark, drizzly night. I swallowed a few gulps of moist air before climbing into the maw of a black maria.

After spending several hours in one of the already familiar Lubyanka boxes, I was taken up a few flights into a commodious office with armchairs upholstered in burgundy leather, a large desk, and a side table covered with a green felt pad.

Major Porunov, my interrogator, and Lieutenant-Colonel Boyarinov, the surveillance prosecutor, were present, the former standing in a far corner, the latter slumped in an armchair, his myopic spectacled eyes glued to the open page of a bulky folder. The presence of the prosecutor signified that the interrogation had attained a crucial point. A young clerk entered and took a seat at the side table. There was a fourth man in the office, his back turned to me.

The interrogation that followed surpassed all the previous ones in sheer nonsense. Somebody must have switched off the ceiling light, because the figures of my interrogator and prosecutor appeared shadowy and sketchy, like the backdrop designs on a darkened stage. The man whose back was turned to me swung around; in the full glare of the large desk lamp, his insignia told me he was a lieutenant-general.

He paced in sharp, impatient steps back and forth in front of me. And he fired at me the same question Major Porunov had kept asking at Lefortovo: did I know Anna Louise Strong? His baldness, mean eyes, and pink skin, along with an enormous paunch, recalled an ill-tempered hog.

After I repeated over and over again that I had never been personally acquainted with Anna Louise Strong, he boomed: "What about her husband? You knew him!"

"Yes, I knew Comrade Shubin. I worked for him at the *Moscow News*."

Suffering from shortness of breath, the general was now panting into my face.

"Well, well, how could you know the husband and not know the wife?" he bellowed.

I made no reply. I was stunned by the general's logic. What a farce! I had not the least idea at the time that interrogation by a general—a leading man in the Directorate—signified a turning point in the legal proceedings of my case. The charge of treason was dropped. But I was to realize this only much later.

I was taken down into the Lubyanka courtyard, hemmed in by walls and gates. A van stood out from the shadows, waiting for me; in its pitch dark I sat numb, dazed, a castaway from life.

Back in my cell in Lefortovo I experienced a sensation that perplexes me to this day. It also proves the spiritual resilience we gradually build up to preserve life and sanity when they are threatened as I felt they were.

When an agonizing blow is dealt us, we squirm and tingle with the pain and injury of it. All we want is to crawl into some hole, a place of seclusion to lick our wounds, out of the sight of our torturers. That hole becomes a haven to us.

That was the way I felt about my cell on at last finding myself in it after the almost four-hour interrogation in Lubyanka, where I had had to hold out against a blast of verbiage designed to wear me down and wrest a lying confession from me, where I had encountered an unwarranted animosity, a desire to crush me out of existence as though I were some annoying insect. If there was not a shred of honesty or justice in the way my interrogator and surveillance prosecutor were conducting the case, the general was the epitome of brutality in dispensing with human lives.

No wonder I was glad to be back in my Lefortovo cell; if only for a short while, it offered protection from my tormentors. The four damp walls smiled upon me with a warmth I had not known since I had been hauled away from home. A faint strip of dawn broke into the cell from the tiny barred window up at the ceiling. It cheered me greatly.

I did not hastily slip under the coarse prison blanket to snatch the twenty minutes of sleep allowed me after interrogation. I wished to prolong this sweet sensation of safety in my Lefortovo dungeon. I had a strong premonition of worse things to come, and I prayed that I might serve my entire term within these walls—in my cell, away from the interrogation office, where the charges against me were so senseless and the whole world was made to stand on its head instead of its feet.

How odd it seemed that the dark, damp cell had the power to suffuse me with this homey warmth, to protect me from the wanton hostility of my fellow creatures, from the pain of their blows. I realized that a little privacy for even a short time can have a salubrious effect, indeed bring one back to sanity; to think that this should have been borne in upon me in Lefortovo, one of the most awesome prisons of Europe. Interrogators at Lubyanka and Butyrki were constantly using the threat of Lefortovo to their prisoners: "I'll send you to Lefortovo and you'll turn into an old woman in no time—and sign away your mother's life."

Although that early morning before dawn, when I returned from an especially traumatic questioning, I had a warm feeling for Lefortovo, it was indeed a terrifying place—gloomier, damper, more unhealthy, and with worse food, than any other prison in Moscow. It was used mostly as a place for interrogation. Prisoners were not kept long in Lefortovo, for it required blooming health to endure even a year's incarceration there.

Every morning at six, the hour of reveille, the orderly brought in the prisoner's daily half-loaf of soggy black bread, some herb coloring for tea, and six tiny square lumps of sugar. The bread tasted awful; after two or three hours it was coated with a greenish-white mold. The main meal was a skilly of split barley with a few rusty herring tails floating in it. Day after day, it was exactly the same fare, food— if you could call it that—designed, like everything else in Lefortovo, to wear down your morale, to degrade you: if that is what you eat, you cannot be a human being.

Hence, when I was brought to Lubyanka shortly before my case was closed, the better bread, a meal of real cabbage soup and a second course of *bona fide* potatoes, the kind commonly eaten by human beings, put me in an almost euphoric frame of mind. As I ate the potatoes with an aluminum fork—a fork! I had not seen one for three months and would not see one again for almost three years!—in the tiny Lubyanka box, sitting on a shelf bed, I told myself that surely a prisoner fed the kind of food normally eaten by any other human being was going to be released. Of course, I was in a kind of trance. But such is the psychological impact of food on the mind: I really believed at the time in a happy dénouement. My hopes were up. I would be released, would walk out of the Lubyanka gates.

III My interrogator

"If I declare you innocent, I take your place," my interrogator blurted out in the semi-gloom of his office on the downstairs floor of the Lefortovo Prison. The words had slipped from him at a moment when he must have felt that he himself was trapped in a situation from which there was no more escape for him than for me. There was no escape because he had accepted the role of inquisitor, working night after night to secure my conviction when he was aware even before I was apprehended that the case against me was a fabrication.

He spoke the truth. Any leniency, any attempt on his part to see justice done, would land him in jail.

But why had he not at some point in his career changed—as others had—to a different job? It was not impossible to achieve that, especially for a man with a good legal education. He was not a born hangman, not a confirmed *chekist*, not one who could be brainwashed into thinking that persons like myself or my mother were a danger to the regime. Why then did he participate in a tragi-comedy that invariably ended in the destruction of human life?

He belonged to a generation among whom there were no political fanatics, as there had been at the time of the revolution, or in the twenties and even thirties. Ideology hardly entered at all into his work, and he rarely had the satisfaction of outwitting and eliminating ideological opponents, for the simple reason that they did not exist.

He was doing what he was, obviously, out of the most sordid motives, for paltry material gains—a better apartment, a fur coat for his wife, a vacation at an exclusive place, a privileged education and jobs for his children.

My interrogator was certainly not the worst of the lot. A doctor in camp, a prisoner like myself, told me that the hundreds of young women arriving from jails in the Western Ukraine bore the marks of their interrogator's boots, sometimes across their breasts, and sometimes over their pregnant bellies.

Major Porunov was most correct with me. I was never sent to a punishment cell. Only once did he hurl an obscenity at me. I was shocked, but presumed he did it simply to put down in the reports he handed to his superiors that he had resorted to that common "method" too. Only once did he make an offensive allusion to my nationality.

And this was at a time when in my cell I could hear strings of the typical Russian obscenities from the interrogation department on the floor below. At the top of their voices the interrogators yelled out at the prisoners the three-letter Russian word for the male organ, and it was always your mother this and your mother that—the supreme insult, dating back from the Mongol-Tartar invasion when the conquerors gloried in telling their Russian victims that they had raped their mothers. To my cell window was carried the venom slung at Jewish political prisoners: *Zhidovskaya morda*, beloved yell of the Black Hundreds and the Cossacks during the pre-revolutionary pogroms. And now it reached me from the lips of Soviet interrogators, with Communist Party membership cards firmly pinned to their breast pockets, next to their hearts. (The loss of a membership card could mean expulsion from the Party.)

Major Porunov was about my age, that is, in his mid-thirties. He was blond, ruddy, athletic, with a steely glint in his eyes, which at rare moments softened, perhaps suggesting the stirring of some scruples.

A man and a woman thrown together night after night for several hours at a stretch; there was some chemistry at work between us. Had it been a normal reality in which we found ourselves, and we met socially, we might have been attracted to one another. Instead we were trapped in a bizarre predicament from which there was no way out but for him to crush me and for me to meekly accept my fate at his hands.

The surveillance prosecutor in my case, Boyarinov, was a squat, formless man in his fifties, bullet-headed, with a small snout of a nose and scared eyes behind spectacles that were strangely askew, as was everything else about him. In sharp contrast to my interrogator, about whom there was a suave, leisurely air, the prosecutor was always tense, impatient, in a great rush.

And now too, sitting on the right-hand side of the interrogator's desk, a few yards away from the tiny prisoner's table, he was impatient to get it all over with. The accusation of "anti-Soviet agitation among friends," no matter how hard he and the interrogator endeavored to procure evidence to support it, hung in the air.

At this stage in the interrogation—and the presence of the prosecutor indicated that some decision was pending—the two men had to decide if it was to be pursued or not. Right there in front of me, they carried on a whispered conference. For all I knew, they might have decided beforehand to drop the charge, and I was now present at what legally could be termed an acquittal.

I was handed a bulky folder with a complete record of all the statements I had signed; this was in conformity with Article 206 of the Criminal Code. For more than an hour I sat perusing the depositions. There was no proof whatever of my guilt, no evidence to support it, no witnesses. The charges were utterly unfounded. I told myself that no court in any country of the world, even one where the worst lawlessness existed, could sentence me on the basis of it.

Breathing a sigh of relief, and well gratified with what I had read, I inquired: "Will there be a trial?" I had asked the question before, had indeed been turning over in my mind what I would say to the judges.

The answer was one I had already heard.

"Yes, of course, I hope you are prepared."

The interrogator was merely amusing himself at my expense. For all my naiveté, I knew I could not hope for release. Yet after I read the summary my spirits rose. Perhaps, I thought, I might be lucky enough to get a term of exile to a locality not far from Moscow. I suddenly recalled all the unfortunates I knew who for years had lived a hundred kilometers from the capital and had to sneak in, risking rearrest, to see their families and friends. I shuddered. It was a grave injustice. But people lived with it, accepted it.

"Am I correct in thinking that the charges of treason and anti-Soviet agitation against me have been dropped?"

"Yes," replied Major Porunov, smiling and looking into my eyes as though expecting to find in them gratitude for the credit due him.

He had been standing just a few steps away from me. Now he walked back to his desk, picked up a paper from it, and once again approached me.

"Read and sign this. It is the conclusion of your case. You are charged under Article 7, Section 35."

I failed at first to grasp the meaning of his words— until I read the conclusion. "The accused is charged with contacts with American and French intelligence agents." What insane grounds were there for this new charge? I could only speculate that my visit to the American Embassy with a tourist and my friend Vera Schwartz's liaison with the French Havas Agency correspondent were vaguely related to it.

I now came under a more mild political article as a "socially harmful element."

The interrogator stood over me with a benevolent smile.

"You are very lucky indeed to get off with this mild charge."

I hardly heard his words. So it was all over! There would be no trial. And I had been rehearsing speeches in my defense. What a fool I was to hope for justice.

It turned out that there was yet a third document for me to sign. After the prosecutor had waddled out of the office with his bursting briefcase, the interrogator took out of his desk a bundle of papers and placed them in front of him.

"I have here your personal papers, letters and photographs," Major Porunov said in a soft voice. "You will not need them where you are going," he purred. "You will not be allowed to take them with you, nor can they be returned to any of your family."

He rose from his seat and came as close to my prisoner's table as, I suppose, security permitted. "The usual procedure," he continued, "is for the prisoner to agree to the disposal of such papers."

A chill settled in my heart. The bundle on the interrogator's desk contained photographs and letters I treasured. But what did it matter now? What was the point in having regrets about mementos when my own life was finished?

It shocked me to hear the interrogator echo this very thought in the same honeyed tone into which he had suddenly lapsed.

"Your life is finished. It's all over for you. Forget the world you have been living in . . ."

"Dispose of everything as you please," I said indifferently, with an even stronger sensation than ever that all this was happening not to me but to another person.

Major Porunov returned to his desk and presently handed me a sheet titled "Affidavit of Burning." I signed it.

Years later I learned that it had been within my legal right to refuse to sign it. But prisoners were never apprised of an alternative. Whatever rights the prisoner had—and these were few enough—they were craftily concealed from him.

"I shall not be seeing you again. The interrogation is over."

IV Butyrki Prison

I found myself in the solitary confinement tower of Moscow's Butyrki Prison. Located on the outskirts, walled in from all eyes, far away from the Metro, Lefortovo was a top-secret prison; few were even aware of its existence. But Butyrki was well known to Muscovites as a place of detention for all criminals. In times of mass political arrests—in 1937 and 1938, and in the period beginning with 1947 right until Stalin's death—Butyrki was packed to overflowing with men and women charged with or convicted of political crimes.

With its scuffed but clean linoleum floor, fair-sized window, and freshly painted walls, my cell in this wing of the prison was quite cheerful compared with the gloom, chipped concrete, and damp of Lefortovo. The food was more palatable. The millet gruel and thick soup were inviting and savory after the herring-bone slops of Lefortovo, but ravenous as I was, there was no way I could get the oversized wooden spoon issued me into my mouth. How I struggled with it, poking sidewise, working in the tip! Having failed, I ended up lapping the prison fare with my tongue like a cat or dog. Humiliated and exhausted, I flopped down on the bunk and wept.

Next day I plucked up the courage to ask the warder for an aluminum spoon. He returned with a wooden ladle. It was small, and I was grateful.

With no books allowed, the hours, the minutes, even the seconds dragged interminably. The day seemed to stand still, confronting me with a mocking immobility, a leer. I had no idea that months later, in camp, I would think back wistfully to the peace and privacy of solitary confinement—and with regret that I had not diligently searched my mind for resources that could transform emptiness into motion and activity.

How could I not have seen, not valued the advantages of solitary confinement? Perhaps it was these gradual changes from bad to worse that enabled prisoners, in the long run, to adjust and survive in the bizarre world into which they were thrust.

Although the interrogation, according to Major Porunov, was supposed to have been closed, it was pursued sedulously during my solitary confinement. It appeared that "for lack of evidence" my case was returned from the prosecutor's office for further substantiation. I was interrogated about friends who had been apprehended in 1937 and 1938, all of whom, as the questions showed, were dead. My contacts with these "enemies of the people" were to be set down in my record as further proof that I was indeed a "socially harmful element." But there was yet another objective behind the nightly questionings: to extract compromising information about friends, co-workers, and acquaintances, even neighbors.

Major Porunov was getting impatient. His tone grew more menacing. Nervously he paced his office, demanding that I tell him what anti-Soviet thoughts my friends entertained, how they viewed the arrests. I must have heard them vilify Soviet literature and art. Such talk, he persisted, was common. My obstinacy would get me nowhere. There were hosts of other reports on what people I knew were saying.

"We trust nobody," he burst out.

Indulging in a bit of histrionics to break up the tedium of the almost six-hour nightly questioning, he let loose a spate of abuse against the intelligentsia.

"Take Moscow University professors. They are a political liability, undependable, traitors in the making."

After pausing to see what effect his words had on me, he continued: "We have on record the anti-Soviet sentiments of the intellectuals. They're rotten to the core, the whole lot."

I was shocked by what he said, knowing it to be a lie. Soviet intellectuals were dedicated, hard-working, though grossly underpaid compared to him with his high salary and the many privileges he enjoyed.

"We'll isolate them from the rest of society—in prisons and camps," he concluded, yawning and stretching himself.

I tried to put in a remark about the loyalty of the intelligentsia.

As though anticipating what I wanted to say, Major Porunov warned: "Don't attempt to whitewash the intellectuals. I want exposures, exposures only!"

For three months now I had been allowed no more than a half hour's sleep a night, and none whatever during the day. I often recalled the Russian proverb: "Sleep is more precious than a mother and father."

Choosing a moment when I felt most weary and had hardly any control over my drooping lids, he barraged me with questions about Merkurov. The sculptor was a big catch, and to obtain information that could discredit him would add a brilliant feather to my interrogator's cap.

"For your own good, you had better describe what anti-Soviet conversations you overheard at Merkurov's."

"I heard nobody talk against the Soviet system at his home."

"And Merkurov himself?"

"Never. He was most loyal in thought and deed."

"Don't imagine you'll get away with shielding that sly fox and his entire subversive household. I demand you tell the truth."

Whenever the word "truth" crossed my interrogator's lips, I squirmed in my prisoner's bench. Truth was as remote from him and the institution he represented as freedom and a normal life were from me.

"Why give a hang for Merkurov and his family, when *your* life is finished? You'll go to a camp from which you'll never come back." How often he reiterated these words, as though he derived satisfaction from the picture of urbanites like myself vegetating in the dark womb of Siberia.

"Forget the world you have been living in," he went on. "You are doomed, so why play the noble lady? Can you deny that anti-Soviet jokes were told by Merkurov, his family, and guests?"

"They were never told in my presence!"

Major Porunov lost his temper. "Who is Merkurov to you, that you are protecting him—a father? Look, he is enjoying his freedom, his women, the best of food, while you will rot away, lose your health, your child . . ." He stopped short and turned his head away. Did I witness some human stirring in him?

My eyes filled with tears. I was thinking of my little daughter, longing for her, fearing for her.

My interrogator had not subjected me to the torture by means of which lying accusations against their best friends were extracted from prisoners. I said nothing that could slur the loyalty of Merkurov or other friends.

Merkurov was indeed a dear person to me; he had time and again reinforced my faith in the goodness of human nature. I loved him for what he was, a man of talent and resourcefulness, a highly successful artist who never looked down his nose at another human being. I loved the tickle and French scent of his graying beard when he kissed me, as he did every friend on greeting and parting.

I could imagine what fat dossiers the MGB kept on Merkurov and other prominent artists. And although I provided no "evidence" against him, so perverse were the practices of the Stalinist security police that for a person facing grave political charges to speak highly of Merkurov could in itself be compromising for the sculptor.

Death, however, outwitted the security police. A few months after I was interrogated, for several nights running, about him, Merkurov passed away from a heart attack.

V Cellmates, a poem

From the solitary confinement tower at the top of the Butyrki Prison I was moved to a cell on the second floor at the end of a long wide corridor with tiled walls and a red linoleum floor. Stone at Lefortovo, parquet at Lubyanka, linoleum at Butyrki.

The cell was in a part of the prison that seemed to possess the acoustics of the Bolshoi Theater. It was resonant with sounds I welcomed happily after the muteness of solitary confinement. There was the jangling of the keys on a huge ring snapped to the warder's belt, when prisoners were escorted to and from questioning; the clatter of aluminum cauldrons, trundling back and forth in the prison hallways; even the trilling of birds departing to warmer climes. Outside a large window with a grate I caught sight of a few russet leaves and heard them being swished off the trees by gusts of wind.

It is astonishing how the little attributes of civilization, like a tea kettle, give one a sense of belonging to the human race. That is why, I mused, sitting down at the well-scrubbed wooden table in the middle of the cell, such pains are exerted to deprive the prisoner of the utensils, the technology, that played so important a role in man's transition from the brutal to the human state. Back to the brute, to the dumb animal—that was the strategy employed against the political prisoner.

It was a long time since I had seen or heard anyone speak, apart from my interrogator. Now the sight of several women sitting around the table and chatting warmed my heart. After asking a few of the usual questions directed at newcomers, the prisoners picked up the thread of their interrupted conversation.

I was astonished to catch the name of a well-known writer whom I had frequently seen at the bookkeeping office of the Soviet Information Buro during the war, when he dropped in to collect fees for articles. I remembered him as a man of unstriking but pleasant appearance and a rather happy-go-lucky air, which contrasted sharply with the harried, preoccupied look we all had during the war, or the glum, dour Ilya Ehrenburg who also dropped—rather swept— in, to cavil over the English equivalent of a word or sentence in his crisp style and have it out with the translators. The wife of the writer my fellow-prisoners now mentioned was a tight-lipped, sharp-featured Moscow Art Theater actress, who had made a brilliant career for herself. He himself had risen to the position of General Secretary of the Soviet Writers Union, which gave him power over the lives of many of his confrères—and not them alone.

"Yes, it was the Writers Union's General Secretary who turned them in, " said one of the prisoners.

"Are you sure?" asked another doubtfully.

"She herself will tell you!" The speaker pointed to a swarthy woman in her sixties, but the subject was dropped. The prisoners' animated chatter died down; a brooding silence settled in its stead. The women sat spiritlessly, each a prey to her own dismal thoughts.

I now eyed the dark-complexioned prisoner. She was small and hump-backed, apparently a cripple from birth. Her face was deeply creased and weather-beaten, yet with a dignity and hauteur that intrigued me. Dusky Russian faces mostly suggested Mongolian or Tartar ancestry. The mold of her features, however, was distinctly European, and I attributed her swarthiness to perhaps a strain of gypsy blood. That she had been a migrant most of her life I was soon to learn from Maria Alexandrovna herself.

Bit by bit, I was able to form an opinion of this woman's fate and character. When, after a three-hour nightly interrogation, she was led back into our cell by the prison guard, I was startled by the transformation in her; her eyes blazed with a mystical, almost joyous light, her hollow cheeks burned, and she held her head so high over her dumpy body that it half-concealed her hump. She was as elated and triumphant as a player who had swept all the stakes off the gambling table. This change puzzled me.

It was not until days later, when I had seen her arrive after each questioning in this very exhilarated mood, that I hit on an explanation for her irrational behaviour. Of course, it could well be said that our entire existence was irrational. I realized that what gave Maria Alexandrovna this uplift was that for once in her life her person counted for something. She was happy for a relief from her drab and wretched existence—even if it was happening in prison and would surely end in her conviction.

At last there was someone willing to listen to her views and her life story, who indeed hung on her every word. The feeling that she was a somebody after all gave Maria Alexandrovna this moment of exaltation.

With the interrogator she could talk about everything and everybody. She held forth on her beloved poet Nadson, and he was ready to discuss him with her.

"I'm a pessimist like Nadson," she told me. "I cannot conceive of any thinking person not being one." It was from her own lips that I heard her story, which she had also told at different times to other cellmates.

Maria Alexandrovna came of a well-known St. Petersburg family. I knew her surname—Lopukhina—to have been common among the old Russian nobility. About her face and whole being, notwithstanding her deformity, there was a touch of arrogance and pride that could well suggest aristocratic origins. Her sister had been a celebrated beauty and a maid-in-waiting at the Imperial court. According to Maria Alexandrovna, she herself was the least educated and pampered in the family; she was the ugly duckling.

She trained for a nurse and served with the Red Cross during World War I. A brief liaison with an army surgeon had resulted in the birth of a son. Maria Alexandrovna had been a nurse in World War II as well. But for most of their lives she and her son were homeless, half-starved derelicts. They were not idlers; they worked hard for their living. Having never acquired "housing space," and not being able to afford to rent even the tiniest living quarters privately, they roamed from town to town, penniless migrants taking whatever job came their way. "We were really gypsies," Maria Alexandrovna said. And for this reason it had taken the security police two years to fall on their tracks.

In their misery the pair clung to one another. Perhaps from his mother, the son had inherited a love of poetry, and soon he thought himself a poet. It was their undoing. He wrote a poem ridiculing Stalin. Maria Alexandrovna knew this and other of her son's poems by heart. But we did not want to hear them. It would have been dangerous even to listen to anything that denigrated Stalin. However, she managed to recite the first two lines. If I can trust my memory, they ran something like this: "A Georgian pauper sits on the Russian throne, / To throat-cutting, treachery, and torture prone."

This poem, written in his own handwriting and consisting of about fifty lines, the son had mailed to the influential head of the Writers Union, its General Secretary. He sent it anonymously, giving no intimation of his address. (He had none.) The poem was directed to the secret police and they did not rest content until they had traced the handwriting to the proper source. Both the son and the mother were arrested.

To trust the Secretary of the Writers Union with anything as self-indicting as a poem vilifying Stalin was a mad thing to do. And the interrogator had indeed tried to prove that Maria Alexandrovna's son was insane. For this reason he spent hours discussing both their lives with her. The interrogator knew he was expected to show that only a mentally deranged person could dare to blaspheme against "the greatest genius of mankind." Not that it absolved the prisoner of responsibility: he would be sentenced (Maria Alexandrovna herself received ten years) without the least clemency and ordered, perhaps, to be locked up in one of the psychiatric huts of which the infirmary-camp compounds were full.

A different kind of inmate was a round-faced, pink-cheeked girl with long amber braids. She was the same age—not yet sixteen—as I had been when I was expelled from Baron Byng High School. Her name was Galya Smirnova.

Galya was one of only a few persons I met for whose incarceration there was at least a pretext. She had attended a single gathering of an incipient children's organization joined by a few brave school kids whose parents were serving terms or had been shot for so-called political crimes. Over a period of no more than a few months these teenagers met in utmost secrecy, in small groups.

They were soon tracked down by the secret police, arrested, brutally interrogated, and sentenced to long terms. The organization was called Leninskiye Krylya (Lenin Wings) and it opposed in words only—not even in the actions for which I had been arrested in Montreal, such as the distribution of leaflets and participation in demonstrations—Lenin's ideals to Stalin's repressive policies. The organizer of Leninskiye Krylya was a boy called Felix. He was sentenced to be shot; later the sentence was commuted to twenty-five years. Though released a few years after Stalin's death, these children were never cleared of their crimes, as were other political prisoners, and have had to suffer the cruel consequences.

To keep up their spirits, my cellmates would think up all kinds of rumors, like pending amnesties, pardons on important revolutionary holidays, and other nonsense. Superstitions were rife. If you spilt water while pouring it from a kettle, a calamity was in store for you, which could indeed be. If you were called for interrogation on a Monday, an unlucky day, you could expect the worst. And so it went, on and on. Dreams were swapped every morning and diligently searched for omens. New inmates arrived with fresh rumors.

One of the strangest myths afloat at Butyrki had to do with Fanya Kaplan, the woman who had fired a shot at Lenin in 1918. Two or three prisoners I met insisted that she was alive. They assured me they had been in the same cell with women who swore they had actually seen Fanya when she was taken out for walks in the Butyrki prison yard. Some described her as a wispy, half-crazed woman; others said she looked well, adding that, needless to say, in prison you stood a better chance of surviving, even of looking well-preserved, than in the brutal conditions of the camps.

Yet it was well known that Kaplan was executed directly after her unsuccessful attempt on Lenin's life. Prisoners argued that Lenin had ordered her life to be spared; she was given a life sentence; Lenin had not wanted capital punishment for her since, after all, he had not paid with his life. That may well be true, but she was shot all right.

How can the prison legend that Fanya Kaplan was alive be explained? I know how astonished I was when it was told to me—yet I gladly accepted it as the truth, against my better judgment. I can only ascribe this to a kind of wishful thinking.

We clutched at every straw, every shred of hope. If Lenin had ordered that Fanya Kaplan's life be spared, it was because he was human. Lenin epitomized the best in the Soviet society. He could show mercy. A human heart beat in his breast. Therefore the prisoners, practically all of them totally innocent, could hope for clemency, for a general pardon. The arrests were a mistake, but after a while things would be set right again. The Soviet system was a humane system.

VI My sentence is read to me

There was no trial. My sentence was read out to me in a small elevator at the Lubyanka Prison by a major in an immaculate uniform who was the same height and looked about the same age as my interrogator. He was my last encounter with the world from which I was shut out; he smelt of fragrant soap and freedom.

He had an Armenian's hatchet face, with dark hair brushed back from a frowning forehead, and a petulant blur of a mouth. In his well-cared-for hands he clutched a folder. Hastily he opened it. It was full of loose sheets of paper. After riffling through them impatiently and finding what he needed, he reeled off the words:

"In the name of the Union of Soviet Socialist Republics you are sentenced by a Special Board to five years' imprisonment to be served in the corrective labor camps."

"Five years!" It was a harsh blow. "For what?"

The elevator kept creaking in its upward or downward course—I did not know which. The major now honored me with a glance in which I read a mixture of astonishment and annoyance. He had almost stumbled over the word "five" when he read out the sentence. Later I understood why: because five years was an unusually short sentence—a "kindergarten term," the prisoners called it. And so instead of being shocked, I suppose the major expected me to jump for joy.

Slowly the elevator pulled to a stop. With a squeamish sniff as though I were a leper and he had sullied himself by contact with me, the major drifted out, never turning his head or giving me a second glance. A few minutes later I found myself in the paved Lubyanka courtyard. I was the sole passenger in a black maria. Five years! The knowledge that Soviet political prisoners' sufferings did not end with the termination of their sentence heightened my despair.

The faces of Victor and Mikhail hovered before my gaze in the black emptiness, between the bench I occupied and the one across from me. Victor was long dead. And Mikhail? How many people had emerged alive from the clutches of the security apparatus? Practically none.

I felt remorseful. All too easily I had put both these men I loved out of my mind. Life must go on, I told myself. And now, as though in a kind of retribution, life had stopped for me. Never had I imagined that I too would be arrested. I had been so careful, so circumspect, trying never even to think thoughts that might be construed as disloyal to the regime, let alone articulate them.

Seeing so many people around me mowed down by the security machine, the one thing I dreaded and wished to avoid was their fate. Why is it that we never believe the misfortunes befalling others could overtake us? Blindly I hoped not to share the fate of Victor and Mikhail and the millions of others of whom, in my selfishness, I had tried not to think. And now I was in the same boat—though not quite, for I was not going to be shot. I would live, hateful as that life might be.

The black maria pulled up in front of the Butyrki Prison. Once inside the building we did not have far to go. The guard who escorted me paused in front of a huge door on the ground floor. In a matter of seconds I found myself in a cell for the convicted. I saw before me about twenty women, noisy and agitated, with a dozen questions on the tips of their tongues—the same ones that greeted all newcomers. My mother was among them.

"What is your sentence?" were my mother's first words.

I told her.

"Good, *you* will survive."

I looked long at her. She had aged at least ten years. She was all skin and bones but still erect. My mother had beautiful hands, rather small for her height, and the fingers were not long but perfectly shaped. The hands were still lovely, white, smooth, unravaged except for the nicotine stains. I sat down beside her on the iron cot, the tears coursing down both our faces. And I took one of her hands into mine. It fitted snugly in my clasp. As I stroked it, pity for her and impotent rage against our persecutors stuck in my throat.

She told me that with her, too, the charge of espionage had been dropped, but not the accusation of "anti-Soviet agitation among friends." It was on the strength of the evidence provided by her boss Pavlov, at the cartography department for which she worked, that she was convicted on this charge. During a confrontation with him at the interrogator's office, he repeated my mother's words: "I would go to Palestine if it were a socialist country." She did not deny them.

But the most painful part of her interrogation was the reference to her capture by General Denikin in Kharkov during the Civil War. "So, you say Denikin arrested you, sentenced you to death, and you got away?" the interrogator said. "Who is going to believe a cock and bull story like that?"

He rose from his seat and approached the corner prisoner's bench where my mother was sitting, yawned, offered her a cigarette, and lit it for her. Hungrily she took a quick draw.

The interrogator yawned again and in a voice of great boredom continued, "Even as early as that you embarked on your treacherous activities against Soviet power."

Another yawn. My mother did not suspect that he was merely asking routine questions, that it was all in the day's work. How could she know?

He was now working himself up into a frenzy—perhaps to keep from falling asleep.

"What did Denikin promise you?" he thundered. "Your freedom? In return for what? For becoming an Okhranka* agent?"

My mother ought to have perceived at once that it was all a comedy. Instead she took his words seriously. His cruel accusation cut her to the quick—she had herself many a time been a victim of the Okhranka agents—and she flung the burning cigarette into his face. A mistake! Perhaps a little thing like that cost her her life. The interrogator possessed great powers: the severity of the sentence could depend on him. And had she received a sentence of five years instead of ten, she might have survived and lived out her natural span of life.

My mother and I were among the thousands of close relations sentenced and deported to camps. Since prisoners were being perpetually moved from one prison to another, and from one overcrowded camp compound to the next, close relations, owing mostly to an oversight on the part of those who drew up the lists for transports, were almost bound to meet in the course of these peregrinations.

There were, however, express orders to avoid such encounters; if they occurred, separation was to be immediately enforced. And so it happened with my mother and myself. After spending only two days together in the cell for the convicted we were separated. We said goodbye, both of us wondering if it was forever. (It was not: several weeks later we met at the Taishet transit prison in Siberia.)

My sentence read clearly: "to be served in the corrective labor camps." But already, in the cell for the convicted, there were rumors that we would be going to camps quite different from those that came under the corrective labor system. We were held to be beyond redemption. In addition to our basic sentence, our punishment included complete isolation from society for life—even from the non-political prisoners, so that we would not contaminate them—and a speedy death. The "special" camps were a new penal institution, known as strict-regime camps—and that was where we were going, though we chose not to believe it.

The warder strode into our cell and, standing with his back to the door, yelled out names from a list.

"Get ready—pack your belongings. Quick!"

We guessed that we would be leaving Moscow. Despite all the fearsome talk about the "special" camps, most of us cherished the hope that life in camp would be more tolerable than in prison. In Lefortovo

* Secret police under the Tsar.

I was taken out for twenty-minute walks in a tiny yard with high timber walls around it, always alone, the guard either walking at my side or standing a few paces away; I never caught sight of another prisoner. At Lubyanka and Butyrki prisons these short exercise periods were denied me. I was starved for fresh air, for the outdoors, and above all for work. Outdoor labor would strengthen me physically, I thought. Having led a sedentary existence and engaged only in mental work, I would at last get a taste of physical labor. It would do me good.

The thoughts of other prisoners took the same course, for we could not imagine anything so destructive to the flesh and spirit as hard labor with continual exposure, sometimes for sixteen hours and more a day, to the biting frosts of Siberia in winter and the black swarms of mosquitoes in the short, scorching summers.

On the night of my arrest, apparently on instructions from my future interrogator, the two men who searched my home allowed me to pack a valise.

"Put in some warm things, you will need them," they said.

And now as we regained possession of our bags from the prison lockers, I saw that I had packed the elegant fall coat my friend Tina had made for me out of an old English blanket she had dyed black. It had a snug seal collar and cuffs.

Snow blew into our faces when we emerged into the prison yard. Tina's coat was poor protection against the winter blast, but for a brief moment it made me feel attractive and stylish.

Among the thirty or more prisoners jammed into the van were, to our great surprise, several men. They sat huddled together on a small bench against the wall of the driver's cabin. They hardly raised their heads or shifted position when we occupied the four benches across them, defeat staring out at us from every bend and curve of their crouched figures.

Like myself, many of the women in the van had arrested husbands. Did they look as crushed as these men? How I longed to talk to them, to ask questions! Perhaps one of them had shared a cell with my husband or heard from others about him, knew what accusations had been brought against him, what his sentence was . . .

"No talking! No communication of any kind between prisoners!" was our guards' strict injunction. And we sat in the van as mute as animals, averting our gaze from one another, ashamed of having been reduced to this state of submission. We had not the guts to utter a single word. None of us!

The prison van rumbled through the dark streets of the city. The guards sat at the windows. As we drove into Komsomolskaya Square the Kazansky Station, with its quaint oriental turrets and flaming colors, loomed from the shadows. Our van veered to the left, skidding into a pitch-black lane where a few railroad cars were shunted close to what I guessed to be the Yaroslavsky Station.

The faint gleam of the headlights illuminated the figures of the men sitting across me, shoulders sagging, thin legs crossed. What humiliation, what torture had been used to crush their spirit? I longed to breathe to them a few heartening words but, fearing to enrage the guards, tightened my lips. If we were not to move our lips, even in the semi-gloom we could still communicate with our eyes. This was how I conversed with one of the prisoners, very handsome, with a sensitive face, over which now passed a succession of thoughts whose meaning I endeavored to translate into words to myself. I too spoke to him with my eyes.

He may have been a few years older than I, but we were both of that age when sexual activity advances towards its apex. It must have been a long while since we had experienced or perhaps even thought of sex. Our mute communication had no room for sexual longing, yet it was illumined by a romantic thrill, an unrealistic hope for a meeting, a chance to get to know one another.

With our eyes we conveyed the need to maintain a philosophical detachment in our plight. Months later I received a verbal message from this fellow prisoner: "Remember the inscription on King Solomon's ring!" It was delivered by an imprisoned nurse on her return to our camp after work at a male sick bay. Knowing that my husband was arrested, she took it for granted that the message was from him.

Our van pulled up at a railway siding and hastily, in the black of the night, we were loaded into a train carriage with three tiers of bunks; on the next stages of our journey we would be packed into cattle cars. We were on the train for a few days. Every morning the guards brought in our food ration for the day: a loaf of bread and a dry salted herring. Water was given to us only once a day, in a slimy, rusty pail with a big jagged hole in it. There were no mugs: we drank the water directly from the pail, spilling much of it, so that soon the floor of the unheated carriage was covered with slippery frozen puddles. Many of the prisoners suffered from upset stomachs; those who had not managed to get a drink were tormented by thirst, while others who had had their fill of water had to cope with bursting bladders. We were allowed to go to the toilet only under escort and never more than twice a day.

Such treatment was calculated to break the prisoner's morale, add to his indignity. I vowed to myself never to eat herring, though it was the sole protein the prisoner could count on—and a very rare treat, as I was to learn later. Sometimes on these journeys I refrained from eating altogether, thus reducing to a minimum the shame of relieving myself like an animal in front of the guards.

The first stop was the big city of Kuibishev on the Volga; our destination, as it turned out, was southeastern Siberia. At Kuibishev too we got off the train at an obscure sidetrack, away from the city and all eyes. We were brought into a common cell packed with about five times as many people as it could hold. There were no bunks, and several dozen women huddled on the floor, knees brought up to the chin, shoulder to shoulder, body crammed against body. How we squeezed in I cannot say, but we did.

At Kuibishev I was for the first and only time thrown in contact with people convicted on non-political charges. Soon after the war a number of harsh laws had been promulgated. One was a penalty of seven years for minor thefts, such as stealing a loaf of bread, a bushel of potatoes, or a small bag of flour. Strict laws against abortion also were enforced. Among the prisoners was a gynecologist, a mother of three, who had succumbed to the pleas of a cousin to perform an abortion. The cousin could not stand up against questioning by the police and gave away her benefactor. She now sat rocking back and forth, shaking with sobs, and repeating, "What will become of my children?"

Novosibirsk, one of the rapidly growing Siberian cities, was our next stop. Here again we arrived at a sidetrack, well hidden from the local inhabitants. The prison and transit quarters were so overcrowded that a few of us were locked up in the strict disciplinary shed. I shared the back part of this ice-cold shed with the wives of three top Leningrad Party bosses who, five years after the war, had been confronted with the insane charge of having made secret advances to Hitler and had been shot.

Outdoors it was minus thirty degrees centigrade. The wooden structure in which we were confined, with half-decayed rafters for a ceiling and just one platform of naked boards, raised about a foot above the floor, to serve as bunks, was unheated. We slept huddled against one another to keep from freezing to death. I removed my Moscow sealskin hat and tucked my cold feet into it; in the morning I found that my hair had frozen to the wall. I was to see the three companions with whom I shared the platform bed in Novosibirsk many times, later, because the four of us were bound for the Taishet camps.

They were Anna Bubnova, wife of the former chief of the Leningrad security police; Popkova, married to the editor of *Leningradskaya Pravda*; and Anna Vasilyevna Voznesenskaya, the first, long-abandoned wife of Voznesensky, rector of Leningrad University. Popkova, a tiny, homely woman, retired into her shell and hardly communicated with us at all. Anna Bubnova, on the other hand, gabbed incessantly. To me she kept saying: "I cannot understand it! The men who came to arrest me stuffed their briefcases with my foreign lingerie. What would my husband have said to that?"

Anna Bubnova was in her early forties, a robust, well-fed, handsome woman. I had noticed that prisoners who had been connected with the security bodies were better treated by the camp bosses than the rest of us. No sooner did she find herself in camp than she managed to avoid hard physical work and got a trusty's job. She was put in charge of a small sewing shop that made clothes for the camp administration and their families.

Considerably older than Anna Bubnova and of very frail health, Anna Vasilyevna was to go along with me on the general labor assignments, determined to show in camp what a good and loyal citizen she was. With all her strength and all her heart she would haul her end of the heavy logs balanced on our two shoulders, from the felling site—and she did not survive. But all this happened months later, when we met at a Taishet camp.

It was in the same cattle car in which we travelled from Kuibishev to Novosibirsk that we continued our journey to the strict-regime camps dotting the territory between Taishet and Bratsk, where later rose the pride of Soviet industrial complexes, the Bratsk Power Station. These camps were known as Ozerlag, the Lake Camps—a pretty name. But since we had long been living in a topsy-turvy world, we knew that words did not mean what they said, that like ideas they could be twisted and distorted out of all proportion.

VII Taishet, Ozerlag

At the transit camp of Taishet, in the heart of the Siberian forest belt, I was cheered by the sight of open spaces. Fresh air at last! The buffeting of the harsh Siberian gales made me feel alive again. My mood of despair snapped.

Thousands of prisoners had now been herded into Taishet, in barracks so congested that many had to sleep on the ice-cold floor under the two-tier bunks. From here, after being equipped with proper clothing to enable them to work without freezing to death, they were sent on to the Ozerlag Taishet camps. The clothes consisted of padded cotton jackets, lined pants, cumbersome oversized felt boots, footrags, and caps with earflaps, all of which had belonged to army conscripts and been written off as unwearable. The threadbare, sweat-smelling garments made the women prisoners look like scarecrows.

And yet it was not easy to transform once beautiful and cultivated women, as many of the prisoners were, into drab, downtrodden slaves. With all their resourcefulness, the imprisoned women struggled to retain some semblance of their former selves. They managed to conceal little pieces of colored cloth for scarfs or belts, and with these "touches" relieve the ugliness of their uniforms. They tried to keep clean and neat. It was a pathetic battle for their humanity and femininity.

When my turn came to change into prison clothes, along with three other young women from Moscow, I had an unexpected stroke of luck in the person of Colonel Grebelsky.

"Allow me to introduce myself: Colonel Grebelsky," the prisoner in charge of the transit-camp wardrobe announced with a chivalrous air. His manner was so very courteous that I half-expected him to say, "Nice to see you here."

Colonel Grebelsky! The name was familiar to all who read the newspapers during and shortly after the war. Whenever foreign visitors or allied commanders arrived in Moscow, the newspapers noted, "the distinguished guests were welcomed at the airport by Colonel Grebelsky and other officials of the Ministry of Foreign Affairs."

"The camps around Taishet were built and lived in by Japanese prisoners of war," Colonel—or rather, convict—Grebelsky told us. "The Japanese government sent their prisoners fine overcoats. A few have been left behind. They're as warm as toast, and certainly more suited to pretty women like you than ragged soldiers' jackets."

That is how I came by this treasure—a coat so roomy that it served as a soft bed and blanket by night and kept me warm during the dreary Siberian winters. I was questioned about this coat by our overseers and warders. Was it my personal property? No, it was prison issue. No matter how envied I was, especially by the women warders, it could not be taken away from me. On the back of the coat I sewed a gray cotton number patch, and another on the knee of my snow pants.

My Moscow clothes went back into my suitcase. I put on the Japanese coat, the decaying pants, and the crude felt boots, one two or three sizes too big, the other even larger, and both intended for the same foot. I was all set for a work detail: I was handed a shovel to clear camp paths.

Blue shadows swayed across the darkening snow. Never have I seen such beautiful skies as in Taishet, always in a dramatic upheaval of some sort, turbulent, alive. And now the sky reeled with clashing shades and colors, from a blaze of vermilion to bands of amethyst and crimson. It was good to be outdoors. I looked around at my partners and did not know whether to laugh or cry.

They were the glorious warriors of the Wehrmacht, the generals' stripes distinctly visible along the outer seams of their threadbare trousers. Bundled up to protect themselves as best as they could from the frost, they had badly frayed mufflers wound around their heads and their feet were encased in sackcloth and newspapers.

The remnants of the German Reich! They were gaunt, cadaverous, hardly able to keep erect, drained of all their former arrogance. These pitiful, unmanly Germans were now smiling playfully at me, even admiringly, for apparently I still possessed the bloom and soft contours of womanhood. The sky turned a sinister purple. There was a phantasmagoric quality about the scene. I smiled back. I was, after all, a human being, and the ritual of returning a smile in a place where no one smiled recalled the fact to me. Dusk had fallen; after shovelling a path in the snow we were taken under guard to our respective barracks. This was my last encounter with male prisoners.

Next morning the women convicts were ordered to line up in front of the barracks. We formed a marching column of about three hundred in close ranks of five abreast. The infirm and elderly, among them my mother, composed the front rows. It was a gesture of mercy to allow the aged to set the pace. And as a further kindness, when they could no longer drag their feet and dropped in the snow from fatigue, as my mother did, they were assisted into a horse sleigh in which the guards and their dogs took turns resting.

The prisoners' march: columns of convicts trudging through the deep snows of Siberia, cutting a path for the mail coaches. How familiar the scene was to people raised on the Russian classics!

"Link arms! Close in!" the guards yelled. "One step out of the ranks and we shoot without warning."

We trudged along the banks of the Angora, its polished surface gleaming with silver and coral. Beautiful Angora, the Siberians fondly call this long and turbulent stream. It was a day of azure sky, flaming sun, and merciless frost.

We gasped for breath, hardly able to keep on our feet. The short

Siberian day waned. The black gun towers and sagging barbed-wire entanglements of a camp at last loomed into view. Cheered by the thought that shelter was close at hand, we quickened our step and all but broke into a trot as the gates opened to receive us, the new penal draft.

It had grown dark. We staggered into the gloomy wooden hut. Tiny wicks floating in oil were set alight with splinters. A fire was hastily started in the rude clay stove in the middle of the hut.

The few doctors among the prisoners immediately set to work. There were about ten cases of third-degree frostbite. My mother's was one of the worst. Her beautiful fingers were an ugly magenta color; the little finger on her left hand was charcoal black. When her turn came to be treated the flesh was cleared away, and there, jutting from the flat of the darkened hand, was the finger's ivory bone.

In the dim hut where everybody was milling around, lining up for the doctor's attention, or rubbing their hands and feet with snow, I averted my gaze from my mother's fingers. I must toughen. My mother understood. She did not approach me. Bartering her bread ration for some loose shag and a scrap of old newspaper to roll a cigarette, she retired to a hut for the aged and disabled.

Camp 022, of the Irkutsk Region in Siberia, where my mother and I were now domiciled, was one of the most brutal under the Ozerlag administration. Its inmates were resigned, listless creatures, their grimy jackets riddled with forest-fire holes hanging loose from scrawny shoulders and kept together with rag belts, their wizened faces hardly visible from under the gray winter caps; they seemed strangely amorphous, unsubstantial. Their sentence was twenty years of *katorga*, hard labor. It was painful to think that *katorga*, that horror of the tsarist regime, had been reintroduced by the Soviet government. "Assisting and abetting the enemy in wartime" was the charge. We landed in this camp because Ozerlag was overflowing with newcomers. Three planks of sleeping space per person!

It was December, 1950. But for us the clock had been set back many centuries. The primitive wooden shacks, the night buckets, the almost total absence of metal except for the guns, of water taps, of water itself, of radio and newspapers, the coarse oatmeal fed us three times a day—all spoke of an assault on our humanity. Civilization had slipped away, retreated into the shadows of the mind.

I was hitched to a sleigh, which I had to load in the forest with fallen wood. At that early phase in my camp life I could still see the humorous side of things. I was in my second incarnation! A draught horse! I almost snorted as I inhaled deep breaths of the invigorating air.

The moment of levity passed. Even the pine branches were too heavy for me to lift, let alone the logs. Among the other prisoners in the forest was Lilli Semyonova, youngest and most beautiful offspring of the notorious General Semyonov who tried to stop the Red Army from capturing Siberia in the Civil War and then fled abroad. His five grown children, three daughters and two sons, were in the Taishet camps, paying with sentences of twenty-five years for the sins of their father.

Lilli gave me a helping hand. Aware that I knew English, she addressed me in that language. Her English was flawless, as was her Russian, for she was born and reared among the White Guard émigrés in Harbin, China. Lilli, who worshipped her father, questioned me about mine.

I told her he was killed in the Civil War.

"Fighting on the side of the Whites, of course?"

"No, on the side of the Reds."

If in prison and during interrogation I felt I had been cast into a freakish world, this sensation was magnified a thousandfold in Taishet.

To preserve my grip on the normal world, I clutched at a straw. It was the beauty of the forest. The forest smells, the play of light and shadows were real. I thought what a perfect etching the interlacing of snowy boughs and dark bare twigs, with random patches of pale daylight, made. Perhaps it was this involuntary comparison of nature to art that recalled to me Renoir's full-length "Portrait of an Actress." Bluish-pink, translucent, so very sunny, it blotted out the insanity around me. As I often did later with other famous paintings, I strained my memory to recall in what museum and what hall I had seen it. I now remembered the walls in the Moscow Museum of Western Art where the Renoirs had hung and, too, how upset I was to learn that, along with other Impressionist paintings, they had been removed and the famous museum closed, a casualty of the policy to keep Western influences at arm's length from the Soviet people.

NINE

I Christmas Eve

The warped door gave way easily. I entered the hut for the disabled, where my mother was quartered, and edged forward into the shadows, groping my way between the sodden log wall and the double tier of plank platforms.

Midway I paused, surprised to see that women from other sheds were assembled here in small knots. The murk was pierced by the low flame of wooden splinters. Heads were bowed in prayer. In the group close to the door were a few Lithuanians, in another I recognized a Polish girl and a prisoner she called her aunt.

Now I recalled it was Christmas Eve. Inmates had chosen this hut for their clandestine service, because there was less danger of discovery by the jailors, who did not burst in as frequently on the aged as they did on the able-bodied work force.

The praying women were Catholics, mostly from Eastern Europe and the Baltic states. There was also a sprinkling of Russian Orthodox believers; many were peasant women wearing long black homespun skirts and handkerchiefs drawn low over their foreheads. They spent their days in the Disciplinary Barracks, locked up for refusing to work for the Anti-Christ, as they called the camp commandant.

My mother was sitting on the edge of the lower sleeping shelf, leaning against a support post. I sat down beside her. She kept silent, eyeing the praying inmates with a perplexed look.

"I could never turn to religion," she said after a while. "It would mean crossing out all of my past life."

We were too downhearted, too wary of stooges, to talk openly about anything or even dwell on our sad plight. An incautious utterance could bring great disaster upon us, add years to our term, if it were reported.

However, as she went on sitting, looking so fragile that it broke my heart, she added suddenly and with vehemence: "People like myself, who had such faith in the revolution and the justice it would bring to all, must go—die, in fact—to leave the stage to a new, entirely different breed of people."

Today I know how right she was.

The gong sounded for the head count. Hastily I left with the worshippers, who had extinguished the improvised candles and like myself were now struggling through the deep, shadowy snow to reach their sheds in time for the count. To be late could earn the guards' curses or a day in the punishment cell. When I got to the front of my shed, the women were just beginning to line up. I joined them in silence.

All camp regulations, I soon learned, were designed to demean the prisoners. One of the most abusive was the head count.

Gray clouds rode the leaden sky. A vicious ground wind kept blowing the snow from under my feet, momentarily piling it up on the flank of the column. I welcomed the drifts; they put a barrier between me and the patrolling jailors. I had already begun to foster in myself a detachment, a kind of protective armor.

When the count was over I breathed a sigh of relief—alas, prematurely.

"On your haunches!" rapped a guard who replaced the counting jailor.

We squatted, after a while forced by the cramps in our legs to plump down on the icy ground.

"Stand up! Stand!"

We remained standing, hoping this last command would finish the muster. We were wrong. There now followed the most dreaded order of all.

Several guards were parading up and down the column. They wore short sheepskin coats, warm, well-fitting felt boots, and fur-lined caps.

"Lie down! Face to the ground!" Their voices cut through the frosty air threaded by the gray vapors of our breath.

We lay prone. When the counting lasted that long and prisoners were ordered to lie in the snow, it was usually in retaliation for some misdemeanor or breach of prison rules. On that Christmas Eve we were kept in the humiliating position of prostrating ourselves before our jailors in reprisal for the few scattered religious services in the camp.

But, that very evening, the horror of the head count was offset by a happy announcement: it was our barracks' turn to go to the bathing-shed. Except for the snow outside, there were no washing facilities. I had not bathed now for several weeks, not since I left the Taishet transit camp.

Like other camp structures, the bathing-shed was a squat hovel made of ill-fitting timber. A few barrels packed with snow stood by the wall. These and the wash buckets were of wood. Hot bricks were dropped into the barrels to melt the snow. With wooden dips we drew the tepid water to wash ourselves.

Our prison clothes and underwear were sent out to be fumigated, and then there was yet another delousing measure, carried out by a male barber, a prisoner, with a lathered safety razor poised for action. The older inmates let him shave their armpits and pubic hair without a murmur. I recoiled and pleaded with him not to touch me. How relieved I was when he waved me aside.

"You could not pull that one off in a German camp," said Yulya, who was behind me and with whom I shared barracks in this camp, as I would in several more.

Later, when she was washing at my side, I noticed the scarred tissue of a big burn on the back of her hand.

"I spent two years in a German camp," said Yulya offhandedly, catching my questioning glance. "The hard work was killing me. One morning in the washroom I let the hot water run and kept my hand under the scalding flow till I was certain I had got a third-degree burn. My reward was a couple of days off work."

Strangely, I was less struck by the fact of self-mutilation than by the availability of a washroom, a tap, and running water in camp. They were amenities out of reach of most Siberians, even outside the barbed wire of a prison camp.

After our bath Yulya and I were sitting across from one another at the long bare table in our barracks, sipping hot water and dunking our bread in it. A few others joined us, among them a woman in her thirties. She coughed a great deal. In the bathing shed I had noticed how emaciated she was; with her, as with other inmates, hard work had resulted in a prolapse of the female organs so that they were nestled in between her legs like oversized testicles.

Proudly she told us she had been a German general's mistress: "He treated me like a princess!" She paused. "I got twenty-five years. It was worth it."

A ravishing long-haired blonde, known as the Countess, now emerged from the shadows and sat down at the end of the table.

"Twenty-five for one general, while I had a go at the whole blasted garrison and got away with a tenner," she bragged.

For once she avoided swear words. In the short time that she slept in our barracks, she would wake us up in the morning with a string of obscenities and round off the day with just as choice an outburst. Nimbly she jumped on the bench and let the huge, hand-knitted grayish-black shawl around her naked body slip to the floor.

"Look at me!" she said, stretching herself to her full height.

Her satin-skinned, pearly pink body, with firm, rosy-nippled breasts, was an apparition of female beauty as incongruous in the murk and stench of our shed as would have been a sparkling crystal chandelier had it suddenly materialized over our heads.

A mischievous twinkle came into her eyes.

"Hut warden," she cried, "get word to the commandant, I have some important information for him—political, mind you."

She gave us a wink. "Don't worry, I'm no squealer. That's my way of getting the commandant's attention. There's not a man who won't go to bed with me."

Prisoners who had been with her in the labor camps confirmed her boast. On arriving at a camp she would immediately lure the commandant with her beauty. She never worked, thus preserving herself while other prisoners withered and aged. To avoid scandal the seduced commandant would send her off to another camp where she fared just as well. But, as it soon proved to be the case, what had worked in the labor camps got her nowhere in the strict-regime camps.

The Countess, she told us herself, had been a hooker in the Odessa harbor area; most of her clients were the men who came ashore from foreign ships. Later she made herself agreeable to occupation officers, which landed her a charge of treason.

But most of the women I met in this camp were ones who had distinguished themselves as Soviet officers in World War II or served in the Medical Corps. Among them were a few Moscow doctors. One was still wearing an army greatcoat when I first saw her, because she had been picked up at a reunion of the regiment with which she had served during the war. She was a long-standing Communist Party member, greatly shaken by her arrest and fearful to the point of hysteria of the repercussions it might have on her only daughter and son-in-law. A few days before she was apprehended she had become a grandmother.

I noticed—and with good reason, I suppose—that survivors of the Nazi camps were less despondent than the rest of us, stronger in spirit and more optimistic about our plight. One of these was also a Moscow doctor, who now wished good luck to the Countess as she swept out of our barracks. This doctor, sentenced to twenty-five years, punctuated her story with little bursts of ringing laughter and ironic gibes.

At the very beginning of the war she found herself encircled by the enemy, was captured, and, after eighteen months in a German war-prisoners' camp, worked at a hospital in occupied Crimea. Four years after the war she was charged by the Soviet security police with poisoning Russian infants in wartime. For her, a Jew, to have escaped death in the Nazi gas chambers was in itself incriminating in the eyes of the MGB. Her name was Maria Anisimovna. Prisoners were drawn to her because of her sunny disposition. Through the whole period of my captivity I was fortunate to have her as a companion; I drew courage from her.

I had apparently just fallen asleep when I was awakened by the unbolting of the door. The Countess returned, escorted by a jailor.

Her tactics had failed. A "special" camp commandant knew the penalty for cohabiting with prisoners. Seeing what she was up to, he ordered her locked up in the punishment cell.

"Get into your clothes, quick, you whore," yapped the jailor.

She cast off her shawl; teasingly, trying the jailor's patience, she slowly began to draw on her prison dress over her naked body.

I noticed that the jailor kept glancing at his watch. I had not seen a watch or heard a clock tick for more than half a year, nor would I until my release.

The Countess left. I dozed off thinking of clocks, promising myself that if I was ever released and a free woman again, I would keep as many clocks in my home as I could, a promise I eventually fulfilled. What joy to sit back and listen to the ticking of a clock! Time spurs you to get things done, regulates your life and associations. You could be master of your time. In camp you served time.

From this state of half slumber I was jolted into full consciousness by a sudden commotion. A prisoner from the camp office had arrived and was calling out names. We were leaving the *katorga* camp. Luckily my mother and I were on the same draft.

Two hours later a warder arrived: "Pack your things!"

In the middle of the night! Night was the favorite time of the state security system: arrests after midnight, nocturnal interrogations, cattle cars shunted to remote, shadowy sidetracks for the loading and unloading of prisoners, convoys of transports by night from camp to camp.

Disentangling myself from the mass of wasted bodies and gray rags on the upper shelf, I slipped down onto the damp plank floor. I took a last look at the sleeping unfortunates with whom I had spent a month in the same shed. Nightmarish creatures, ageless as though in death. The woman who had been sleeping pressed to my right side opened her eyes. Empty eyes, creased gray skin, gray rags covering her. No word, no whisper escaped from her. The *katorga* women! Meek, sexless, mouths opening only at mealtime. I never heard their stories. Their lips were sealed with terror.

II I part with my mother

Transports were the blight of the prisoner's existence. In fact, prisoners tried one hoax after another to dodge postings to new camps. They rarely succeeded, but if they did, the game was worth the candle, because it meant staying on in a place where you had already spent a few months or years, acquired friends, learned to cope with the conditions. It was change, the unknown, that was most dreaded.

The policy of the administration was to keep prisoners on the move from one camp to another, one desolate part of the land to the next, to increase the rootlessness of their lives. Normality, accustomed ways of thinking and understanding, the world as we knew it, had been knocked out from under our feet. There was, as I saw later, a vagueness and impermanence to our existence. Did we exist at all?

But at the start of camp life, with little experience to go by, the prospect of change was not at all frightening. It was therefore with a sense of relief that I left behind me the *katorga* camp and its almost four hundred mute and passive inmates. Surely, I told myself, in that camp we hit the bottom of despair, and now we could look forward to more tolerable conditions of captivity. But I was mistaken. In the new camp I came as close to my end as I ever would, and, moreover, was compelled to make the bitterest choice of my life—between survival and separation from my mother.

Our transport arrived at Camp 032 in the early morning, long before reveille. Searchlights from the guntowers swept the compound, revealing a landscape no different from the one we had abandoned the night before. There were the same smoke-blackened shanties, huddled against the icy ground, as in Camp 022. Inside were the familiar two-tier sleeping platforms and barred windows, the same stench rising in vapors from the wooden bucket that served as a latrine after the prisoners were locked up for the night. But the inmates proved to be somewhat sturdier, less resigned, of a tougher fiber, sullen but not silent.

That very morning we were rushed to the medical hut. Behind a table in a tiny office sat Major Golovko, one of the Ozerlag medical officers; "the worst bastard of the whole lot of free doctors," I heard him called. After giving my naked body a glance from under a pair of grizzly eyebrows, the major muttered to a clerk who stood at his side: "First Category." This work category, dreaded by all prisoners, pronounced me fit for the hardest physical labor.

I was assigned to a tree-felling team. A few months later, when I suffered from badly inflamed varicose veins and was running a temperature, I had a second encounter with the major. Every step I took was agony. I hoped for at least one day off after working non-stop on the felling-site for weeks. No chance. The major was sitting hunched over the table. As at the medical commissioning, he hardly looked up. His stubbly cheeks and purple nose contrasted sharply with his immaculate tunic and shining army boots, looked after by a prisoner who had the good luck to be his servant.

He dismissed me impatiently: "Everybody around here runs a temperature and all women who carry babies have varicose veins."

I rejoined the column of about a hundred and fifty prisoners ready to start on a four-mile tramp to the forest.

"Heads down! No talking!" Meekly we lowered our heads—which we would have done anyway, to avoid the sting of the wind—and we were certainly not inclined to chat. In fact, I noticed that whole days would pass without any of us exchanging even a few words.

Our column heaved forward, straggling through almost waist-deep snow, cutting a path for the convenience of the free lumberjacks and the few vehicles that would follow in our tracks later that morning. We were the human snow-ploughs.

Day in and day out of that long winter I plodded to and from the felling-site. Never on these marches did I catch sight of a human being or an animal, hear any other sounds but the commands of the guards and the snarling of their dogs. How foolish I had been to think that camp would be more tolerable than prison. In prison my mind worked; here my brain and spirit had become numb. In prison you were not as cut off from the familiar world as you were in camp. The warders who brought the smell of normal life, the hateful prison itself, the cells and corridors, the flagstone stairs of Lefortovo, the parquet floors of Lubyanka, were part of the civilized world you knew. But in camp there were only the hostile elements.

My survival now depended on learning to fell the towering pines and larches of the Siberian forest. How could I, when I had never in my life done any hard physical work? I could not even keep the saw moving at a proper angle. My partner, Adele Hermann, was a young German who had worked as an interpreter at Nazi army head-quarters on Soviet territory. She was about my age, her black eyes and bird-like face recalling Goebbels. Adele had the bizarre advan-tage over me that, raised in the Hitler Youth, she had been well trained in outdoor life and sports.

She wielded well both the crude hand bow-saw and the axe. Her movements were smooth and rhythmic, while mine were jerky and forced. The saw kept slipping out of my hand, and I cursed myself for my clumsiness. Fortunately Adele was very patient with me—though, as the German prisoners roused the animosity of the others, she would not have dared to utter a word of reproach even if she wanted.

My attitude to the forest changed. I abhorred its lofty indifference, its ceaseless mocking murmur. Danger lurked in every falling tree. If you miscalculated the direction in which the sawed tree would descend, you could be trapped into death. There had already been a few casualties.

For my poor performance I was on a penalty ration and hungry most of the time. But on returning to camp I could not drag myself to the feeding hut for my half-bowl of oatmeal. It was a battle between hunger pangs and aching muscles. Often I found my mother waiting for me. It was miserably cold in my barracks and I was glad to see that she wore, under her prison uniform, a long brown knitted coat, bought many years before in Canada. Despite the strict orders to leave all personal belongings for safekeeping in the store-room until our release, she had somehow managed not to part with this coat. Her cold hands were tucked into its capacious sleeves.

Silently she handed me her day's portion of bread, which I devoured unashamedly, knowing that the bread I ate was the sole means of her obtaining tobacco, without which life was a torture to her.

Sheer physical exhaustion was paralyzing my will to live, to retain the most elementary human habits. With no water available, we never washed the aluminum spoon with which we ate but licked it clean. I had even ceased to do that, stopped washing myself in the snow or removing my work clothes. Still wearing the sodden padded snow pants I had on in the forest I would climb up to my upper shelf and before I knew it fall into a deep sleep. At five in the morning, at reveille, I awoke unrefreshed, aching all over and filled with self-disgust.

"I know the signs," Yulya said to me. "You can't last much longer unless you're taken off the logging team."

"I don't see how that can be done," I said.

"I do. Your mother's fine knitted coat is the answer. I could tempt a trusty with it and you might be put to lighter work."

Yulya's words brought me out of the stupor in which I had now been going about for weeks. Take away my mother's coat? I could never do that! And the trusties? A privileged caste set above the other prisoners. I wanted nothing to do with them.

Soon we were squelching through the mud beneath the absurdly hot Siberian sun. Spring brought two rumors to the camp. One was that women prisoners in future would not be employed as loggers and ditch-diggers. Another concerned the launching of "Communist Hydro-Electric Projects." One of these would be the Bratsk power station, on the fringe of the Ozerlag territory. To supply it with insulation material, a mica factory was being opened close to Camp 027. It would be staffed by prisoners.

"There are bound to be drafts from the surrounding camps to 027," Yulya, always well up in camp affairs, said. "Mostly of young prisoners with good eyesight. You certainly stand a chance."

Shortly afterwards we learned from prisoners who worked in the camp office that lists for a transport to Camp 027 were being drawn up. I knew I must go and talk to my mother at once.

Her face lit up when she saw me. Did she know what I came to talk about? She looked more spectral than the other women, who also were in their late sixties. But her voice was clear and sonorous as she lapsed into her lifelong habit of rhetoric.

"The dark ages have descended on Russia," she declaimed.

I half listened to her words, trying to sort out my thoughts and to quench my anger at the choice I was forced to make. Deep down in my heart I nursed a resentment against her. Had she not, with the communist dream that brought her to the Soviet Union, got us into this trouble?

She smoothed a scrap of newspaper, dropped into it a few grains of coarse tobacco, and rolled a cigarette.

"I know what you came to talk about," she said softly. "I know, too, that your mind is made up. Yes, you must not miss the chance. By all means go to the mica camp. It's for the best."

It was far too painful to pursue the conversation. I cut short my visit and quickly left. My barracks was abuzz with the excitement of the coming draft. I could hardly believe that my lumberjack days would soon be over. But the price exacted—the cruelty of having to part with my mother—filled me with remorse. Tired as I was that night, I could not sleep. My mother's face, the lips compressed to hold back her tears, stood before my eyes.

III The need for love

It was a relief to work indoors, to sit on a bench with my elbows resting on one of the eight long plank tables arranged in two rows across the width of the factory barracks. With a short-handled blunt knife I broke loose the rock crystals and then split the mica into feather-light laminae with a long sharp one.

We worked in two shifts of one hundred and fifty women each and trudged six miles a day to and from the factory. Splitting mica was child's play compared to logging. It was absorbing work and we loved it. As with deft piercing motions I cleaved the mica, the flakes on my left-hand side grew into an iridescent mountain. I was tantalized by the mica's rainbow hues. Time flew. After our shift of ten hours I would have liked to stay on and work at the factory rather than return to the congested barracks, with its barred windows, frequent searches, and rude intrusions by the jailors.

Mica made life bearable for us in other ways too. We now saw less of the guards and jailors. They brought us from the camp and took us back. But for the duration of the shift we "belonged" to the factory manager and forelady, from whom we never heard an unkind word. These two may have been ex-convicts, as were many of Siberia's inhabitants. For this reason, perhaps, they addressed us as one human being to another, although they were scared to ask any personal questions or show the least interest in us apart from our work.

Since we no longer felled trees and battled with the elements, the three bowls of oatmeal, along with our bread ration, sufficed to still our hunger. I had begun to give thought to my appearance. Not being one of the fortunates to receive the rare food parcels allowed from home, I begged my friend Yulya for a little butter. Rather than eat it, I nourished the skin of my face with it. Yulya also presented me with a toothbrush. I worked it vigorously to strengthen my scurvied gums; my teeth were loose and a few had already fallen out.

Not for a moment did we forget the lawless and brutal way in which the state had treated us. And yet it was a comfort to know that we were engaged in useful work. The mica laminae we split would help to electrify Siberia. An existence devoid of reason and purpose, I found, was what human beings dreaded most.

The camp bosses were well aware of how we felt about mica and kept threatening us with postings to Kolyma, and other camps, if we did not increase our output. But hard as we tried, we could not meet the inflated quotas. Before long, sad days came upon us again.

The food was almost impossible to eat or digest. Gone was the oatmeal gruel to which I had grown used and even ate with relish. The soggy rye bread too had vanished. Instead we were given a bitter skilly of unripe corn and unleavened greenish bread baked of the same corn. The bread was bitter and crumbled before you could stuff it into your mouth. The camp had run out of water. We drank last winter's supply of melted snow, odorless, with a cloying sweet taste.

All summer through we worked with no days of rest, leaving the camp at dawn and returning at dark. At the head count we were plagued by black flies, which swarmed in dark dense clouds over our heads. Because of these biting pests the windows of the unventilated factory remained closed. Like pads of jet moss, the flies stuck to the panes, blocking out the daylight. The silicate haze was thicker than ever and we choked and coughed.

There were several deaths. Prison doctors who performed the autopsies told us they were blinded by the glint of the dead organs, so heavily coated with iridescent mica dust were they. And we came up against strange ironies. Two prisoners alone of our shift succeeded in filling the mica quota; the rest of us lagged far behind. These two were as different in background, education, and convictions as any two human beings could be. One was a tense, emaciated woman of forty who had a Ph.D. degree in philosophy. Before her arrest she was a lecturer in Marxism-Leninism at the Leningrad University. The other was Lilli Semyonova, with whom, after our first meeting in the forest, I stayed in the same camp for almost two years. Coached by fine tutors in languages and music, she knew nothing of the theory of Marxism-Leninism, while her acquaintance with its practice was derived from prison and camp alone. These two were our "labor heroines."

At the end of the summer I was tormented by a rash; my chest was covered with itchy bleeding sores. I went to the medical section. The same major who had ordered me back to the felling-site when I could hardly walk or keep on my feet was in charge. He pronounced the sores to be eczema.

A fortnight later we were at long last granted a day off work. A blessed Sunday all to ourselves. We could rest our aching bodies. Daylight streamed through the barred windows of the barracks, replacing the gloom of months. What luxury it was to be able to lie down or sit on our narrow bunks. We attended to our personal needs, mostly the mending of our prison garments. Since few of us possessed needle and thread, we took turns borrowing them.

The itching was driving me crazy. But for what followed after I removed my coarse black cotton brassiere, I was quite unprepared. It was crawling with lice!

Most of the other prisoners had made the same discovery. We spent half of that precious Sunday ridding ourselves of parasites. Our heads itched too. Word of our lousy state had reached the camp bosses. A few days later we were issued fine combs and on the following Sunday had our first bath in months.

Happily, we now learned that we would be allowed two off-days a month. This was a luxury indeed. However, the camp bosses in their vicious way turned these days into a veritable hell for us. They hired us out like slaves to extinguish forest fires, which raged with a mad fury that hot and dry summer, or to weed fields on farms miles away from the camp. Also, to prevent us from resting, we were assigned such meaningless tasks as hauling rubble in hand barrows from one corner of the camp compound to another.

I can remember a Sunday that ended badly for me. One of my oversize boots had slipped off my foot as we retreated from the flames of a forest conflagration we were powerless to fight. At the evening head count, a notoriously mean wardress noticed my unshod foot and had me handcuffed and sent off to the punishment cell. The next morning I was released. But even one night in the crammed wooden cell, with barely standing room for one person, made me realize what courage it took to defy the strict regime of the camp. Throughout my term I was a meek prisoner, never daring to answer back, let alone disobey prison rules.

Two off-days that summer I spent digging graves, both small trenches for five or six bodies and long ones to hold fifty or more. We guessed that the common graves were for men prisoners, who were treated more brutally than the inmates of women's camps and among whom there was far greater mortality.

We were glad when Sunday was over and we could look forward to our week at the factory. Despite the high quotas we were unable to fulfil, no matter how hard and conscientiously we toiled, and the worsening of conditions at the camp, our love affair with mica continued. Of an evening we still had some time we could call our own— no more than an hour, but it allowed us to chat a little. We were drawn closer together, and our tempers were not as frayed as when we did strenuous physical work.

There were two attitudes that crystallized among my fellow prisoners, typical, perhaps, of that harsh form of human captivity of which we were the victims. The first attitude, common among prisoners like myself, was a desperate clinging to the world we knew before our arrest, to memories of our loved ones, of friends, of the books we had read, the works of art we had seen in museums, the plays and movies that had most impressed us. They mattered greatly to us because they helped to keep that other world alive in our minds. The second attitude, mostly held by the camp veterans, was expressed by them as follows: "We know only one world, the prison world. Here we live and here we shall die. We must adapt to our captivity as best we can." I found such thinking painful and alarming, but I was compelled to admit that it was justified by the long terms to which so many of the inmates had been sentenced and the little hope they had of being released even after having served their full term—or of surviving.

In keeping with this attitude, and appalled by the harsh conditions of the strict-regime camps, many of the older inmates longed desperately to be back in the labor camps. All agreed there was a better chance of survival under the corrective system. There the state had not given up on you. You were not as completely isolated from the outside world as you were in the strict-regime—also called strict-isolation—camps. You could hope in some ways to be treated on a par with the thieves, murderers, rapists, and embezzlers, all regarded as rehabilitation material, while you were not.

Regulations were more humane in the labor camps. Prisoners were paid a few roubles for their work. And those convicted on political charges who worked by their side could not be entirely discriminated against.

In the strict-regime camps under Stalin, no matter how hard and what long hours you toiled, you received no pay, and the food consisted of nothing but oats (almost as crude in form as those fed to horses), bread, and only occasionally sugar. Labor-camp inmates were permitted to write and receive more letters than the two a year we could count on in strict-regime confinement.

Visits by relatives were practically never allowed under "strict isolation." No individual prisoners, as in the labor camps, could ever set foot outside the camp zone. Barracks were locked up by the guards for the night, from lights out to reveille. A suffocating stench rose from the huge decaying bucket, which usually overflowed in the morning with urine and excrement; windows were heavily barred and never opened. The guards were far more brutal and hostile than in the labor camps, for they were certain we would never return to the normal world.

One of the women who often spoke to me nostalgically of the labor camps was Marina Spendiarova. She had served the larger part of her sentence in them.

"My dear, you've never been in the labor camps, so you can't judge," she would say. "They're quite humane, compared to the camps we're in now!"

Prison camps humane? It was a little too much, even from Marina, actress, linguist, singer, everybody's darling, the daughter of the composer Spendiarov (after whom the opera theater in Yerevan, the Armenian capital, was named).

"The great thing about them was that there were men around," Marina went on. "I don't mean the criminal riffraff, but refined, sophisticated persons like ourselves. You pick one out, talk to him on any subject, you could fall in love. Despite our wretchedness, loving made you human, romantic, lifted you above the odious, unjust, primitive jungle around you."

No one dared contradict Marina. She was too lovable, too kind— one of the few who shared the food she received in parcels with others; too influential. She had set up a cultural brigade and did everything in her power to make life a little easier in camp for people like myself. But how could I agree with her? Corrective or "special" camps, they were all a horror, an obscenity designed to crush and destroy human beings, innocent ones at that, and in numbers never before known in history.

But Marina had struck a deep chord when she spoke of love as a humanizing factor. No matter how wretched we were, how devoid of hope, the need for love, sexual or other, was great. Among women prisoners for long years completely cut off from men, over and over again I witnessed the emergence of that need and its satisfaction, at times by a lesbian bond, but more often by a surrogate mother-and-daughter or aunt-and-niece one.

Many prisoners had been disowned by their families. Others had of their own accord severed contact with their relatives to save them from losing their jobs, being thrown out of university, or, worst of all, facing arrest. In captivity the gap left by the former normal family was filled by the adoption of "camp daughters," "nieces," or "husbands" in lesbian relationships, or in sexless "marriages."

With the strong taboo against homosexuality—it was regarded as a criminal offense, punishable by prison or camp—only the very daring among the inmates, mostly those in positions of power, like the overseers or team leaders, embarked on lesbian unions.

In our barracks were two four-bunk structures. Occupied by team leaders, they stood a little apart from the rest and were curtained off with rags to prevent prying. One of them resembled a big canopy bed; by night it heaved and rocked and rattled, but no one cared or showed the least curiosity. We were too engrossed in our woes, too listless, too shocked by the hell into which we had been cast. The lesbian couple who shared the canopy bed made no secret of their relationship. But the only time the prisoners gave it a thought was when they were disturbed by the noisy rows of these two intensely passionate women.

Though such relationships satisfied the need for sex, unfortunately, they often erupted in ugly quarrels and violence. It was generally the couple's promiscuity, and the jealousy and bitterness it caused, that made other prisoners recoil and opt for the sexless marriage, a more placid attachment, usually with one partner who was stronger in spirit, more protective and solicitous, but without the clearly defined male and female roles.

There were no smiles and no laughter in our camp, but the pleasure of the giving of oneself to another human being shone in the faces of those who lived in couples. There was a mutual dependency, as well as a tendency towards generous behavior as opposed to the bestiality of the state's secret police. To an older woman the young girl with whom she formed a close bond represented the loved one she had left behind in that other world and with whom often she had no communication, and the younger clung to her as she would to her own blood.

Such couples could be seen together, sharing their bread or, on those rare occasions when a sugar ration was issued, enjoying it with the steaming water we called "tea." In the feeding shed they sat side by side. There were tears and heartbreak when two such people were forcibly torn apart and sent off on transports.

As I saw them, these emotional bonds were a cherished reminder of family and other relationships of which the women had been part in their lives before captivity.

IV Non-Soviets

Among the inmates at Taishet were large groups of prisoners from outside the Soviet Union. They were entirely ignorant of the ways of the Soviet system. Many had been picked up right off the streets of European cities at the end of the war or in the late forties and early fifties.

There were even a few teenagers. They felt much more lost and bewildered than the rest of us. Among them were two high-school kids kidnapped in West Berlin and a defiant, beautiful Polish girl who was in and out of the punishment cell most of the time I spent in the same camp with her.

These girls did not know a word of Russian. I tried addressing one of the two Berlin teenagers, Louisa by name, in German, but she hardly responded. She was in a state of shock. A sensitive, aristocratic-looking girl, she could not cope with the situation in which she found herself. She went stark mad. The last time I saw Louisa she was an inmate of the overcrowded, tumble-down psychiatric hut in the Taishet hospital compound.

Among the aliens were several mistresses of men in high positions. One told me she had a long-standing liaison with Popovic, a well-known Yugoslav communist. He had been critical of the Soviet Union and provoked Stalin's wrath.

In the Taishet camps I kept meeting too the paramours of Soviet public figures—of an admiral and a general, both war heroes; of a famous actor and a writer. What better way was there to intimidate and get back at the men than to victimize the women they loved?

This selfsame blow Stalin dealt the composer Sergei Prokofiev, whom he hated and whose music the great connoisseur of all the arts termed "unsuitable for the Soviet public, mere snobbery." In 1948 Prokofiev's enchanting, Spanish-born wife Lina was thrown into prison and sentenced to twenty-five years.

Prokofiev had met her when travelling with Sergei Eisenstein and Grigory Alexandrov, for whose film, set in Mexico, he was writing the music. I had visited the Prokofievs in the late thirties at their home in the newly-built state apartment house for composers on the fringe of Sadovaya Ring. The composer, with his usual preoccupied look, was seated at the piano, his domed forehead gleaming with perspiration, oblivious to everything except the score in front of him. Lina, in a clinging black sheath—she seemed to have a predilection for black—which showed to advantage her perfect petite form, busied herself with preparing coffee; the aroma of the freshly ground beans soon pervaded the entire modest apartment. Where was she, I wondered. Most likely in one of the Taishet camps; she must have been classed as a foreigner. And their two sons?

The prisoners from foreign countries were in many ways worse off than Soviet citizens, to whom the state's policies of repression were not unfamiliar, who were able to communicate, if only twice a year, with their families and receive parcels, and who had no language barrier to grapple with.

Of one of these aliens I have the most vivid recollection. This was Dolly—I cannot quite recall her second name. With Dolly, prima ballerina of Budapest, I spent one and a half years in Taishet. She was arrested by the secret police soon after the Soviet troops liberated her country. Dolly's mother was Hungarian and her father was Jewish.

"I rejoiced when the Soviet armies marched into Budapest and the Nazis fled," Dolly told me. "A few months earlier my father, whom I dearly loved, had been put into a Jewish prisoners' camp. I wanted to find him, hoping he was among the few lucky survivors.

"The first place I went for help was the Soviet army headquarters. A captain heard me out and was sympathetic. He offered to take me in his car to places outside Budapest where a few Jews, it was rumored, had been in hiding. Our efforts came to nothing. I could find no clue as to what happened to my father. But I went on seeing the Soviet captain; we became lovers."

Dolly paused. Her eyes saddened. "One day when I was expecting him, he never showed up. Two months later I was arrested, kept for six weeks in a Budapest jail, then after a long train journey under guard was brought to Lubyanka in Moscow. My interrogator claimed that the Soviet captain was an American spy, and I, his mistress, was assisting him in obtaining important intelligence. In my wildest dreams I could imagine no such thing. No testimony was produced to corroborate these lying allegations."

At the time I met her she had served almost all of her eight-year sentence and expected to be released in sixteen months. But Dolly's health had become so poor that we all feared for her life. Among the younger women tuberculosis was the great scourge, and Dolly seemed to have all the symptoms; she was pronounced tubercular by the medical section.

Dolly had the sweetest disposition. Perhaps for this reason she was one of the few women who had retained her beauty. Her skin was pearly, unlined; goodness of heart softened the contours of her face, shone out of her eager, wide-open round eyes. She had the look of an angel. Marina Spendiarova, who had been with Dolly in the labor camps and loved her dearly, racked her brain for a way to help her.

"We must save Dolly!" Marina cried. "To get her away from the mica dust, I shall put on a concert. Dolly will dance; she'll get a few days off for rehearsals."

Save Dolly! The call swept the entire camp, and no one who was in a position to do something failed to respond.

Our emotions and thoughts were raw, unadorned by the veneer and little stratagems that serve so effectively in the normal world when we are eager to show ourselves in the best light. Our common wretchedness made us more sensitive to the sufferings of each one of our fellow prisoners. We took Dolly's condition very much to heart. Our redoubtable Marina persuaded a camp official to permit her to get together a team of camp talent and rehearse for a show.

Although Dolly was uppermost in her mind when Marina pleaded her cause, she also hoped to make life a little more bearable for a few of us. Her plans for the evening's entertainment included a scene from *The Forest* by Ostrovsky, a nineteenth-century Russian playwright. Marina generously assigned me the lead part of Madame Sadovskaya, the rich owner of many acres of forest land.

The rehearsals soon revealed that I was no actress. Marina urged me "to enter into the role" (she knew the Stanislavsky method inside out). But the fact that Sadovskaya's troubles were much too remote from me, and my own too erosive, proved an insurmountable barrier. The part finally went to another prisoner.

Dolly was practicing the dance of the captive Maria from the *Fountain of Bakhchisarai*, fluttering across the barracks rehearsal room with airy grace, whirling, gliding and extending her shapely white arms in a prayer for freedom. Yet we saw that the strain of the rehearsals was telling on her. Too often she paused for breath; once she actually fainted and had to be carried back to the barracks.

On the evening of the performance, however, she was splendid. Maria came alive to us, less a character from Pushkin than a real person, like ourselves inexorably approaching her doom. I was grateful to Dolly that evening for the brief moment of elation her art gave me.

A nurse at the camp's medical station, a prisoner like ourselves, managed to smuggle a thermometer into our barracks. In this way we could keep track of Dolly's temperature; the high fever persisted for days. Through our camp doctors we learned that a new drug said to be very effective in treating tuberculosis had been discovered. The camp's medical section lacked the simplest of medicines, let alone wonder drugs. It was through prisoners who received parcels from Moscow, through bribery and other means, that an ample supply of this drug was procured. Dolly would be saved!

Frequently now Dolly talked to us of what she was going to do after her release. Knowing well that she would not be allowed to go back to Hungary, and not having a soul to turn to, she pinned all her hopes on the man with whom she had had a love affair in one of the labor camps.

"We thought ourselves as good as married," she said. "I hope to be reunited with him."

Everybody knew about Dolly's camp husband, a young man from Soviet Georgia, convicted on a charge of embezzling funds at his job. Dolly was separated from him when, as a political prisoner, she was shipped to the Taishet strict-regime camps. He, in the meantime, having served his term, was released. It had been arranged between them, Dolly told me, that when he got settled he would write to her so that she could join him. But long months had gone by without her having heard from him.

Marina was indignant: "He's a bastard, a cad, I knew it all along. He's got himself another woman, I'm sure. He could have at least had the decency to write or send a parcel. That would do Dolly more good than the medicine."

All of a sudden Marina's eyes lit up. "My, what a fool I've been, why didn't I think of it long ago?"

Two weeks later when the parcels were handed out, Marina collected little donations for Dolly from the prisoners, packed a parcel for her, printed Dolly's name on it, and brought it over to our barracks.

"It has no return address," Dolly remarked surprised. "Yet it must be from *him*. Who else would be sending me parcels? Perhaps he has no permanent address as yet." She offered her own explanation.

We were relieved and put in hastily:

"To be sure, that's the reason, Dolly."

Personally I do not think she was deceived. Dolly saw through our little game, but being an unusually tactful person, she did not wish to let on and disappoint us. Instead, gratitude illumined her lovely smooth face.

Dolly was taking the new medication, but far from improving, her health deteriorated. She was transported to the Taishet camp hospital, about thirty miles away, to everyone's sorrow. A week later I fell very ill and found myself in the same hospital, in the bunk above Dolly's. For her noonday meal somebody had brought her a big dish of meat, mostly enormous bones, of what animal I could not tell. In the two and a half years I was in Taishet, it was no more than twice that meat, mostly bones, was doled out to us.

Dolly nibbled at the bones with relish. "That's real meat," she said. "It's sure to give me strength."

That night I was awakened by Dolly's long fit of hiccups, after which she seemed to fall asleep. In the morning I bent over the side of my bunk to look down at her. Her white face was lifeless. I listened hard, but there was no sign of breathing. Dolly died just three months before she was due to be released.

That day there was yet another death, of a sixty-six-year-old Russian émigrée from Shanghai. In 1949, at the time the Chinese People's Republic was proclaimed, Russians who had emigrated right after the revolution were assured by the Soviet government that they were welcome to return to their native land.

"My husband and I were happy to be repatriated," this lady told me a few months before her death. "We dreamed of the day we could set foot again on our beloved Russian soil, where we hoped to live out the last years of our life. Shortly after our return, we were arrested and charged with anti-Soviet agitation. My husband died on his way to prison camp."

She was a tiny, frail lady, who spoke a quaint, old-fashioned but beautiful Russian. She had managed to make it through almost three years of captivity, never comprehending why she had been imprisoned. "It is peacetime, not war," she would say with a perplexed lift of her eyebrows.

A few days later I was back at the mica factory in Camp 027. Two prisoners, freshly arrived from the maternity camp, brought the news that Lilli's sister Tatyana had given birth to a baby boy. So there were not only deaths, but births too, in our far-flung prisonland.

It was one of the ironies of life that Tatyana, or Tata, as her sister called her, second daughter of General Semyonov who, in addition to his hatred of the Soviets, was notorious for his anti-Semitism, should have married a young Jew shortly before the arrest of the entire family in Harbin. Along with all the Semyonov offspring, he was apprehended, though he ended up with a much milder sentence—eight years to their twenty-five. Tatyana was allowed two meetings with her imprisoned husband over the years of their Taishet captivity, which accounted for the birth of their two children.

There was yet another group of prisoners at Taishet who could be classed as non-Soviets. They were women from the Baltic countries, from Latvia, Lithuania, and Estonia, which became Soviet republics in 1940. Many of the professional and well-to-do people in these countries who did not wish to live under the Soviets fled. But the Baltic Jews were trapped. They had the choice between Hitler's "final solution" and "safe harbors" in the Siberian forestland.

There were two women from Riga at Taishet with whom I became quite friendly. Both of them came from middle-class Jewish families and had already spent four years in deportation and six in prison camp. They were as close as mother and daughter, and did everything they could to keep their spirits up. Both in temperament and in appearance they were opposites. The younger, Faina, was blonde, blue-eyed, and apathetic; the older, Rabinowitz, was swarthy, thin as a reed, and full of fire. Tragedy had not crushed her spirit. She had two grown-up daughters, about whom she often talked to me. One was married in Siberia to an exile like herself, had two children, and led a wretched, poverty-stricken existence. The other, a girl of nineteen, was a prisoner in a nearby camp. Faina, Rabinowitz, and her daughter were serving ten-year sentences as co-defendants in a case of group anti-Soviet agitation. Each one's testimony on allegedly anti-Soviet utterances (one being, as Faina told me, a complaint about the high collective-farm market prices) had been used by the interrogator to incriminate the other.

V The dreaded Article 58

The state security set-up, whatever names or organizational forms it has taken, has always been regarded with fear by the citizens of the country. Throughout its history it has engaged in mass arrests, mass terror, and prying into the private lives of the citizenry. The less people know of what goes on behind the doors of that institution the happier they are. Therefore, because ignorance is bliss, the secret police have been successful in keeping concealed their methods of interrogation, their abuse of the law, their prison-camp system and executions.

Not until my own incarceration, when I was thrown into contact with other prisoners, did I have any idea of how ramified with subclauses was the political article 58 under which we were all charged. There were clauses on "slander" of Soviet literature, the security organization itself, the "leader of the peoples" (lese majesty). There was also the "with intent to" sub-clause 17. The adding of this subclause to your main charge meant that you had not committed the crime for which you were arraigned, but had had the *intent* to do so. Often this sub-clause was appended to such grave charges as treason, clause 1, and terror, clause 8, of the same article.

A fellow prisoner working with me at the mica factory in Camp 027 was the daughter of a well-known Swedish communist. Having quarrelled with her husband, she snapped at him: "I'll go to Sweden and live with my father." She loved her husband and two children and did not mean a word she said. But the MGB had gotten wind of her "intent" to leave her motherland. She was charged with treason via the mitigating sub-clause of "intent to" and was sentenced to ten instead of fifteen or twenty-five years.

My friend Tina's husband, Nikolai S., a successful architect, faced the ludicrous charge of "the purchase of a house in London," which, of course, turned him into a British spy. No "intent to" there; it was treason plain and simple, and he was sentenced to twenty-five years.

Most prisoners I met who were convicted of terrorist acts were, oddly enough, sedate elderly ladies from Leningrad, with a peculiar St. Petersburg air of good breeding about them. One of them, quite out of character, while watching over her pot of cabbage soup in a shared kitchen, muttered under her breath, "I wish that sonofabitch was dead!" A neighbor reported the remark and she was arrested, for whom else could she have meant but Stalin? After a stiff interrogation she got off with a mild sentence—eight years for "the intent to assassinate the leader of the peoples."

"A son does not answer for his father!" Stalin had said in a speech. People breathed with relief. Descendants of the former bourgeoisie or nobility, as well as the children of shot "enemies of the people" could now hope to be treated, if not on a par—because no decision could be quite interpreted to mean what it said—with the offspring of "proletarian stock," or of unimprisoned parents, then in any event far more leniently than in previous years.

But the truth was that you never knew where you stood in regard to these utterances; another utterance would come from the lips of a Stalin or a successor of his that would contradict the former one, or, worse still, a secret instruction would follow to replace the leniency by even more stringent measures. This was a well-tried policy that dated back to tsarist times and served its purpose only too well. Put a few wise words on paper to appease the public, wave the carrot, and then go back to your black deeds.

It was exactly what happened this time, too; no sooner had the enthusiasm abated around this wise utterance than a new interpretation of a law that had already been in existence was added to the long list of political offenses. Called the "member of a family" law, it allowed for not only the spouses of arrested persons but also other relatives to be packed off to prison camps. It was under this law that the grown-up daughters and sons of General Semyonov, as well as his in-laws, were arrested and sentenced. It applied, too, to the many relatives of those tried and executed in the Leningrad Case of 1949–1950, which involved almost all of the Party bosses and leading municipal executives of the city. Among the relatives were the three wives of Voznesensky and his two sons who, like the Semyonov family, were serving terms in the Taishet camps. If persons were indicted on such charges, is it any wonder that prison camps were packed with millions of inmates?

Great as the crimes of the MGB and its forerunners against its own citizenry were, perhaps there were no worse felonies than the rearrest, on the same charge, of people who had completed their sentences and been released, as well as the non-release of prisoners after they had served their full terms. Those arrested during the bloody years of 1937 and 1938 were either shot or sentenced to ten years; longer terms, especially the ubiquitous twenty-five years, were instituted during and after the war. This meant that large numbers of political prisoners would have to be released in 1947, and the slave labor force so badly needed for the post-war industrial economy greatly depleted.

An ingenious solution was to rearrest the released prisoners and, ten years later, start a new wave of terror—the 1947–1953 mass arrests—to prevent the shutting down of the camps and to provide the new building projects with penal labor. Politically, too, it was most expedient to keep the innocent victims of 1937 and 1938 in continued isolation, lest they besmirch the good name of the Party. It was killing two birds with one stone.

Many of us were plagued with the fear that we would never be set free. "You are to remain in camp pending further instructions," prisoners were told when their terms expired. To have served your term, to have survived, and then be informed that you will not be released, to see the light at the end of the tunnel suddenly extinguished, what could be more shattering? People charged under Article 58, mostly those tried by a special board *in absentia*, as my mother and I were, came under the system of unspecified sentences.

This is what we all feared—an end forever to our freedom. Our sentences could be extended over and over again so that we would never return to the normal world, never be reunited with our loved ones.

I began having the first variant of a nightmare that to this day I dread. I find myself in the overcrowded prison-camp barracks—gray vapors, gray shadowy figures, and gloom. A few days have elapsed after the end of my sentence. I am on tenterhooks, awaiting the arrival of the guard with the paper for my release. I must not miss him. I must keep my ears pricked up to catch my name when he calls it out. There is pandemonium in the barracks, all the inmates talking at the top of their voices, but I ignore them. Why hasn't the guard come yet? He was due days ago.

The guard arrives. He reads out the names of two prisoners, but not mine. They say goodbye to us. I want to address the guard and ask him: Why not me? I have served my sentence just as they have. But I dare not. I am petrified with fear. As the guard leaves, I grow very articulate. I beseech my fellow prisoners to listen to my grief, to advise me what to do to regain my freedom.

In a later variant of the same nightmare, at this point I praise the Russian people: they are the best in the world, yet treated like dirt. A man—there were no men prisoners in our camp—whispers in my ear: "This talk of yours will be reported. Watch your words or years will be added to your sentence. You'll never be released. You will die here." I am now more fearful than ever.

For about twenty years after my release I had these dreams. It was as though the fear of never being set free and dying in camp had sunk so deeply into my subconscious mind that it could not accept the reality of my freedom.

And the fears that racked us all were never more real, never better founded, than in the winter of 1953.

Early in the year news reached us of the arrest of several Kremlin doctors, most of them Jewish, on charges of poisoning. We feared that the "uncovering of the Doctors' Plot," as the newspapers termed it, could stir up anti-Semitic feeling among the guards and inside our camp. But fortunately we were spared that. My own feeling is that the Russians are no more anti-Semitic than other nationalities. The seeds of anti-Semitism, like those of any other ugly feeling, are sown by the ruling clique to gain their own selfish ends.

The screws of the camp regime were tightening. Searches were more thorough. We were threatened that photographs or letters found on our person would be confiscated. Many prisoners who had been writing the two letters allotted per year now ceased communication with their families. Supplies of the few drugs available for prisoners had run short and were not replenished.

There were several suicides. It was rumored that one of them was the eldest of the three Semyonov daughters. Another young woman in our own camp hanged herself in the outhouse. One of our prisoners had learned that her thirteen-year old son was in a Taishet camp convicted of a political crime; night after night we were awakened by her sobbing. A law existed by which children from the age of twelve upwards were to be tried for certain crimes on a par with adults and could even be given death sentences.

Things seemed blacker than ever. Even the exuberant Marina Spendiarova, always ready to help and cheer up others, went about with
a cowed look on her mobile face. She was worried about her sister
in Moscow and hesitated to write to her when the time arrived for
our first letter of the year.

However, there were two women in my immediate entourage who
waved aside fear and panic. They were my old companion Yulya and
my Moscow doctor friend Maria Anisimovna.

"It will never get as bad as in the German camps, because we have
a different ideology—communist, not fascist—and even if words are
not deeds, they do matter," Yulya said wisely. "Besides, when it gets
that bad," she added as an afterthought, "it is bound to get better."

Linking her arm in mine, Maria Anisimovna suggested we take a
walk. For a while we trudged along in silence, inhaling the icy air,
listening to the crunch of the snow. The moon rode high in the indif-
ferent February sky, dispersing the shadows of the evening, as
though to introduce a little clarity into our somber and eerie
existence.

There was a true friendly warmth between us. Yet we dared not
speak except in the innuendoes and hidden meanings that had
become the habitual way of communicating among the people of our
country.

Wanting to cheer me up, she said: "Nothing goes on forever. The
tightening snaps. I believe that the Doctors' Plot may prove just that
last straw that broke the camel's back."

I made no reply.

"Men do not live forever," she continued. Forever seemed like a
magic word with some deep connotation when she uttered it. A message to me.

My heart gave a leap. I knew what she meant. I had had the same
thought, which I dared not even verbalize to myself: Stalin is bound
to die and then there may be changes, perhaps new hope for all of
us innocent victims of his policies. And obviously he had gone too
far with the Doctors' Plot. It was too medieval, too farcical.

Maria Anisimovna's words proved prophetic. A few weeks later,
on March 5, we learned of the death of the great leader, the Father,
the greatest genius of mankind, the guiding light of the international
proletariat, butcher of my family and millions of others.

VI Amnesty

Three weeks after Stalin's death, news of an amnesty broke upon
the startled Soviet populace. It brought little joy to the camp's
inmates. Hardened criminals, murderers, armed robbers, recidivists

with long terms were cited for release. But pardon for political crimes was confined to a handful of prisoners with sentences not exceeding five years.

None of the prisoners I knew well—Yulya, Maria Anisimovna, Marina, Lilli Semyonova, or my mother—could count on clemency. Out of the five hundred inmates of our camp, only nine had five-year terms. I was one of them.

Clearly though it was stated in the amnesty, our camp commandant and his staff refused to believe that even this small number of Stalin victims would be allowed to return to the normal world.

"The amnesty does not apply to strict-regime camps," these officials repeated. On no account, they reasoned, can political prisoners be set free. They will talk—if only to their close ones—about conditions in the camps, their interrogation and charges. The news will leak out, perhaps even abroad. The Party cannot allow this to happen. It will hurt its prestige.

The camp bosses warned us: "Do not build up your hopes!"

Nor did the guards and jailors imagine for a moment that we would one day walk out of the camp gates free people. And they would lose their lucrative posts? No! They wanted things to remain exactly as they were, as they had been under Stalin.

One evening in late April I dropped in at the medical section. A solitary guard was sitting on the waiting bench. He was a lad of about nineteen, with a flat peasant face twisted into the scowl that all guards wore in the prisoners' presence.

I would never have dared before to make conversation with a guard, but now, heartened by the prospect of release, I said, "I'm going to be set free and will return to Moscow."

If I had hit him over the head he could not have been more astounded.

Recovering from the shock of my words, he retorted morosely, "The likes of you will never be released!"

"Why?"

"Because you are spies, saboteurs, the worst criminals."

The doctrine of lies and hatred! At their weekly political sessions it was drummed into the guards' heads that we were too dangerous ever to be released, which, of course, justified their brutality to us.

Two months went by after the amnesty was made public. We still remained in ignorance of our fate. The waiting and uncertainty were a torment. Night after night I dreamed that I would never be set free and would spend the rest of my life in the squat, damp, wretched barracks that I shared with so many other unfortunates.

At long last I was summoned to the camp office and silently handed a "Certificate of Release," with the words "unrenewable if lost" printed in the upper right-hand corner. Other papers included several receipts from my last place of detention, the Butyrki Prison, for my typewriter, wristwatch, and two government medals, all of which, I was told, would be returned to me in Moscow. Maria Anisimovna lent me the money for a train ticket in a sleeping compartment; that meant I would not have to travel for weeks in a cattle car with former inmates of the labor camps, mostly men with long criminal records.

In the early afternoon of June 11, 1953, a warm, sunny day, I walked through the tall timber gates, out of the camp inferno, dazed and unbelieving. More than myself, the air around me seemed to celebrate my release, sparkling, spinning in playful whiffs, whispering in my ear: Rejoice! you are back in the human world, free to move about as you please. I needed time, and time suddenly underwent a transformation right before my eyes, expanding enormously, every minute swelling into an hour, languorous, deliciously long, not painfully endless as it had been in solitary confinement; throbbing with new life.

I threw a last glance at the solid prison gates. There had been no goodbyes, for the camp inmates were ordered to keep a distance from the lucky nine who had five-year terms, after we had been issued our release papers.

You are still there behind the gates, my fellow sufferers, I thought. Your crippled lives, your deaths, the pain in your eyes, will never leave me.

We squeezed into a horse cart and were driven along the bumpy dirt road to Taishet, where both the westward-bound freight trains and the trans-Siberian express stopped. On arriving I learned that the express for Moscow would be departing the next day. I was put up for the night in the crummy local hotel on the floor in a room with about ten other women.

What did it matter if I slept or not that night? I was free! In a few days I would see my little daughter who, I had learned a year before, was staying with neighbors of mine. I pictured our meeting. But would she, my friends and neighbors recognize me?

In all the three years of my imprisonment I had not looked into a mirror.

"Is there a looking-glass somewhere?" I asked the receptionist.

"Yes, down the hall, badly mildewed, but you'll be able to see yourself in it," she answered kindly.

Steeling myself for the worst, I looked at my reflection in the glass. I was appalled by the expression of my face. The inhuman experiences I had been through showed clearly in it. Remembering that I had once been a light-hearted, rather exuberant romantic, I made an effort to smile, but the result was only a freaky contortion of the features.

Just then a man, whose girth must have equalled his height, advanced towards me, fluttering a fifty-rouble bill in his chubby fingers.

"Take this, cutie," he said tipsily, "and buy yourself some sweets."

Though full of liquor, he knew me for a released prisoner and longed to show his sympathy.

I broke into laughter, the first genuine laughter in long years, waved his bill aside, and thanked him as sweetly as I could. He too, I thought, was Russia, my generous, dearly loved Russia.

Cheered by the sound of my own laughter, I took another look at myself in the mirror. Laughing had relaxed my face a little. Gradually, I told myself, time will blur the horrors I have seen. But it will not blot them out from my memory. I will laugh and smile and enjoy life again, yet always in the shadow of the crippling and needless death of millions of human beings.

In the Moscow-bound train I found myself sharing a four-berth compartment with a camp commandant and his wife. With criminals being released in such great numbers, and camps shut down, that should not have surprised me. But it took much joy out of my return journey to hear the uncouth wife address me in the same harsh Siberian accent in which the guards shouted their commands. Thankfully, the husband, deprived of his post, remained silent and glum through most of our four-day journey.

I do not believe the wife suspected I was an amnestied prisoner, because she chattered on and on about her fears of being attacked or robbed by the freed criminals, complaining bitterly about the amnesty, what a mistake it was, and that the government would live to regret it. Her husband had made good money as a camp commandant, she said, "the best-paying job he ever had." All that money, she soon confided, thousands of roubles, was sewn into the lining of her girdle. Every time she absented herself to go to the washroom or accompany her husband to the restaurant car, she removed her girdle and entrusted it to my care. "So many ex-convicts are at large . . . do keep an eye on it," she begged. I assured her I would not leave the compartment until she returned.

Most of the day, however, I avoided her company. I stood mutely in the corridor watching the shaggy Siberian forest flicker past the train window. At times I was joined by a man from a neighboring carriage. Like me he was an amnestied prisoner on his way to Moscow. This I surmised from the half-syllables in which he spoke. His face was a mask of fear.

I learned nothing whatever about his life or imprisonment; what I shall always remember about him was the shirt he wore. It was good quality, of Western cut; I could tell it by the collar and the cuffs. At some point in the prisoner's life, how and when I do not know, it had been reduced to tatters, riddled with countless holes at the shoulders and sleeves. And then it was made whole again, mended in a thousand places with a minute interlacing of thread, dyed a pleasant shade with tree bark so as to make the darning almost invisible. It must have taken the prisoner many nights of patient toil to make the shirt wearable, and enable him, on stepping out of the camp gates, to resemble the spruce and prepossessing man he must have been before his arrest. Apparently it helped to restore his shattered dignity.

Our trans-Siberian express was pulling into the busy junction of Moscow's Yaroslavsky Station. Track upon track, train after train of passengers and freight cars, many loaded with timber, perhaps felled by prisoners, and presently to be delivered to Moscow's building sites; people roaming about freely, faces more or less relaxed.

Not on a sidetrack, not in the pitch of night, but on this sunny morning of June 17, 1953, just three months after Stalin's death, our train snaked into an open platform. With hardly a murmur of parting to the grim-faced commandant and his surly peasant wife, I elbowed towards the exit, dragging behind me my battered valise. On alighting I caught a glimpse of the man with the mended shirt. The train's "hard" carriages were disgorging amnestied camp inmates by the hundreds. We two were perhaps the only politicals—still too fearful, still too constrained, to wave goodbye.

TEN

I Vicky

Clutching the loose handle of my valise, which contained the clothes I had packed on the night of my arrest, I made for the long line at the taxi stand outside the Yaroslavsky Station. Men and women were scrambling furiously to grab the rare taxi that pulled up in front. I was no match for them, but the scene was poignantly familiar. *My* Moscow.

A violet sky, with filmy clouds drifting far apart, promised a balmy day. Clock faces on each of the three railway stations flanking Komsomolskaya Square showed a quarter to eight.

Parking his car some distance from the waiting crowd, a taxi driver approached and casually inquired if I had far to go. He cocked an ear as I gave him the address.

"Thirty roubles. We won't run the meter."

This was four times the regular fare and, curiously enough, the exact sum I had in my purse. A Moscow taxi driver will in a twinkling spot a customer he can squeeze dry. He sensed immediately that I was not likely to haggle over the price.

Trailing after him as he led the way, I shoved my valise into the back of the car and plumped down beside it, the seat's steel springs prodding into my sides. We were driving down Kirov Street. It was Sunday and the traffic was light.

Stone, glass, concrete—how good they looked after the wooden hovels of Siberia. On our right we passed the Corbusier office building perched on its gray pillars, epitomizing the craving for modern art. We swung into the deserted Dzerzhinsky Square dominated by the lone towering figure of the man who founded the Cheka, then skidded across Moskvoretsky Bridge, the river greeting me like an old friend with the sparkle of a silver salute.

My own Embankment. I climbed the gray stone stairs, worn by so many feet, among them those of Napoleon's soldiers, billeted in this very building in 1812. On reaching my room, Number 171a, on the fourth floor, I put down my valise and stood waiting for someone to show up with the key; before boarding the train at Taishet I had sent a wire to the neighbors who took Vicky in.

Two women in dressing-gowns, their hair in curlers, passed by on the way to the washroom shared by goodness knew how many tenants. One of them turned to say hello.

"Why, you've hardly changed," she exclaimed and walked on. Without waiting for me to be out of earshot, she added to her companion, "I'm sure she slept with the camp commandant. That's what helped to keep her looks."

The remark was like the lash of a whip. My neighbor arrived with the key. She threw me an incredulous, almost baneful look. It was as though my return, or being alive at all, was an affront. Instead of a greeting, she blurted out hysterically: "Only don't take the child away from me!" She did love my Vicky.

On that morning of crimson sunlight, Vicky, almost eight years old now, was standing up in her bed as I walked in. Solemn face, eyes probing, intelligent far beyond her years. No flicker of joy. A dignity and aloofness about her restrained me from what I had so longed to do—crush her in my arms.

I remained glued to the spot, waiting, hoping for some response. Nothing! Her form and proud face stiffened into a question mark: So, you're back, what now?

Added to the crimes of the state in arresting and exterminating innocent people were the wounds inflicted on their children. Left practically alone in the world, after my brother's suicide, Vicky was pushed around from home to home. Taken in by compassionate neighbors, she ran away from them when she was six.

Bundled up in her heavily padded coat, fur hat, and scarf, she waddled in her stiff felt boots and galoshes across the ice-encased Moskvoretsky Bridge, past Red Square, and down Gorky Street, amidst hustling pedestrians, stopping to ask how to reach Bolshaya Bronnaya Street, off Pushkin Square, where her paternal grandmother, aunt, and aunt's daughter shared one room. On arriving there and realizing she was not wanted, she hastily slipped out unnoticed, plodded all the way back, passing her own house and stopping at the home of a friend of mine. There too she was not welcome. Back into the dark night. Her new foster parents were relieved at the return of "the little orphan."

Vicky was growing up with the stigma of a child of "enemies of the people." Tactless adults did not hold their tongues in her presence. They made it clear that she was not likely to ever set eyes on her parents. Nor was she spared the teasing of her peers: "Your mother and father are in chains! They are spies and will be shot."

Longing to disassociate themselves from their arrested parents, such children all the more eagerly proclaimed their loyalty to the socialist regime. On the day of my arrival the words "Stalin is the wisest and the best in the world" hit me in the face. They were scrawled across the wall above Vicky's cot in her childish handwriting.

"We were certain you would never return. We thought it best for Vicky to forget her parents," friends and neighbors told me.

My reunion with my daughter was indeed a miracle. It was the policy of the state to isolate released political prisoners and keep them away from their families. Such people knew too much to roam freely in socialist society or to be allowed to influence the upbringing of their children, who themselves were pressured into disowning their parents.

Traumas of separation and guilt on the part of those who all too readily abandoned their loved ones in misfortune eroded family relationships. Many mothers were less fortunate than I; belated reunions resulted in total wrecks of both their relationships with their children and their children's lives. There are bounds to the capacities of human adjustment.

Years later I was to learn from Vicky that when I turned up so unexpectedly, she did not believe I was her real mother. Perhaps it was an attitude prompted by the need to stifle the guilt she must have felt in closing her heart to me. She put me down as an imposter, reacting to my homecoming in the same way I had myself to my mother's return after her narrow escape from the death sentence passed on her by General Denikin in the Civil War.

This situation between us continued for almost three years. But I was too busy teaching, translating, and picking up the threads of life to brood over it. In prison and in camp we were hungry, desolate slaves; all normal desires were crushed in us. But now, with the first breath of freedom, I began to feel and act like a woman and human being again.

I did not want Vicky to grow up in a fatherless home, as I did. Nor had I ever shared my mother's conviction that a woman should above all value her independence and stand on her own two feet alone. I had my career and was earning more than many other women—and men. But the yearning for love, companionship, also another pair of shoulders to lean upon, propelled me into the search for a life partner.

With the male population decimated by the Stalin terror and the war, it was not easy for a woman of forty to find a husband. Moreover, I could only consider someone I was sure would make Vicky a good father.

One day Vicky tore to shreds a photograph of me. This animosity hurt, but I dismissed it as something a child would grow out of. My main concern was her education. In the face of a stubborn resistance on her part, I taught her English, engaged tutors in French and music, introduced her to the best theater, travelled with her, and converted our one room—divided up into a tiny kitchen where we ate our meals, a "drawing-room" and a bedroom—into a cozy home where we could entertain our friends, sometimes as many as ten guests sitting around our small, oval mahogany table. One afternoon, on going out to a movie, Vicky left me a note ending with the words: "I would do anything for you. I love you."

Pensive, inquisitive, studious, Vicky was treading the road to independent thought. In Chernyshevsky, Herzen, and other great Russians she sought the answers to moral questions, perusing their works from the first to the last page and over again. At one time the poet Mayakovsky was her idol. It was when a new idealism, along with a contempt for philistine small-mindedness, was gaining ground in the hopeful Khrushchev era. Sensitive to my intellectual preferences, Vicky knew I did not share her enthusiasm for Mayakovsky. She had inherited my mother's good memory and also her gift for expressive recitation; her recitals of my own favorite poets were a source of enjoyment to me. I always believed that Vicky would pursue a literary career. Instead she chose my mother's and brother's great love—mathematics.

II The living and the dead

It had, after my return, suddenly grown cold and windy. I walked behind young women in flared, belted coats of good material. Very chic! Young men swaggered in narrow trousers—something never seen or imagined in Moscow before. Many of the people I now saw in the streets I mistook for visiting tourists—until I learned that the fine spring coats were imported from Czechoslovakia. And the hip-hugging trousers, resented by the older generation and even dubbed bourgeois decadence by the writer Mikhail Sholokhov at a congress, were also among the imports from the Soviet Union's new socialist European neighbors.

I've always had a sweet tooth, which made me devour our prison camp's monthly sugar ration of 400 grams, at the rare times we got it at all, in two sittings. And now my love of sweets drove me to the famous bakery and confectionery in Stoleshnikov Street on the third day of my homecoming. I could hardly believe that I was there, feasting on gooey éclairs.

At night I was kept awake by the unaccustomed traffic noises, the strange cooing of pigeons outside my window—and the nightmares bringing back the horrors of prison and camp, making me for years and decades to come wrest myself from them in a cold sweat.

I had to piece my life together again. Special advisers at Communist Party District Committees were assigned to provide employment for amnestied prisoners. I applied to one such party functionary at the Bauman District Committee. Her face set in the stern lines of Stalinist officialdom, she told me outright that the "ideological" field, such as translation and teaching, was closed to me. She proved wrong.

Editors and publishers I had worked with, also acquaintances, shrank from accepting the reality of the release of persons like myself. Statements of mine quoted by my prosecutor and investigator from bulky dossiers revealed how many informers there were in my immediate entourage. Fears surfaced. Most likely, however, it was as hard to explain our sudden reappearance as it had been our arrest.

But the climate was changing, the pendulum swinging away from the bloody Stalin era. Friends and colleagues were now going out of their way to help me. The availability of jobs for all was one of the great gains of the Soviet system. I had more work than I could handle, books to translate and classes to teach.

People around me now began to say that had Stalin lived on, they themselves would have shared my fate. They cited instances of provocation and spying against them by the secret police. I do not know how sincere they were, for they later surprised me by a roundabout turn; they refrained from any mention of the Stalin period. It was the way a new wind was blowing.

In late September of the same year I was released, a parcel I mailed to my mother in Camp 215/023 of the Taishet District, Irkutsk Region, was returned to me. Across the wooden lid were stamped the words, "Addressee dead."

No official notice of her death. No confirmation. Under what circumstances she died, or where she was buried, I do not know. I dared not, nor do I yet dare, make inquiries. No memento, no photograph of her remained. Like myself she had signed the affidavit for the burning of her personal papers. Her file at Lubyanka, "to be kept forever", as the KGB stamp on its cover reads, is the sole proof of her having existed at all.

A few years after her death, when the jailings and shootings of millions of innocent people went by the name of "violations of social-ist legality," cases were reviewed and political prisoners exonerated. Both my mother and I were cleared of our "crimes," my mother post-humously. And so was my husband. On my request my husband's death certificate was issued to me. From it I learned that Mikhail died sixteen months after his arrest. He was forty-two. On the certificate neither the cause of death nor the place were indicated, as they are supposed to be on all such documents. In their stead two blank spaces stared at me.

During an intermission at a performance of Prokofiev's ballet *Romeo and Juliet*, I ran into Marina Spendiarova. Her silver hair shone like a halo around her refined, animated face. Marina was doing most of the talking. It thrilled me to hear her musical voice not in the murk of our foul-smelling prison shed in Taishet, but amidst the red plush and gilt of the Bolshoi. Excitedly she told me she was writing, trans-lating, singing on stage, collecting musical scores to perpetuate the memory of her father, the composer.

From her I learned that Lilli Semyonova had been released and was living in exile in Siberia. She had two children. I recalled her glowing skin, pink cheeks—flushed from tubercular fever—her exquisite fea-tures, sweet temper, and artistic gifts. Lilli was an exotic flower, cruelly transplanted to wither away in the harshness of Siberia.

Maria Anisimovna dropped in a few times. Her ringing laughter had cut through the brittle Siberian frost when she listed the pre-posterous charges brought against her. And now the same laughter tinkled in my room—"very cozy", she commented—as she told me she had been cleared of "poisoning Russian infants in wartime." In the mid-fifties, when Vicky and I were having dinner at the home of a friend, I was delighted to see Lina Prokofieva walk in—wearing a stylish black suit, well-groomed as usual, her cheeks flushed from the Moscow frost. We both knew of each other's experiences but somehow, as in this instance too, we never spoke of them except in the company of fellow-sufferers.

Her face with its dusky complexion and well-proportioned features showed little sign of ravage. Perhaps it was her pride that kept her from bending under the harsh captivity in the strict-regime camps.

One sunny afternoon in August Yulya came to see me. She was getting married and needed to borrow some money, which I gladly gave her. Nothing was too good to repay Yulya for her kindnesses to me in Taishet. The many years Yulya spent in German and Soviet camps had creased her skin and turned her hair gray. But she still looked pretty, though much older than her thirty years.

"There is something I would like you to know, a secret really." She paused, looking around the room and towards the door as though expecting to catch an eavesdropper.

A lengthy tale followed of a summons she had received to report to an office of her District Soviet.

"They wanted me to work for them . . . as an unpaid employee."

They, I guessed at once, were the Committee for State Security, or KGB.

"And what did you say?"

"I agreed—how could I refuse? To safeguard the security of our Soviet country is vital, don't you think?"

I had no answer for that one.

Yulya left soon after this confidence.

A few days later, to my surprise, I received a similar summons. The new beginnings! The room I entered at the District Soviet Committee smelled of fresh paint, as did the rest of the building, and was in a state of disarray, having just been moved into. Chairs and desks were askew; folders with secret files were in evidence everywhere, piled up on the windowsill, cluttered on the desks, spilling over from a chair onto the floor. The folders had names on them in bold print. I recognized a few of them, all of teachers I had worked with at the Army Language Institute. One was Senior-Lieutenant Reiber who, after my husband's arrest, suddenly began showering his attentions on me. His behavior was so crude and transparent that I did not doubt he had a special assignment to sound me on Mikhail's arrest.

In former days the man in charge of this new office would have been in grave trouble for the careless way in which the folders were exposed.

"We are going back to our old contacts, to people like you whom we trust," he said.

Half-pleadingly, he continued, "A family living in your house is expecting a visit from an American uncle." He paused. "We need information about the uncle and this family."

He was callow and inexperienced. I was both amused and infuriated. Information again! More stool pigeons at every step, more prying into the private lives of the citizens. Firmly I made it clear that I would have nothing to do with the security organs.

As I walked out of the building I thought: The monster Stalin is dead. There is a sense of relief. Some warm gusts of freedom ruffle the stagnant surface of our lives. Surely we can hope for better, freer times. But is Stalin really dead? Will he ever cease to turn the tide in his favor? The years to come held the answer to that question, and they would decide my own fate.

III The state and the individual

Two short blocks from where I lived, in the army guardhouse on Osipenko Street, the butcher Beria, recent head of the secret police and Stalin's closest workmate, was tried and executed. Only a few others were slated for the same fate.

In my home, over a bottle of dry white wine, coffee, and rum cupcakes, I was chatting with a few friends. It had suddenly become possible to express political views, a situation that obtained only for a short period.

"What do you make of Khrushchev's policies?"

"He's brought a fresh breeze, revealed Stalin's crimes against his own people, and is trying to bring the survivors of prison camps back to a normal existence," I replied.

"Do you really think that is such a good policy? Consider the way it makes us look to the rest of the world. Khrushchev is a disgrace to our country! Imagine him taking off his shoe and pounding with it on the table at the United Nations!"

Since I owed my very life to Khrushchev, I was happy to hear quite a different comment: "He has opened the road to reform. We must never return to Stalinism!"

A few years would go by, and those who had condemned Stalin would be forced to eat their words. Khrushchev's inconsistencies enabled Stalin's heirs to reascend to positions of power. The opinion that Khrushchev was nothing but a boor, that he had messed up the economy and was an embarrassment to the Soviet Union abroad, persisted. The Soviet people have always been extremely sensitive about the image their rulers and country project to the world. Most truly regard their system as a model for all nations.

To distance himself from the cynical, self-seeking opportunists, of whom there were so many within the Communist Party, Georgi Mikhailov, the man I married in 1959, liked to refer to himself as a "communist of the twenties." He identified with the idealistic type my mother represented, who craved no privileges, no power over their fellow beings, and worked honestly to build what they thought should indeed be a just and good society.

A first-generation intellectual, he owed much to the revolution and the Soviet system. This he repaid with unselfish dedication to the ideological tasks the Party set before him and with combat service from the first to the last day of the war, his many wounds reopening year after year and greatly undermining his health. He was an upright man, industrious and successful in his chosen field, and a devoted husband who, having no children of his own, doted on Vicky.

Party policies affected our lives. An orientalist by profession, Georgi had written a four-hundred-page dissertation towards the coveted Doctor of Philology degree. A portion of his research dealt with Mongolian folklore, much of which had been inspired by Genghis Khan. This bloodthirsty conqueror had become a great hero in Communist China, with which the Soviet Union was eager to establish more friendly relations. Not to offend the Chinese, my husband was urged by the Central Committee to revise his assessment of Genghis Khan and show him in a more favorable light. He refused, and it was not until a few years later, when Sino-Soviet relations remained at the same low ebb, that the censor gave him the green light to promote his book.

Living with my husband and seeing him work, I could appreciate the time and energy many Russians were giving to initiating and advancing scholars and professionals among the Asian and Mongolian nationalities. Georgi not only edited and wrote many chapters of a history of the Kalmyks, but helped other Mongolian nationalities to publish textbooks in their own language, compile grammars, and switch from the ancient alphabets to the less difficult Cyrillic letters. Often I accompanied him to conferences in these republics and was impressed by the speed with which the native population, under tsarism doomed to extinction because of syphilis and other scourges, were acquiring skills and producing their own competent and well-educated intelligentsia. Many had been educated in Moscow, where they often enjoyed preferential opportunities of enrollment in schools of higher learning.

Among the leading cultural figures of these nationalities were many victims of the Stalin terror. There was the poet David Kuguldinov, a Kalmyk, and the Mongolian poet and literary scholar Damdinsuren, a close friend of my husband's. They seemed to have no rancor, perhaps because they felt that the rapid rise of culture in their republics was a compensation for their sufferings.

Out of picture frames from which only a short while ago Stalin, Beria, and Khrushchev had been removed, Leonid Brezhnev stared at us from building façades. After leader worship had been denounced as the root of all evil it was carried to new extremes.

Politicians, scholars, scientists, and writers became maudlin over the genius of the new head of state. He lost no time in making himself twice and thrice Hero of the Soviet Union, titles with which accrue hosts of benefits; he also bestowed upon himself a marshal's baton. He had masterminded, we were told, the battle of Novorossiisk, which decided the outcome of the war. This was not easy to stomach for war veterans like Georgi. Whenever Brezhnev's face came on the screen my husband turned off the television. His outstanding contribution to victory Brezhnev recorded in two volumes, an epochal work that won him the Lenin prize in literature.

Why this literate leader—like, incidentally, Stalin and Khrushchev before him—stumbled over the pronunciation of many words, among them "communism" and "socialism," was quite puzzling and soon became the butt of many jokes. Fortunately, under Brezhnev one did not pay with a ten-year sentence for a political joke.

Still, life was becoming happier and more bearable. Many of the good programs begun by Khrushchev, such as housing construction, could not be discontinued. People in Moscow, as well as a few other lucky cities, were abandoning dingy shared flats and moving into new one-, two-, or even three-room homes of their own. More foods and consumer goods were becoming available. Faces lit up with new joy. My husband and I too were now living in far more comfortable surroundings.

Political life, however, was becoming more rigid and ominous. It was a field day for the bootlicker and the timeserver. No mention was ever made of the 20th and 22nd Party Congresses, at which Stalin's brutalities had been brought to light. It was as though they had never taken place. But this was not new to the Soviet people. What the party had said yesterday could be denied today without batting an eyelid.

Muscovites love to feast and get together. No occasion for merrymaking is missed, and family celebrations are big events. In late August, 1979, on my daughter's birthday, we were all having a grand time, the old generation along with the young. I was in exuberant spirits until a friend of my daughter's, a professor of mathematics at a military academy, said to me, "Surely the people arrested under

Stalin were guilty of some criminal act against the state." I knew this man, who was in his mid-thirties, to be an honest and well-wishing person. I did not answer. His words pointed to the latest trend in political thinking. Stalin's shadow! The clang of steel in the many-tiered galleries at Lefortovo rang into my ears the warning of silence.

A sixth sense told me that among the friends I entertained on Saturday nights, the number of informers was on the increase. In comparing observations with my daughter, I realized we shared the same conviction.

A colleague of mine who had recently returned from a visit to the United States was too open in her praise of American democracy. I drew her aside, into my kitchen, in the new condominium close to Moscow University where we now lived.

"Do watch your words," I cautioned her. "There are bound to be a couple of informers sitting around my table."

"Yes, I know, I was an informer myself," she suddenly blurted out.

I was shocked. I admired and loved this person. Her confession made me sick. I paled. She flushed scarlet.

"The arrest of a dear friend is on my conscience. She never came back from camp. God, how I hate the KGB!"

"Hush! Don't talk that way. We may be overheard."

A spate of articles, novels, and television series had now descended upon us, glorifying the deeds of the Soviet secret police, from the Cheka to the present-day KGB. Not a word about the victims. I did not know that I myself was not yet through with the KGB.

Having married a Canadian (a post-doctoral fellow at Moscow University, and a mathematician like herself), Vicky, her husband, and their three-year-old son were now in Canada. Her absence for even less than a year was a strain on my nerves. We were both obsessed by the fear that for reasons unknown visas might be withheld by the Soviet authorities. Georgi and I applied for visiting permits. We were hopeful.

An old and dear friend of mine had died about six months before, leaving a will in Vicky's favor. By Soviet standards she came into a tidy sum, close to ten thousand roubles. There was no way the assets could be taken out of the country; Soviet currency is not convertible and is of no value outside the U.S.S.R. Georgi and I had no need of the money; we had savings of our own.

Learning at the Moscow Visa Office that Soviet citizens visiting abroad could legally take out a few valuables, I made the rounds of the jewelry shops to see what I could buy. On Arbat Street I stood in line for almost an hour waiting for the shop to open after the lunch break. A youngish man in an elaborate get-up that seemed to come right out of a theater wardrobe approached me.

He addressed me as "Madame," an obsolete form that has not been in use since the Revolution, and proceeded slimily; "If you are after really fine jewelry, I can take you to a private dealer in sapphires, emeralds . . ."

"No, thank you." I cut him short. A woman standing behind me pricked up her ears. "I would be interested," she said in a half-whisper.

"It is this madame that would find what she is looking for," he persisted.

I was suspicious: in making a proposition that was obviously illegal, why was he speaking in a voice loud enough for others to hear? So that, if necessary, witnesses could be summoned?

It took some time for me to brush him off. I believe I saw through his disguise. Months later, after my experience with customs at Sheremetyevo, I recalled this incident, wondering if the man had not been a KGB plant; I am still uncertain.

At the Arbat jewelry shop I bought two rings and a brooch, the value of which did not exceed what I was legally entitled to take out of Moscow. These pieces of inexpensive jewelry would be but a token reminder of the inheritance left to my daughter.

In September, 1980, carrying the new red passports issued for the duration of a visit to a foreign country, Georgi and I were on our way to Moscow's main international airport, holding hands, exhilarated, like a newly married couple. With two pieces of luggage, mostly packed with gifts, we faced customs inspection.

It was at this point that things altogether unforeseen started to happen. My husband was told to move on, while I was detained for more than an hour, with the passengers in back of me hastily melting away and fleeing to other lines. Three customs officials, two young women and a man in his late twenties, rummaged through my things, opening and closing the brightly coloured Matryoshka nest dolls, feeling and ripping the lining of coats, emptying my handbag, carefully examining every item in it. I was both frightened and infuriated, yet dared not utter a single word of protest. There was a man hovering in the background, scowling, watching the whole procedure with eagle eyes. He had the hard, arrogant look and high-handed manner I knew so well. There was no doubt in my mind that he was KGB, probably with the rank of captain or major.

The final humiliation: I was led into a cubby-hole for a body search. It yielded nothing. The KGB was behind the entire ugly masquerade.

When it was over I was told that our plane reservations had been cancelled the day before. But at the last minute, after a whispered conversation between the KGB man and a few other officials, we were allowed to board the plane. Fortunately for us, take-off was delayed because the Soviet ambassador to Canada, who was on the passenger list, arrived late. We made it to our seats in the nick of time.

Instead of feeling elated at the prospect of seeing my daughter and her family, I wept bitterly through the entire flight from Moscow to Montreal. My husband too was upset and puzzled as to why I had been singled out to be so brutally harassed.

To bully and intimidate, to wreck their citizens' plans and lives, is the long-standing practice of the KGB. They sent out signals—an ominous signal to one Jewish emigrant and his wife. They were turned back from the airport, stripped of their exit visas, told they would never be allowed out of the country. No reason was given. Another went to a member of the U.S.S.R. Academy of Sciences who, on his way to an international conference, was ordered off the plane in Moscow and sent home without a word of explanation.

What was the message to me? Since explanations for the government's actions are rarely offered, Soviet citizens must willy-nilly rely on conjecture. The grilling I received at customs was most likely a stern warning to keep my mouth shut about the gross injustices my family and I had suffered at the hands of the secret police. At the same time, the KGB might have hoped to discover a smuggled manuscript or a piece of jewelry, or provoke an imprudent censure of their tactics, any of which would have sufficed to prevent me from boarding the plane.

The message struck home—though not in the way intended by the all-powerful secret police. I was not going to risk a second grilling, or worse, refusal of an exit visa the next time I decided to visit my daughter. After several months' stay in Canada I applied and was kindly granted permanent residence by the Canadian government.

Georgi took my decision very hard, hoping fervently I would change my mind and return to live in Moscow. For him to abandon his motherland was unthinkable. Our attachment was too deep for us to live apart. Georgi came to stay for brief periods in Canada. I made several trips to Moscow in the mid-eighties, each lasting a few months.

In early May of 1985 and 1986 I watched the Victory Day celebrations, the elaborate preparations for which can last for weeks. An atmosphere of triumph and patriotism prevails. War veterans parade through cities and villages wearing their hard-earned medals. Moscow was flooded with these gallant men and women. I saw them everywhere—in the streets, public squares, museums, and theaters.

I thought of Vicky's father and my brother Shurri. They too had been in the war. No mention of them and the hundreds of thousands of other war veterans, nor their reward—prison, death, a bullet in the back of the head from a KGB thug, the latter himself wearing medals, parading in the streets of Moscow, living off the fat of the land with no fear of ever being brought to justice.

Verdant Moscow, with well-dressed crowds of shoppers from all over the land, wide new boulevards, mauve, scarlet, and pearly white tulips swaying in the spring breeze. I was sitting in the airy, well-furnished condominium bought out of my savings twenty-four years earlier.

Georgi had had a stroke, his second. Hastily I had arrived from Canada to nurse and care for him. Vicky too had, the year before, spent her Christmas holidays with him in Moscow. My husband's condition now kept me more at home, at his bedside, than on previous visits. I was tormented by guilt, feeling partly responsible for his rapid deterioration.

A long address by the new General Secretary delivered at the Palace of Congresses in the Kremlin was being broadcast. In it acclaim was given to Stalin. At the mention of Stalin's name, the audience rose as one man, as indeed in his own time, and applauded wildly.

At Moscow movie houses and in television series, again and again, I saw Stalin's face projected on the screen and listened to inordinate praise of his wisdom and deeds.

Another visit to Moscow: slogans, catch phrases, pronouncements! The air is full of them. How familiar they are to me. I have heard them from the lips of Stalin, Khrushchev, Brezhnev. Sadly, I know only too well how casuistic words can be. Tactical utterances: you must search for nuances, fathom ambiguity. The very Party leaders, along with giants in literature and the arts, who only yesterday swore by one idea are now saying and writing practically the opposite.

True to Russian tradition, the public seeks answers in literature and art. Painting, poetry, novels, the theater, and later the cinema, have played their role in disclosing elements of truth, if not the whole truth. But the artist must watch his step. Analogy, allegory, symbols have always been his stock in trade—from Pushkin to the present day. Eagerly Moscow audiences flock to see a movie recreating the dark atmosphere of the Stalin terror. However, disguised by a Hitler moustache and a Beria pince-nez, the protagonist can hardly be identified with the true perpetrator of the crimes of the period.

Many of my Moscow friends are nevertheless ecstatic. Even a crumb of truth is better than nothing. The current wishy-washy attempts to deal with the bloody Stalin era, which took a greater toll of human lives than World War II, somehow recall to me Stalin's magnanimity in allowing the production of Bulgakov's *The Days of the Turbins* in the thirties at the Moscow Art Theater. Then too, everybody was delighted. Doddering grand personalities of Moscow's theater world were known to remark: "How wise and gracious of our dear Yosif Vissarionovich to approve the play. It's getting to be freer and freer, just like before the Revolution."

Georgi was fighting for his life. I was hopeful. He had the best medical care: weekly and sometimes daily doctors' visits from the Academy Clinic of which he was a longtime patient.

Leaning on a cane—which I bought him after phoning about a dozen Moscow drugstores before at last finding one that had some in stock—he resumed his daily constitutional. Frail, his wounded legs giving him more pain than usual, he nevertheless kept up a fast pace. Though he refused to be accompanied on these walks, his sister or I, apprehensive that he might trip and fall, would follow a few steps behind, never letting him out of our sight.

He was now hobbling towards the corner of the block, where our street, Michurinsky Prospekt, began and where a statue to Indira Gandhi had been unveiled and a square laid out in her honor. On that corner stands the University Hotel, accommodating academics and students from foreign lands.

Georgi walked through the hotel doors, perhaps with the intention of glancing at the magazines displayed on the newsstand in the lobby. Presently I saw him start back. I was close enough to hear the doorman's words, flung at all Soviet people who try to go into a hotel reserved for visitors from abroad: "You're not allowed in! Entrance only for foreigners."

My husband turned away. Outrage at this treatment flamed on my face. But Georgi admonished: "Pay no attention to such trifles. Think of the good we have achieved."

I pressed his arm.

"Yes, yes, I will try."

Think of the good that has been achieved. How many times have I tried to do just that. See the Soviet experience in historical perspective, I tell myself. But the perpetual lies, the blood of the victims, of my loved ones and so many others, cannot be shunted aside by positive thinking. Can I forget and forgive? Never! Nor forgive the long silence, or the hypocrisy of the present day.

Yet I try to be fair. I repeat to myself the magic words: Economic security. The right to a job. These outweigh many of the freedoms that democracies claim for their citizens. I keep meeting people, friends, who are sincerely socialist in their views and deeds, working for the public good first and for personal gain second. Yes, and I must not forget my Soviet women friends, indeed all of the country's women. They can be proud of what they have made of their lives, acquiring skills and professions that render them indispensable to society, leading as productive an existence as the men, possessing the same sense of self-worth.

After Georgi passed away before my eyes in July 1986, I fled to Canada. But Moscow as always remained in my heart and my thoughts. In my dreams I saw her green avenues, rushing crowds—and the faces of my own generation, grim, deeply lined. On all my visits I could not tear my gaze away from them in the Moscow Metro. They were part of me, dear and close, for with them I had shared so many hardships, losses, pain. Surly clerks whose rudeness I had endured for decades had their place in my memory, too. Bolder youths—not carefree but intent—sat glued to their university textbooks or world classics. Riding the Metro I had also watched them, searching their faces for the idealism of my own youth. And then there was the constantly baffling ideological see-sawing of the Party and government bosses that had been so integral to my Soviet existence.

Years of life in Canada could not get Moscow out of my system. Nor could I forget my friends, happy now to be living comfortably in two- or three-room flats of their own, not minding the absence of bedrooms, or having to convert the couches sat on in the daytime into beds by night.

Now it is August, 1987—thirteen years away from the twenty-first century, which I fervently hope will be less brutal and tragic than the twentieth. I arrive in Moscow on a Friday night. The cool air is a relief after the heat of the Canadian summer.

In teeming rain I make my way to Arbat Street. Here I lived before my first marriage, on the contiguous Gogolevsky Boulevard. Here I shopped, ran into friends, spent Saturday night dancing and drinking wine at the Praha Restaurant, where gypsies shimmied and, with their soul-stirring, passionate songs, brought tears to the eyes of my Russian escorts.

On my previous visit to Moscow, the year before, Arbat was being transformed into a promenade, with old-fashioned wrought iron lamp-posts; former mansions of the nobility, half-concealed by scaffolding, were being restored. And now, besides the architectural face-lift, the street presented a scene so new to Soviet life and so reminiscent of nooks in Western cities that I had the feeling of not being in Moscow at all. Everywhere were little knots of young people who, though not entirely uninhibited, behaved far more casually than I had ever seen them do before. Poets were reciting their verse, painters trying to sell their pictures and offering to paint portraits for the passing crowds. A breath of freedom. Yet I could not help noticing the large number of "archangels," as, like its predecessors, the KGB has been christened by the people.

To my trained eye groceries and bakeries seemed more poorly stocked than the year before, and there was more queuing up.

"Who cares if we have shortages so long as we can get the books we want to read and the newspapers and magazines at last print the truth?" a friend says. There is a new sparkle in her eyes, a new happy look that I have never seen before. Her father was a victim of the Stalin terror. At last, she feels, she can speak openly of her deep wound and the sufferings of her whole family.

Despite the shortages, I find the table at the home of a neighbor laden with choice dishes. The spread is a credit to Muscovites' ingenuity in the perpetual hunt for foods in short supply.

The conversation around the table is as much a surprise as the Arbat scene. Historians are busy, I am told, writing articles on Bukharin, Zinoviev, and Kamenev—all three shot—to at least partly clear them of their "crimes." Daringly I drop the name of Trotsky. The air grows electric with an almost palpable bewilderment, then clears momentarily like a thundercloud pierced by rippling sunlight. We recall Trotsky's theory of permanent revolution. Time has proved him wrong.

A man who holds a high academic post—and whom I knew always to stress his wholehearted support of every Party policy, also to sing the praises of Stalin and later Brezhnev—suddenly reveals qualms of remorse: "We knew that most of the people shot or deported to camps in Siberia were innocent. But what could we do? Stick our necks out, lose our own freedom or even life?"

A lull in the conversation. The same man continues: "Most of those responsible for the crimes under Stalin are dead."

Convenient self-deceit! Nazi criminals who operated from 1939 to 1945 are being hunted down and brought to trial, while the Soviet Communist Party members who signed and counter-signed thousands of lists of people to be shot and arrested, and the secret police assassins who executed their orders, are presumed to be dead.

Such hypocrisy has its harmful effect on Soviet youth, who squirm at the lies and half-truths fed to them daily. I read the report of a trial held in one of the Soviet Caucasian republics. The offenders are young men, some even teenagers, charged with car theft, trafficking in drugs, and burglary. They want a taste of the good and easy life, they say.

"Where did you acquire such pernicious ideas in our socialist society?" the judge inquires. He does not have to wait long for an answer. Insolently the young offenders fling at him: "Where did those who set themselves up as an example to us acquire their villas, their Mercedes cars, their diamonds?"

Young people, as well as many of my own generation, long desperately to know the truth. Alas, the glaring contradiction within Soviet society is that there are millions who have become so accustomed to lies and lying that they would go to any lengths to continue living in the old way. The truth is feared.

Truth! *Pravda*! Russia has been the land of truthseekers, *pravdaiskateli*. Among the truthseekers were some of the greatest and noblest minds the country has produced. But perhaps truth was so diligently sought because it was, and still is, so rare.

EPILOGUE

This happened at the beginning of our century, just after the celebration of the New Year. The day was bitterly cold. Snow lay deep and hard on the ground. The Russian landowner's family felt dull after the Christmas and New Year merrymaking.

Annoyed by the boredom, the landowner hit on an idea to liven up things a bit.

"Fetch Ivan," he commanded one of the servants.

Ivan arrived. He paused in the doorway, crumpling his cap in his hand.

"How would you like to own twenty-five *desyatins* of land?"

The family and servants pricked up their ears. They knew the landowner was a great joker. Curious, they waited to hear Ivan's answer.

"I would like nothing better," replied the peasant. "But how will I get the land, when I have no money to pay for it?"

"I'll give it to you free—on one condition."

"And what is that?"

"See that hill over there?"

Ivan nodded.

"Remove your bast shoes and footcloths. If you can stand barefoot on it for twenty-four hours, the land is yours."

"That I'll do, because I want the land badly. But I too have a condition to make."

"And, pray, what is that?"

"Light a fire a little distance from the hilltop so that I can watch the flame."

"Very well," agreed the landlord. "But we won't use up more than just one pile of firewood."

The pile to which the landowner pointed seemed big enough to Ivan, and he nodded assent.

Hour struck after hour. The family kept staring out of the window, amazed to find Ivan still standing there in his bare feet. A wind rose, it was getting frostier, but Ivan did not stir. He seemed glued to the spot. Twenty hours had gone by. He was still on the hilltop, never taking his eyes off the flame.

The last log was fed into the fire. At the end of the twenty-second hour, the flame died out. Ivan fell flat on the ground. A servant ran out to see if Ivan was dead. Ivan was alive, unharmed, except for his feet. He was brought to the village hospital and there his feet were cut off.

Hearing the story, the doctor asked: "Why in Heaven's name, Ivan, did you do a foolish thing like that? Twenty-two hours out in the cold in your bare feet! In such weather! You must be mad!"

"Doctor, I would have stood on the icy ground all of the twenty-four hours," said Ivan. "And the land would have been mine. If only the flame were alight. Watching it was what gave me courage."

Will the flame be rekindled? People like myself who had faith in the dream of a new society have been destroyed and betrayed over and over again.

Index

Editor's Note

Suzanne Rosenberg died in London, Ontario in 1988.